The
Garland Library
of
War and Peace

The
Garland Library
of
War and Peace

Under the General Editorship of

Blanche Wiesen Cook, *John Jay College, C.U.N.Y.*

Sandi E. Cooper, *Richmond College, C.U.N.Y.*

Charles Chatfield, *Wittenberg University*

War-What For?

by
George R. Kirkpatrick

with a new Introduction
for the Garland Edition by
Scott Nearing

Garland Publishing, Inc., New York
1971

Introduction

George Kirkpatrick's War, What For? *was a social-ist agitator's contribution to the peace-war contro-versy which immediately preceded the outbreak of the European war in July, 1914. During those turbulent years, when war was a prime issue in Europe, economic problems were still in the forefront of American thinking. The "hard times" of the early eighteen-nineties, followed by recessions in 1907 and 1913, had punctured the "prosperity-progress" myth of complacent American capitalists.*

War with Spain in 1898 and the British-Boer War in South Africa, which broke out the next year, were minor episodes for millions of American dollar-a-day wage earners whose lives were plagued by poverty, unemployment and insecurity. Upton Sinclair's The Jungle *and Robert Hunter's* Poverty *and other protest writings highlighted the issues facing Americans in the first years of the present century.*

George Kirkpatrick learned his socialism during those bitter years. As a speaker and organizer he went from one socialist meeting to another, preaching the gospel of human brotherhood and urging his listeners to line up with their fellows in a massive protest against the big business trusts which were taking control of the United States, and against the war-

menace threatened by the arms race of the chief European capitalist empires.

Socialists were not alone in their appeal for solidarity behind the slogan "Save America for the People." Woodrow Wilson, running for the Presidency in 1912, reminded his fellow-countrymen that "an invisible empire has been set up above the forms of democracy," and Theodore Roosevelt warned United States citizens against "the malefactors of great wealth."

Eugene V. Debs, heading the Socialist ticket in the presidential election of 1912, polled almost a million votes. This showing gave substance to the slogan: "Make America Socialist."

Not a few of those socialist votes were the result of George Kirkpatrick's arduous speaking tours. Traveling by night and talking day after day, sometimes to a handful of unsympathetic listeners on a street corner, sometimes to large sympathetic mass meetings, he carried it verbally. Then he put it into writing: leaflets, pamphlets and books.

The first printing of War, What For? *appeared in August, 1910. A second printing followed in October, and by the end of the year fourteen thousand volumes had been printed. About 150,000 copies had been printed when World War I began. The classic Marxist indictment of war for American socialists, it charged capitalists with preparing for and waging war in order to protect and increase their profits. International war, borne by the working class, was the product of economic rivalry for the benefit of these who had expropriated wealth.*

In the seven years between the first printing of War, What For? *and the United States' declaration of war against the Central Powers, George Kirkpatrick and his fellow socialists saw their country transformed from a peaceful democratic state into a hectic, frantic belligerent which finally recrossed the ocean to take part in a military conflict that was not of its own making.*

The American people had been largely on the fence. "I did not raise my boy to be a soldier" was a song popular among Americans opposed to entering European conflicts. President Wilson even won his second term in the 1916 election largely with the slogan, "He kept us out of war." Much of the United States was strongly isolationist. Radicals – the Industrial Workers of the World and the Socialist Party – were adamantly against intervention.

Long before April, 1917, American businessmen had invested heavily in the Allies. President Wilson was pro-British; he extended economic credit to the Allies and tried to gear up for defense. When the pro-Ally business interests opened the preparedness campaign, with J. P. Morgan marching along Fifth Avenue in a parade, most Americans never dreamed that within months their country would be sending not only armament by the billions but also young men by the millions to weight the stalemated war on the Allied side. Nor did they imagine that at the end

*of a war fought ostensibly "to make the world safe
for democracy" President Wilson would be the key
figure at a Peace Conference that excluded representatives of the defeated Central Powers and revolutionary governments. The turbulence of the
times, to which Kirkpatrick had pointed, had
swamped the idealism beneath which he had probed.*

*With other socialist spokesmen and many non-
socialist Americans who agreed with them, Kirkpatrick had tried to rally anti-war forces. Upon the
involvement of the United States the Socialist Party
passed strong anti-war resolutions at its party convention in St. Louis. The People's Council of America
for Peace and Democracy, founded after the declaration of war with the backing of socialists and
liberal pacifists, agitated and lobbied for a negotiated
peace and civil rights.*

*It was to no avail, as a vicious pro-war sentiment
swept the country. People who a few months earlier
had been against fighting were turned into pro-war
fanatics who tarred and feathered, rioted, and even
lynched their anti-war fellow countrymen. President
Wilson took advantage of this war fever to push
through a Conscription Act and an Espionage Act.
Both laws ran counter to American traditions of civil
liberties. Both were opposed by substantial sections
of American opinion. Both laws gave the Administration the legal means of smothering dissent, radical
as well as anti-war, while putting the United States on
a war footing.*

INTRODUCTION

The Conscription Act swelled the ranks of army and navy manpower. The Espionage Act dealt a body-blow to the opposition. Passed as a means of deterring enemy spies, the Espionage Law was used to indict, try, convict, and sentence to long terms of imprisonment leaders and prominent figures opposed to a total war for victory.

The Industrial Workers of the World were opposed to both war and capitalism. Their headquarters were raided by police-protected mobs, and were looted. Their officers were arrested, tried, and sent to prison for terms up to forty years. Socialist Party leaders met the same fate. Their national spokesman, Eugene V. Debs, was sent to the Atlanta Penitentiary for making a speech critical of the conduct of the war. Victor Berger, Socialist congressman from Milwaukee, was tried with other socialists for opinions he expressed.

War, What For? *had played an important role in the anti-war campaign. It was not a sophisticated book in its denunciation of war as arising from economic causes and as a crime against humanity. But there was nothing sophisticated about the war. It was brutal. George Kirkpatrick and his book became a storm center. Wherever he went he was hailed by anti-war crowds as a leader in the struggle for socialism and peace; and he was denounced by fervent patriots as "pro-German" and a traitor to the United States.*

He insisted simply that the war was the outcome of

INTRODUCTION

*economic rivalry between the leading capitalist
powers. The more radical elements among the
socialists had taken this position before 1914. After
the war began some held fast to it under the
leadership of Lenin in Russia, Liebknecht and Lux-
emburg in Germany. Ironically, after the war's end
Woodrow Wilson acknowledged a measure of truth in
the argument when he said that "of course it was a
commercial war."*

War, What For? *is dated in that it was published
more than a half century ago. But in a world which
has known no year of all-around peace since 1910,
where conscription of young men for killing is all but
universalized, where brush-fire wars are reported from
all over the planet, where economies feed on conflict,
and where the solution for domestic and international
problems is to grab a gun, this book should be
circulated and read by all people who look forward to
a warless human society.*

Scott Nearing
Harborside, Maine

10

INDUSTRIAL DESPOTISM, SHREWDLY CALLED FREEDOM

WAR—WHAT FOR?

BY

GEORGE R. KIRKPATRICK

"The cannon's prey has begun to think, and, thinking twice, loses its admiration for being made a target."—*Victor Hugo.*

"A nod from a lord is a breakfast—for a fool."—*Proverb.*

"The poor souls for whom this hungry war opens its vast jaws,"—*William Shakespeare.*

PUBLISHED BY THE AUTHOR,

WEST LA FAYETTE, OHIO

WAR—WHAT FOR?

SINGLE COPY, $1.20

Liberal discounts in clubs of 3, 10 and 25 or more.

Chapter Two, with two pictures and other selections, printed separately in 16-page pamphlet form.

By the same author:

THINK—OR SURRENDER

About 100 pages of elementary economics, politics and organization—for the propaganda of Socialism. (Nearly ready.)

THIS book is dedicated to the victims of the civil war in industry; that is, to my brothers and sisters of the working class, the class who furnish the blood and tears and cripples and corpses in all wars—yet win no victories for their own class.

CONTENTS

PREFACE.

Justice soothes.

Justice heals the wounds and sores in the social body.

Justice strikes down all robbery—illegal and legal.

Justice calms.

Injustice stings.

Injustice burns, irritates—kills sociability and creates conflict.

Injustice prevents brotherhood.

Injustice is unsocial—anti-social—and is thus a social sore.

Injustice, organized injustice, is the soul of all *class*-labor forms of society.

The purpose of all class-labor forms of society is ROBBERY.

The robbed resist—sometimes.

The robbers are ready for resistance—always.

In all *class*-labor forms of society the ruling class always have:

FIRST, AN **ARMED** GUARD—READY:

> ready to serve as tusk and fist of the robber ruling class,
> ready to suppress protesting chattel-slaves,
> ready to suppress protesting serfs,
> ready to suppress protesting wage-earners,
> ready to defend the class-labor system,
> ready to extend the class-labor system,
> ready to defy and defeat and hold down and kick the robbed working class.

SECOND, AN **UNARMED** GUARD—composed of prideless purchasable human things, social chameleons, moral eunuchs, political flunkies—intellectual prostitutes—READY:

> ready to make laws in the interest of the ruling class,

ready to interpret laws in the interest of the ruling class,

ready to execute laws in the interest of the ruling class,

ready to cunningly cajole and beguile the toil-cursed working class,

ready to cunningly teach meekness, humility and contentment—to the working class,

ready to cunningly teach servility and obedience—to the working class,

ready with grand words to cunningly dupe and chloroform—the working class,

ready to bellow about "Law and Order" when the unemployed call loudly for work or bread and when hungry strikers open their lips in self-defense,

ready "for Jesus' sake" (and a salary) to glorify war and scream to the "God of Battles" (also the "God of Peace") for victory; ready to baptize wholesale murder and flatter the blood-stained conquerors; ready to whine and mumble over the shell-torn corpses of the victims and hypocritically sniffle and mouth consolatory congratulations to the war-cursed widows and orphans—ready thus to mock their own ruined victims—for a price; ready to preach—to the workers—that they must fight like hell to "get a home in heaven."

Many of my brothers—my betrayed younger brothers—are soldiers: they have been seduced to serve as Armed Guard. They have been deceived. And they are abused. Many of them are even driven insane. Insanity ranks *third* in the long list of disablements for which our betrayed brothers are dismissed from the service. (Report of the Department of War, 1908, p. 21.) A whole car-load of insane soldiers were shipped through Pittsburgh—home from the Philippines—December 11, 1909.

These men are indeed betrayed and abused—and ashamed. They even destroy themselves to hide their shame and escape abuse. TWENTY-SIX TIMES AS MANY enlisted men *committed* *suicide* in 1908 as in 1907; AND THIRTY-NINE TIMES AS MANY of them committed suicide in 1909 as in 1907.*

More and more the boys in the Army are *disgusted* with the whole vile business, but as the boys become increasingly sick of the service and would like to run away, the War Department more and more prepares to hold them *like rats in a trap* —just as the Secretary of War *boasted* in his Report for 1908 (p. 19) that he *now* finally had "an elaborate system . . . almost perfected well calculated to secure swift and certain apprehension and punishment of deserters, and will . . . have a marked effect in reducing the crime to a minimum." Thus the boys are trapped and stung,—and some of them kill themselves.

The working class men *inside and outside the Army* are confused.

They do not understand.

But they will understand.

AND WHEN THEY DO UNDERSTAND, their class loyalty and class pride will astonish the world. They will stand erect in their vast class strength and defend—THEMSELVES. They will cease to coax and tease; they will make *demands*— unitedly. They will desert the armory; they will spike every cannon on earth; they will scorn the commander; they will never club or bayonet another striker; and in the legislatures of the world they will shear the fatted parasites from the political and industrial body of society.

But these things they will not do and *can not* do till they are *roused*—roused *because* they understand.

Therefore, I "rise to a point of order": The most important thing on the program in the politics of the world

---

* Reports of the Department of War for the years 1907, '08, '09, pp. 17, 21, and 18 respectively. The Reports of the Secretaries of War include no losses by suicide from 1901 to 1906 inclusive. The suicide record reported by the Secretaries of War for 1907, '08, '09, are: 1, 26, 39 respectively. Fifty-eight per cent. of all desertions in 1906 were desertions by men (boys) in their first year of service; over half of these in first half year of their service. See Index: "Desertions."

to-day is to rouse the working class to realize itself, to be conscious of itself, to see itself and also see distinctly the age-long conspiracy of the ruling class; the first thing is to rouse the working class to unite socially and unite industrially and unite politically and seize all the powers of government in all the world—for self-defense; the supreme business of the hour is to rouse the working class for the crowning victory in the evolution of mankind—for the industrial freedom of the working class, for the peace and the calm born of justice, for the beauty and the glory of the brotherhood of man.

This book is written to help instruct and rouse the working class; and if in some small measure this unpretentious book carries light to the brains of my younger brothers on the big steel battleships, in the barren gloomy barracks, and to my abused and cheated brothers (and sisters) in the mills and mines and on the farms—and thus helps *stir my class* to a consciousness of their class and thus helps *advance the demand for justice and the demand for a reconstructed, socialized society,* my reward will seem abundant.

GEORGE R. KIRKPATRICK.

July 4, 1910,

The pictures in this book add much to its interest and usefulness. Those on pages 31 and 33 were made by Mr. Ryan Walker, of New York; all the others were made by Mr. John Sloan, also of New York. The author is genuinely grateful for their kind cooperation.

Ready.

The Roman slave-owners of two thousand years ago with their armed slave-drivers; also the slave-owners of sixty years ago with their hireling slave-drivers, armed with black-snake whips and pistols, on horseback in the cotton fields of the South—the ancient and the modern chattel slave-owners thus were ready—*ready* to murder the *slave* working class.

The lords of serfdom with armed hirelings housed near their castles were also ready—*ready* to murder the *serf* working class.

Recently, in 1907, when the number of the unemployed wage-earners in the United States numbered over three millions, it was promptly planned by the War Department serving the Caesars of industry that one machine-gun company with six rapid-fire guns of the Maxim or some similar type should be added to each of the thirty regiments of infantry and fifteen regiments of cavalry now constituting the Army—a total of two hundred and seventy of the most terrible murdering machines ever invented. With these guns, each firing eight hundred shots per minute, eight million six hundred and forty thousand cold steel nuggets of "law-and-order" and "unparalleled prosperity" could be handed out to the unemployed in just forty minutes,—to lovingly show the working class how, under the wage-system—the present *class*-labor system,—"the interests of the capitalist class and the interests of the working class are practically the same."

Thus the capitalists of our day are also ready—*ready* to have wage-paid soldiers, militiamen and policemen murder the *wage-earning* working class.

"Although the conventions of popular government are preserved, capital is at least as absolute as under the Caesars. The aristocracy which wields this autocratic power is beyond attack, for it is defended by a wage-earning police, by the side of which the [Roman] legions were a toy—a police so formidable that, for the first time in history, revolt is hopeless and is not attempted. The only question which preoccupies the ruling class is whether it is cheaper to coerce or bribe."—Brooks Adams: *The Law of Civilization and Decay,* p. 292.

An Insult from the Commander-in-Chief:

"The fact can not be disregarded nor explained away that for some reason or other the life of the soldier as at present constituted is not one to attract the best and most desirable class of enlisted men. . . .

"The [military] service should be made so attractive that it would not be difficult to obtain intelligent and desirable men and to hold them."—William H. Taft, Secretary of War (now President and Commander-in-Chief of the Army and Navy) : Annual Report of Secretary of War, 1907, page 14. Mr. Taft repeated this insult in a public speech. (See New York *Times,* April 26, 1908.)

In the Report of the Secretary of War, 1907, page 79, is the following from the General Staff:

"The bulk of recruits come and must always come from the agricultural, artisan, and laboring classes."

How long will strong men of the working class accept a kick as a compliment—from so-called "great" men?

CHAPTER ONE.

A Confidential Word With the Man of the Working Class.

BROTHER!

Whoever you are, wherever you are on all the earth, I greet you.

You are a member of the working class.

I am a member of the working class.

We are brothers.

Class brothers.

Let us repeat that:—Class Brothers.

Let us write that on our hearts and stamp it on our brains:—Class Brothers.

I extend to you my right hand.

I make you a pledge.

Here is my pledge to you:—

I refuse to kill your father. I refuse to slay your mother's son. I refuse to plunge a bayonet into the breast of your sister's brother. I refuse to slaughter your sweetheart's lover. I refuse to murder your wife's husband. I refuse to butcher your little child's father. I refuse to wet the earth with blood and blind kind eyes with tears. I refuse to assassinate you and then hide my stained fists in the folds of *any* flag.

I refuse to be flattered into hell's nightmare by a class of well-fed snobs, crooks and cowards who despise our class socially, rob our class economically and betray our class politically.

Will you thus pledge me and pledge all the members of our working class?

Sit down a moment, and let us talk over this matter of war. We working people have been tricked—tricked into a sort of huge steel-trap called war.

Really, the smooth "leading citizens" tried their best to flim-flam me, too. They cunningly urged me to join the militia and the army and be ready to go to war. Their voices were soft, their smiles were bland, they made war look bright, very bright. But I concluded not to train for war or go to war—at least not until the brightness of war became bright enough to attract those cunning people to war who tried to make war look bright to me. I have waited a long time. I am still waiting. Thus I have had plenty of opportunity to think it all over. And the more I think about war the more clearly I see that a bayonet is a *stinger,* made by the working class, sharpened by the working class, nicely polished by the working class, and then "patriotically" thrust into the working class by the working class—for the capitalist class.

The busy human bees sting themselves.

If I should enlist for service in the Department of Murder I should feel thoroughly embarrassed and ashamed of myself. It is all clear to me now. This is the way of it, brother:—

In going to war I must work like a horse and be as poor as a mouse, must be as humble as a toad, as meek as a sheep and obey like a dog; I must fight like a tiger, be as cruel as a shark, bear burdens like a mule and eat stale food like a half-starved wolf; for fifteen or twenty dollars a month I must turn against my own working class and thus make an ass and a cat's-paw of myself; and after the war I should be socially despised and snubbed as a sucker and a cur by the same distinguished "leading citizens" who wheedled me to war and afterward gave me the horse-laugh;—and thus I should feel like a monkey and look like a plucked goose in January.

Indeed I am glad to see it all clearly.

I want you to see it clearly.

The "leading citizens" shall never have opportunity to laugh at me for doing drill "stunts" they would not do themselves and for going to a war they could not be induced to go to themselves. Moreover, no member of the working class can ever say that I voluntarily took up arms against my own class.

If, however, years ago, I had joined the militia or the army I should have been entirely innocent of doing voluntary wrong against my class, because I did not understand—then. But it is different now. All is changed now—because I do understand now. And I want you to understand this matter. Indeed we members of the working class should help one another understand. And this book is for that purpose. You will permit me to explain very frankly—won't you?

You will notice that this is a small book*—very much smaller than the vast subject of wholesale murder called war. But kindly remember that this book of suggestions—chiefly suggestions—is written for those, the working class, whose lives are too weary and whose eyes are frequently too full of dust and sweat and tears for them to read large and "learned" works on war. This book is indeed written in behalf of the working class—and the working class only. The lives and loves of the working class, the hopes and the happiness of the working class, the blood and tears of the working class are too sacred to be viciously wasted as they have been wasted and are wasted by the crafty kings, tsars, presidents, emperors, and the industrial tyrants of the earth.

This book contains no flattery.

We are flattered too much—by cunning people.

Flattery confuses most people. Flattery blinds us, and that is why business men and their unarmed guardsmen flatter the working people.

A multitude of intelligent honey bees can be confused, hopelessly confused, at swarming time, simply by beating an empty tin pan or drum near them and calling loudly the almost patriotically stupid word, "Boowah! Boowah! Woowah! Woowah!" And, indeed, down on the old home farm in Ohio

---

* The present wholly unpretentious book has a distinct purpose (announced in the Preface and also on this page), and has, too, it is hoped, an effective plan and method for the realization of that purpose. Readers in search of conventionally elaborated theses on war are referred, for suggestions, to Chapter Twelve, Sections 8 and 9.

we often "brainstormed" our swarming bees by just such simple means—in order to hold them in slavery and thus have them near and tame. We wished to rob them when they worked—later on.

This device works perfectly in human society also. The capitalist class use this method with great success on the human honey bees, the working class.

Millions of intelligent working men can be confused—and more easily robbed later on—simply by flattering them carefully and then beating a drum near them and cunningly calling out the pleasingly empty words, "The Flag! The Flag! Patriotism! Patriotism! Brave boys!"

Bewildered moths rush into a flame of fire because it *is* bright. Bewildered working people rush to war and singe their own happiness, snuff out their own lives—like moths— because war is *painted* bright. In the shining candle flame moths virtually commit suicide. In the glittering "glory" of war multitudes of the working class practically commit suicide. This will be clearer to you as you read these chapters.

Brother, let me help you tear the mask off this legalized outrage against the working class, this huge and *"glorious"* crime called war. At this horrible "Death's feast" we working people spit in one another's faces, we scream in wild rage at one another, we curse and kill our own working class brothers, we foolishly wallow in our own blood and desolate our own homes—simply because we are craftily ordered to do so. Thus we are both savage and ridiculous. Ridiculous did I say? Yes, ridiculous. That word ridiculous sounds like a harsh word—doesn't it? But, remember, in *all* wars the working class are always meanly belittled, wronged—outraged.

We are the plucked geese in January—patriotically.

When we working people hear a fife and drum and see some handsomely dressed, well-fed military officers and see their long butcher-knives called swords—our confused hearts beat fast, our blood becomes blindly and suicidally hot and eager. . . . Look out, brother! Take care! Remember: Always in all wars everywhere the working class are confused, bewildered—then shrewd people make tools, mules, fools, and foot-stools of us!

"Follow the flag!" sounds good—but strikes blind the working class.

"Follow the flag!" sounds brave and grand. Very.

"Follow the flag!" is wine for the brain—of the working class.

"Follow the flag!" makes millions of our class blind and useable.

"Follow the flag!" stirs a savage passion cunningly called "patriotism."

"Follow the flag!" *never* confuses a man wearing a silk hat.

"Follow the flag!" is bait laid for fools, "rot" fed to mules, by every tyrant king, tsar and president at the head of governments used by the industrial ruling class.*

Governments—to-day under capitalism—are composed of "leading citizens."

These "leading-citizen" governments quarrel over business —markets and territory.

Being proud, these "leading-citizen" governments pompously decide to "protect their honor"—their alleged honor— "at *any* cost."

Lacking sufficient brains, they can not settle their quarrel with brains.

Reverting to savagery, they decide that "might makes right."

Being brutal, they decide to "fight it out."

Being cowards, they decide to avoid personal danger—to themselves.

Knowing the working class are gullibly useable, these "leading-citizen" governments decide to use the *workingmen* as fists.

Being crafty, they decide to *seize the brain* of the toiler— to *teach* the working class:

To follow the flag—automatically—that is, patriotically

---

* "An' you'll die like a fool of a soldier.

Fool, fool, fool of a soldier."—Rudyard Kipling: "The Young British Soldier," in *Ballads.*

To follow the flag—blindly—tho' "leading citizens" do *not* follow the flag into bloody danger

To follow the flag—blindly—cheered by silk-hatted cowards

To follow the flag—blindly—*no matter where it goes, no matter how unjust the war may be*

To follow the flag—blindly—tho' the working class fighters are to be given no voice in declaring the war

To follow the flag—"patriotically"—like slaves defending masters who buy and sell them as chattels—"patriotically"—like ancient serfs defending the very landlords who robbed the serfs, insulted their wives and raped their daughters

To follow the flag—brainlessly—like dumb cattle following a "trick" bull to the bloody shambles of the slaughter house

To follow the flag, brainlessly, as a frog will swallow a bait of red calico loaded with a deadly fish-hook

To follow the flag, automatically, to the horrors and hell of the firing line—automatically, to the flaming cannon's mouth and there butcher other workingmen and be butchered by other workingmen who are also—automatically—following another flag—like fools used as fists for cowards.

And the leading citizens have indeed succeeded in doing what they decided to do. They have had us taught DISASTROUSLY.

Patriotically we have worn the yoke throughout the centuries—centuries sad with tears and red with blood and fire.

Patriotically for thousands of years we have stormed the world with the cannon's roar—but never won a real victory for *our* class.

And for a hundred years—when we could vote—we have stupidly followed the political crook to the ballot-box, and then we have meekly teased for laws, whined for relief, and humbly coaxed the "reformer."

Gullibly we swallow the traducer's lies that paralyze our brains, bind our wrists, and lay us under the employer's lash.

Deafened and stunned with a fool's "hurrah," we wade

in our own blood while those we love are broken in the embrace of despair.

And when on strike for bread and for the betterment of the women and the little children, blindly on horseback we ride down and club one another, blindly we bayonet one another at the factory, blindly we crush one another at the mines, blindly with Gatling guns we sweep the streets and hills with storms of lead and steel, and in a thousand ways blindly our class destroy our class in the bitter and stupid civil war in capitalist industry—cheaply we lend and rent ourselves for our own ruin.

Ah, my friend, there is a political earthquake coming which will swallow up the political prostitutes and the industrial parasites and Caesars of society—when our class open wide their eyes and see the great red crime—not only on the battlefield, but around the factory and before the miner's cabin door. Not blindly but proudly and defiantly the workers will then—but not till then—defend THEMSELVES.

This book is not a parasite's platitudes, nor a hypocrite's pretenses in a Fakir's Parliament; this book is not a tearful lament about war nor a long-winded essay on militarism, nor a coward's whine for peace.

This book is not intended to be harsh; it is frankly intended to be a short, shrill call: "Danger!" and also a guide-board for the producer's road to power.

Too long, too madly and sadly, too gullibly the flim-flammed working class have broken their own hearts and wet the earth with their own blood and tears; too meekly and weakly the toilers sweat themselves into stupidity and then—like cheated children—gullibly hand over the choicest culture, clothing, bread, wine and shelter to the robbers and rulers who despise them and betray them.

What for?

They have the habit.

O, my brothers of the working class, no matter what language you speak, no matter what God you worship, no matter how bitterly you would curse those who would teach you and rouse you—wherever you are, in the barracks or in the mines, in the armories or in the mills, in the trenches at the front or in the furrows on the farm—let us clasp hands— *as a class.* Let us talk over this matter. And in talking it over among ourselves let us be frank. We must be very frank. And let us be friends. Even as I write this, mighty fleets of gun-laden ships of steel are steaming up and down the seas provoking, insulting, challenging war; and in several parts of the world thousands of our working class brothers are slaughtering one another in wars *they* did not declare, and they do so simply because they do not understand one another; and they do not understand one another because THEY HAVE NEVER TALKED THIS MATTER OVER AMONG THEMSELVES in friendly frankness—like brothers, without flattery and without bitterness toward one another.

As you and I consider this matter now by ourselves and for ourselves, we may for a moment—just for a moment—disagree somewhat; but if we do disagree, let us disagree without bitterness toward one another. Let us remember that we are class brothers, and permit nothing to injure our friendship or class loyalty. Some things concerning war must be said plainly—even bluntly—things neither flattering nor complimentary to anybody. Remember, too, that a flattering friend is a dangerous friend. Therefore I refuse to flatter you.

Stamp this into your brain: The *working* class must defend the *working* class. In national and international fellowship we must stand together *as a class* in *class* loyalty.

And now, first thing, let us get an idea of what war (one phase of the great class struggle) is—for *our* class. But before reading the next chapter on "What Is War?" examine the photograph of hell here following:

"They say there are a great many mad men in our army as well as in the enemy's. [In the Russian and the Japanese armies.] Four lunatic wards have been opened [in the hospital]. . . .

"The wire, chopped through at one end, cut the air and coiled itself around three soldiers. The barbs tore their uniforms and stuck into their bodies, and, shrieking, the soldiers, coiled round like snakes, spun round in a frenzy . . . . whirling and rolling over each other. . . . No less than two thousand men were lost in that one wire entanglement. While they were hacking at the wire and getting

entangled in its serpentine coils, they were pelted by an incessant
rain of balls and grapeshot. . . . It was very terrifying, and if only
they had known in which direction to run, that attack would have
ended in a panic flight. But ten or twelve continuous lines of wire,
and the struggle with it, a whole labyrinth of pitfalls with stakes
driven at the bottom, had muddled them so that they were quite
incapable of defining the direction of escape.

"Some, like blind men, fell into funnel-shaped pits, and hung upon
these sharp stakes, twitching convulsively and dancing like toy
clowns; they were crushed down by fresh bodies, and soon the whole
pit filled to the edges, and presented a writhing mass of bleeding
bodies, dead and living. Hands thrust themselves out of it in all
directions, the fingers working convulsively, catching at everything;
and those who once got caught in that trap could not get back
again: hundreds of fingers, strong and blind, like the claws of a
lobster, gripped them firmly by the legs, caught at their clothes,
threw them down upon themselves, gouged out their eyes and
throttled them. Many seemed as if they were intoxicated, and ran
straight at the wire, got caught in it, and remained shrieking, until
a bullet finished them. . . . Some swore dreadfully, others laughed
when the wire caught them by the arm or leg and died there and
then. . . .

"We walked along . . . . and with each step we made, that wild,
unearthly groan . . . . grew ominously, as if it was the red air, the
earth and sky that were groaning. . . . We could almost feel the
distorted mouths from which those terrible sounds were issuing
. . . . a loud, calling, crying groan. . . . All those dark mounds
stirred and crawled about with out-spread legs like half-dead lobsters
let out of a basket. . . .

"The train was full, and our clothes were saturated with blood,
as if we had stood for a long time under a rain of blood, while the
wounded were still being brought in. . . .

"Some of the wounded crawled up themselves, some walked up
tottering and falling. One soldier almost ran up to us. His face
was smashed, and only one eye remained, burning wildly and terribly. He was almost naked. . . .

"The ward was filled with a broad, rasping, crying groan, and
from all sides pale, yellow, exhausted faces, some eyeless, some so
monstrously mutilated that it seemed as if they had returned from
hell, turned toward us.

"I was beginning to get exhausted, and went a little way off to
. . . . rest a bit. The blood, dried to my hands, covered them like a
pair of black gloves, making it difficult for me to bend my fingers." *

* Andreief: *The Red Laugh*, passim. (Russian-Japanese War
literature. Published by J. Fisher Unwin, London.)

Would it not be a strange thing to see a banker, a bishop, a railway president, a coal baron, an anti-labor injunction judge, and a United States Senator all hanging on stakes in a pit with scores of other men piled in on top of them—all clawing, kicking, cursing, wiggling, screaming, groaning, bleeding, dying—*"following the flag"*—patriotically?

Such would indeed be a strange and interesting sight.

Strange and interesting, extremely so—but *absolutely impossible.*

And there is good reason.

Let me explain.

CHAPTER TWO.

What Is War?

WAR is wholesale, scientific suicide for the working class under orders from their political and industrial masters.

War is:

For working class homes—emptiness,

For working class wives—heartache,

For working class mothers—loneliness,

For working class children—orphanage,

For working class sweethearts—agony,

For the nation's choicest working class men—broken health or death,

For society—savagery,

For peace—defeat,

For bull-dogs—suggestions,

For the Devil—delight,

For death—a harvest,

For buzzards—a banquet,

For the grave—victory,

For worms—a feast,

For nations—debts,

For justice—nothing,

For "Thou shalt not kill"—boisterous laughter,

For literature—the realism of the slaughter house,

For the painter—the immortalization of wholesale murder,

For the public park—a famous butcher in stone or bronze,

For Roosevelts—opportunity to strut and brag of blood, and win a "war record" for political purposes,

For Bryans—a military title and a "war record" for political purposes,

For Christ—contempt,

For "Put up thy sword"—a sneer,

For preachers, on both sides,—ferocious prayers for victory,

For Sunday-school teachers—blood-steaming stories for tender children and helplessly impressible boys,

For bankers—bonds, interest (and working class substitutes),

For big manufacturers—business, profits (and working class substitutes),

For big business men of all sorts—"good times" (and working-class substitutes),

For leading business men, for leading politicians, for leading preachers, for leading educators, for leading editors, for leading lecturers—for all of these windy patriots who talk bravely of war, who talk heroically of the flag, who talk finely of national honor and talk and talk of the glory of battle—for all these yawping talkers—never positions as privates in the infantry on the firing line *up close* where they are really likely to get their delicately perfumed flesh torn to pieces.

Thus war is hell for the WORKING class.*

It is, of course, true that in ancient times the leading citizens did much of the fighting—but that was very long ago, in the days when the machine-gun had not yet been dreamed of. Even two thousand years ago the plutocratic snobs were beginning to show traces of intelligence sufficient to avoid going to hell voluntarily—afoot.

Says Professor E. A. Ross :†

"Service in the Roman cavalry, originally obligatory on all who could furnish two horses, became after a time a badge of superiority. 'Young men of rank more and more withdrew from the infantry, and the legionary cavalry became a close aristocratic corps'. . . . Finally the rich came to feel that wealth ought to buy its possessors clear of every onerous duty. In Caesar's time 'in the soldiery not a trace of the better classes could any longer be discovered . . . . the levy took place in the most irregular and unfair manner. Numerous persons liable to serve were wholly passed over. . . . The Roman burgess

---

* See Chapter Seven ("For Father and the Boys"), Sections 14, 15, 16—"Were not some of the rich men of to-day soldiers at one time?"

† *The Foundations of Sociology,* pp. 220-221.

cavalry now merely vegetated as a sort of mounted noble guard, whose perfumed cavaliers and exquisite high-bred horses only played a part in the festivals of the capital; the so-called burgess infantry was a troop of mercenaries, swept together from the lowest ranks of the burgess population.' "

At present a movement is being promoted by Harvard University authorities to organize in the University "a fashionable troop of cavalry."* It does not seem likely that many members of the labor unions, so heartily despised by scab-praising ex-president Eliot, will be able to join this "fashionable troop of cavalry." The labor unionists on strike, unarmed and helpless, may later come in handy as targets for practice by the highly educated "fashionable troop of cavalry."

After all is "said and done" concerning wars past and present—what is really determined by a so-called great war?

Which of two warring nations is the nobler—is that what a war decides?

Not at all.

Which of the two bleeding nations is the more refined—is the more sensitive to the cry for justice, or has the greater literature, or the keener appreciation of the fine arts, or is more devoted to the useful arts and sciences, or contributes most to the profounder philosophy—which of the two warring nations is the more truly civilized—is that what is decided by war?

Not at all.

Which of the struggling nations is the more wholesomely social? Does a war make that evident?

Not at all.

Which nation has the better cause? Is that, then, what a war decides?

Not at all.

Which nation does more for the progress of mankind? Is that made clear by a war?

Not at all.

A war decides no such questions.

---

* See New York *World*, Nov. 21, 1909. Also Chapter Eight, Section 16.

Well, then, what is determined when two nations go to war?

Simply this:—*which can make the better fight.*

That is all.

And that is exactly what is determined when two sharks fight, or when two tom-cats, or two bull pups fight, or when a cruel hawk and a sweet-throated song bird fight: which is superior *as a fighter.*

War is the ignoble trick of slitting open the blood vessels of the excited working class to "satisfy" the "honor" and save the pride and business of crowned and uncrowned cowards of the ruling class. There never is a war and never can be a war till the *working* men are willing to do the marching, the trench-digging and the actual fighting, bleeding and dying. And the working men are never willing to butcher and be butchered wholesale till influential but coarse-grained people of the capitalist class or "highly educated" panderers to the capitalist class, craftily or ignorantly *excite* the humble toilers to the fiend's stupid mood of savage hate. First come the "powerful editorials," the "great speeches," the "eloquent sermons," and ferocious prayers for the war; then the fife and drum; then the brain-storm of the humble, humbugged working men; then the recruiting; then the hand-waving and "Good-bye, boys, good-bye, good-bye"; then the butchering and the blood; then the tears and taxes.

It is, of course, true—grandly true—and is here gladly, gratefully acknowledged—that some educated influential people are too highly civilized, too finely noble, to stoop to the shameless business of rousing the slumbering tiger in the human breast. Some of them proudly scorn the vicious rôle of throwing fire-brands into the inflammable imagination of the weary toilers. These have courage—true courage. These we greet with profound gratitude.

But every lily-fingered snob, every socially gilt-edged coward, every intellectual prostitute, every pro-war preacher, every self-exempting political shark, and every well-fed money-glutton, who dares help excite the working class for the hell of war—these, every one of these—in case of war, should be forced to dance on the firing line to the hideous music of the cannon's roar till his own torn carcass decorates a "great battle" field.

And to this end—as part of their own emancipation—the working class should make all haste to seize the powers of government, and thus be in position, by being in legal possession of the power, to make and enforce all laws concerning war. Beginning *now,* always hereafter, the labor unions, the working class political party, and all the other working class organizations should *for future use,* keep a *careful record* of all male editors, teachers, preachers, lawyers, lecturers, and "prominent business men" and politicians and "statesmen," who *speak,* or *write* or even *clap their hands* in favor of war; and in case of a war thus fostered, these, all of these, should be forced by *special draft* to fight in the infantry, without promotion, on the firing line, till *they* get *their* share of the cold lead and the cold steel. Thus let the mouthers do the marching, let the shouters do the shooting, let the bawlers do the bleeding, let the howlers have the hell—force them to the firing line and force them to stay on the firing line—and there will be far less yawping about the "honor" and the "glory" of war, and there will be fewer humble homes of the poor damned with the desolation of war.

But, you see, for all such self-defense the working *class* must as soon as possible capture the powers of government. You see that, don't you?

Friend, don't curse the militiamen and the soldiers. No, no. They are our brothers. Explain—with tireless patience explain—to them that the capitalists seek to make tools and bullet-stoppers of them. Explain it like a brother inside and outside the ranks till our working-class brothers everywhere—inside and outside the ranks—are roused to a clear consciousness of the meaning of a Gatling gun with a working-class "man behind the gun" and a working-class man in front of the gun.

Brother, stamp this into your brain and *explain it into the brain of our brothers:*—The *working* class must themselves protect the *working* class.

If in imagination the mothers, sisters, sweethearts and wives of the world could get the roar of the cannon in their ears and feel the splash of blood in their faces, could see and hear the horrors of the battlefield and the agonies of the war hospital, they would never again be fooled into smiling caressingly upon the haughty and jaunty "higher officers," when, like peacocks, these gilt-braided professional human butchers strut through the ball-rooms and through the streets on military dress parade, and these women would also regard the pro-war orator with complete contempt.

The women of the world owe a great debt of gratitude to the writers of some powerful pen pictures of war. The terrible but accurate realism of some of their descriptions of war makes one hate the word war. Emile Zola's story, *The Downfall,** is crowded with these pictures. *The Downfall* should be in a million American private libraries. Following is a page of Zola's flashlights from the battlefields of the Franco-Prussian War, 1870-71 :†

"At no time during the day had the artillery thundered more loudly than now. . . . It was as if all the forces of the nether regions had been unchained; the earth shook, the heavens were on fire. The ring of flame-belching mouths of bronze that encircled Sedan, the eight hundred cannon of the German armies . . . . were expending their energies on the adjacent fields. . . . The crash that told of ruin and destruction was heard. . . . Some lay face downward with their mouths in a pool of blood, in danger of suffocating, others had bitten the ground till their mouths were full of dry earth, others, where a shell had fallen among a group, were a confused, intertwined heap of mangled limbs and crushed trunks. . . . Some soldiers who were driving a venerable lady from her home had compelled her to furnish matches with which to fire her own beds and curtains. Lighted by blazing brands and fed by petroleum in floods, fires were rising and spreading in every quarter; it was no longer civilized warfare, but a conflict of savages, maddened by the long-protracted

---

* Excellent English translation published by The Macmillan Company, New York. Excerpt printed with kind permission of publishers.

† In Chapter Five, "Hell," Section 1, "Modern Murdering Machinery," is plenty of proof that since the war of 1870-71 the slaughtering equipment has been improved *horribly*—more than a hundredfold. See Index: "Franco-Prussian War."

strife, wreaking vengeance for their dead, their heaps of dead, upon whom they trod at every step they took. Yelling, shouting bands traversed the streets amid the scurrying smoke and falling cinders, swelling the hideous uproar into which entered sounds of every kind: shrieks, groans, the rattle of musketry, the crash of falling wall. Men could scarce see one another; great livid clouds drifted athwart the sun and obscured his light, bearing with them an intolerable stench of soot and blood, heavy with the abominations of the slaughter. In every quarter the work of death and destruction still went on: the human brute unchained, the imbecile wrath, the mad fury, of man devouring his brother man. . . . Horses were rearing, pawing the air, and falling backward; men were dismounted as if torn from their saddle by the blast of a tornado, while others, shot through some vital part, retained their seats and rode onward in the ranks with vacant, sightless eyes. . . . Some there were who had fallen headlong from their saddle and buried their face in the soft earth. Others had alighted on their back and were staring up into the sun with terror-stricken eyes that seemed bursting from their sockets. There was a handsome black horse, an officer's charger, that had been disemboweled, and was making frantic efforts to rise, his fore feet entangled in his entrails. . . . Of the brave men who rode into action that day two-thirds remained upon the battlefield. . . . A lieutenant from whose mouth exuded a bloody froth, had been tearing up the grass by handfuls in his agony, and his stiffened fingers were still buried in the ground. A little farther on a captain, prone on his stomach, had raised his head to vent his anguish in yells and screams, and death had caught and fixed him in that strange attitude. . . . After that the road led along the brink of a little ravine, and there they beheld a spectacle that aroused their horror to the highest pitch as they looked down into the chasm, into which an entire company seemed to have been blown by the fiery blast; it was choked with corpses, a landslide, an avalanche of maimed and mutilated men, bent and twisted in an inextricable tangle, who with convulsed fingers had caught at the yellow clay of the bank to save themselves in their descent, fruitlessly. And a dusky flock of ravens flew away, croaking noisily, and swarms of flies, thousands upon thousands of them, attracted by the odor of fresh blood, were buzzing over the bodies and returning incessantly."

But let this fact burn its way into your brain to save you from hell and rouse you for the revolution—this fact:

NOWHERE ON ALL THAT BATTLEFIELD AMONG THE SHATTERED RIFLES AND WRECKED CANNON, AMONG THE BROKEN AMBULANCES AND SPLINTERED AMMUNITION WAGONS, NO-

WHERE IN THE MIRE AND MUSH OF BLOOD AND SAND,
NOWHERE AMONG THE BULGING AND BEFOULING CARCASSES
OF DEAD HORSES AND THE SWELLING CORPSES OF DEAD MEN
AND BOYS—NOWHERE COULD BE FOUND THE TORN, BLOATED
AND FLY-BLOWN CARCASSES OF BANKERS, BISHOPS, POLITI-
CIANS, "BRAINY CAPITALISTS" AND OTHER ELEGANT AND EMI-
NENT "VERY BEST PEOPLE."

Well, hardly.

Naturally—such people were not there, *on the firing line*
—up where bayonets gleam, sabres flash; flesh is ripped, bones
snap, brains are dashed and blood splashes.

WHY NOT?

Note carefully bottom of page 28.

CHAPTER THREE.

The Situation—Also the Explanation.

The situation, the "lay of the land," must be clearly seen by every member of the working class who wishes to help himself and his fellow workers avoid the vicious sacrifice of the working class by the capitalist class.

In Chapter Ten of this book the unsocial nature of the present form and structure of society is explained more fundamentally; but just here notice the clash of *class* interests in a war. War is a "good thing" for one class and war is simply hell for the other class.

Who *want* war?—What for?

Who *declare* war?—What for?

Who *fight* the wars?—What for?

Get these questions straight in your mind. First study the Situation; then the Explanation. Now for the Situation. Here it is:

CAPITALISTS—"CAPTAINS OF INDUSTRY"—"LEADING CITIZENS":—

"We *want* war.

"Mr. Wage-Earner, it is none of *your* business *why* we business men want war. You are impudent even to inquire about such things. Little boys and working men should be seen and not heard. You poor deluded wage-earner, you just keep right on working and sweating till *we* have *you* ordered to the front.

"Ha, ha, when we business men want a war we have a war—whether the working people like it or don't like it. We just show them some bright-colored calico and urge them to *follow the flag.* Then they promptly get 'behind the gun' (also in front of the gun). They like it all right—we have 'em taught to like it.

"They are so easy."

S<small>TATESMEN</small>—P<small>OLITICIANS</small>—"L<small>EADING</small> C<small>ITIZENS</small>":—

"We *declare* war.

"Mr. Wage-Earner, don't you ask any impertinent questions about *why* we statesmen declare war. That's *our* business. Attend to your own business—working—just working and sweating—till we statesmen order you to the front and 'sic' you on some other working people somewhere. When we conclude to declare war, we don't consult the working men's wishes. We simply don't have to.

"They are so easy."

W<small>ORKING</small> C<small>LASS</small> B<small>ROTHERS</small>—O<small>FF</small> <small>FOR THE</small> F<small>RONT</small>—T<small>O</small> K<small>ILL</small> "<small>THE</small> E<small>NEMY</small>," T<small>HEIR</small> W<small>ORKING</small> C<small>LASS</small> B<small>ROTHERS</small>:

"We *fight* the wars.

"Friend, please *don't ask us* to explain why we fight the wars. We really do not know why we fight the wars. We modern wage-earners do just as the ancient chattel slaves and serfs did. We meekly do as we are told to do by the 'best people.' The sleek, glossy folks tell us to 'rush to the front'—so we meekly march right to the front and blaze away. We furnish the tears, blood, cripples and corpses. We are dead easy—and we don't understand it at all. Of course, we don't like to shoot and bayonet one another. It seems so strange to us that the working men should always be ordered to shoot working men;—but our 'betters,' our 'social superiors,' the 'men with the brains,' tell us to 'show the *stuff* that is in us' —so it must be all right. Great business men tell us frequently, 'What this country needs is confidence.' Well, we working people have the confidence—also the blisters and the lemons and the cold lead.

"We are so easy."

THE EXPLANATION.*

(A)—C<small>APITALISTS</small> <small>WANT</small> <small>WAR</small>—<small>BECAUSE</small>—
War sends up prices—of most things.

* On the historical *origin* of war and of the working class, see Chapter Eleven.

LEADING CITIZENS: "WE *want* WARS"

War stimulates business—makes business brisk;—the more blood the more business.

War means more investments and more profits;—the more blood the more bonds, more interest; more land and more rent;—more unearned income.

War helps solve the problem of the unemployed. Simply have the surplus workers go into a big field and kill themselves off—butcher one another. It is so simple and easy.

War makes the working people clap their hands and yell so loudly they can't think, and as long as the working people don't *think,* it is *easy* to keep the bridles and saddles on them. It is surely a thoughtful scheme;—really, it is successful.

War—to advocate war, sometimes makes newspapers vastly more popular and therefore more profitable; for recent example, the Hearst papers for the Cuban war and the English jingo papers in the Boer war.*

War makes a larger home market for toys; that is, for fifes and drums with which the working people excite one another and get themselves into a butchering mood,—"ready to die for their homes and country," the United States, for example, in which far more than half of all the people have

---

* "The modern newspaper is a Roman arena, a Spanish bull-fight and an English prize fight rolled into one. The popularization of the power to read has made the press the chief instrument of brutality. For a half penny every man, woman and child can stimulate and feed those lusts of blood and physical cruelty which it is the chief aim of civilization to repress and which in their literal modes of realization have been assigned . . . to soldiers, butchers, sportsmen, and a few other trained professions. . . . The most momentous lesson of the [Boer] war is its revelation of the methods by which a knot of men, financiers and politicians can capture the mind of the nation, arouse its passion and impose a policy."—John A. Hobson: *The Psychology of Jingoism,* pp. 29 and 107.

"The Bourses [the European Wall Streets] of the West have made Cairo and Alexandria hunting-grounds for their speculation. Their class owns or influences half the Press of Europe. It influences, and sometimes makes, half the Governments of Europe."—Frederic Harrison: *National and Social Problems,* p. 208. See also John Bascom: *Social Theories,* pp. 100-116; and W. J. Ghent: *Our Benevolent Feudalism,* Chapter 7.

OUR LAWMAKERS.

LEADING CITIZENS: "WE *declare* WARS"

no homes of their own and live in rented houses, and more than one-eighth of all the people live in mortgaged homes,* and in which nearly all of the working class are kept so poor that they can't even have cream—real cream and plenty of it —for their cheap coffee. The fife and drum and some patriotic wind stampede the working class easily.

"A nod from a lord is a breakfast for a fool."

War—you see in a war soldiers produce nothing, but they consume and destroy vast quantities of many things. Thus soldiers in war create a larger market—though they create nothing whatever for that market. This is fine for those capitalists whose puny souls can hope and plan for nothing higher than more markets—and thus have more opportunity to sweat more wage-earners simply in order to make more profits. Funerals look good to the coffin trust and the undertaker, and war looks good to the capitalist class.

War—PREPARATION for war on the huge scale of the present day—furnishes a market for an enormous amount of commodities for sale by the capitalist class, such as steel, clothing, leather products, lumber, food products, horses, and the like. True, these things are worse than wasted; but just as the capitalist class are willing to destroy part of the coffee crop—in Brazil, for example—in order to keep up the price for profit's sake, so also are the capitalist class willing to fan the flames of war and urge "preparation for war," vast and senseless "preparation for war," in order to have a market into which to dump at a profit immense stores of commodities.

"There is money in it."

War is a means of opening up or protecting, for modern capitalistic exploitation, new territory, such as Egypt, Algeria, Madagascar, South Africa, India, Alaska, The Philippines, Borneo, Hawaii, Cuba, Porto Rico, China, Korea.

United States Senator A. J. Beveredge puts the matter thus:†

"Every progressive nation in Europe today is seeking new lands to colonize and governments to administer."

---

* Census Report, 1900. Vol. II., p. cxcii.

† *The Meaning of the Times*, p. 131.

CITIZENS WHO ARE LED: "WE *fight* THE WARS"

J. H. Rose :*

"In short, the crystallization of national existence at home has necessitated the eager exploitation of new lands which forms so noteworthy a feature of the life of today."

Thus John Jay :†

"It is too true, however disgraceful it may be to human nature, that nations will make war whenever they have a prospect of getting anything by it."

Alexandre Hamilton sneers thus at the windy blood-for-profit statesmen :‡

"Has commerce hitherto done anything more than change the objects of war? Is not the love of wealth as domineering and enterprising a passion as that of power or glory? Have not there been as many wars founded upon commercial motives since that has become the prevailing system of nations as were before occasioned by the cupidity of territory or dominion? Has not the spirit of commerce, in many instances, administered new incentives to the appetite, both for the one and for the other?"

Professor Simon N. Patten (University of Pennsylvania) states the case bluntly :§

"Most nations have been formed by conquest, and have therefore started with a dominant and a subject class. The former seize the surplus, and force the latter to work for a bare minimum."

The New York *World* is commendably frank concerning this matter :‖

"Commerce and conquest have always been the main causes of war. Back of most slogans of strife has ever been the commercial watchword—'trade follows the flag.' "

As illustrations of wars due to economic causes, *The World* mentions the wars of Venice and Genoa, The Crusades, our

---

* *The Development of the European Nations*, 1870-1900, Vol. II., p. 333.

† *The Federalist*, Number 4. (The numbering of *The Federalist* papers varies slightly in different editions.)

‡ *The Federalist*, Number 6.

§ *The Theory of Prosperity*, p. 4.

‖ Editorial, Oct. 13, 1909.

French-and-Indian-War, the American Revolutionary War, and the American Civil War.

General Fred D. Grant, of the United States Army, threw this into the teeth of the lard-and-tallow magnates:*

"It is your statesmen and your people that create wars. First the people become irritated, generally through some commercial transaction. The statesmen then take hold of the matter and they compromise, or try to, if the nations are nearly equal. If they are not nearly equal the stronger one slaps the weaker one in the face and the soldier is then called in to settle the matter."

War *tightens the grip* of the industrial ruling class on the working class at home and all over the world.

War—mark this—war absolutely concentrates public attention upon *one thing,* the war, the events of the battlefield. This gives the crafty capitalists a *perfect opportunity to sneak,* to do things in the dark, while the people are "not looking," opportunity to slip into city council chambers, state legislatures and national legislatures, and there get "good things"— charters, contracts, franchises and other profitable privileges.

Here is the substance of the matter:

Under capitalism the worker's *consuming* power is *arbitrarily restricted.* Under a CLASS-labor system the worker's life is always arbitrarily repressed, the worker is FORCED TO PRODUCE MORE THAN HE IS PERMITTED TO CONSUME, leaving a SURPLUS for the ruling class. Under chattel slavery, of course, the slave's life was arbitrarily restricted by his master. The chattel slave was a human animal used to produce his "keep"—*and a surplus.* Of course you see that—don't you? Under serfdom the serf's life was arbitrarily restricted by his landlord-and-master. The serf was a human animal used to produce his "keep"—*and a surplus.* That's easy to see, isn't it? And now under capitalism the *wage*-earner's life is arbitrarily restricted, limited, by his employer-master who allows the wage-earner a reward called *wages.* The wage-earner is used as a human animal to produce his "keep"— a living for himself and his family—*and a surplus.*

* May 5, 1909, Chicago, Illinois, at banquet given by the Chicago Association of Commerce; Press reports.

NOTICE: *wages* will not buy *plenty* of excellent food. *Wages* will not buy *plenty* of good clothing. *Wages* will not buy *plenty* of thoroughly good shelter. *Wages* will not buy *plenty* of high-grade furniture. Though the wage-earner is able and willing to produce and does produce all these things abundantly, yet his wages will not permit him to *consume* these things abundantly. *Wages* will *not* buy as much value as wage-paid labor produces.

Thus there is a surplus.

If you will think about this a moment (if you will *think*) you will understand how it is that a glossy, well-fed employer often smilingly asserts that "there is prosperity—times are good —no cause for complaint," and so forth—even tho millions of the poor are in sore want. You see *he* can smile as gently and fraternally as a hyena—*he feels good;* he can smile as long as there is that surplus. That's his. It's lovely—for him.

Surplus—fascinating surplus.

Surplus—for "our very *best* people."

". . . . . As soon [in the evolution of human industry] as the amount produced began at all to exceed the immediate requirements of life, the struggle commenced for the possession of the surplus. The methods employed were as varied as the human mind was fertile."[*]

Not alone chattel slaves and serfs, but *wage*-slaves also, are used simply, only, *always*, as domesticated *human animals* to produce a surplus for their masters.

Slavery was a surplus game.

Serfdom was a surplus game.

Capitalism is also a surplus game.

By pinching, repressing, restricting the wage-earner's life the capitalist employer skims off a surplus. By *belittling* the wage-earner's life the employer *increases* his own life—with the surplus *legally* filched from the life of the wage-earner.

The wage-worker, under capitalism, is forced by the lash of threatening starvation, forced by the fear of the bayonet, forced by the threat of the injunction court—is forced to produce a surplus.

---

[*] Lester F. Ward, *Dynamic Sociology*, Vol. I., p. 582.

Besides producing the *equivalent of his wages* and all other necessary expenses of production the worker is compelled to toil on for weary hours producing for his capitalist employer THIS SURPLUS. (See Note, end of present Chapter.)

This surplus is the sacred wafer of the capitalist.

This surplus is the capitalist's heart's desire.

This surplus is the lode-stone, the purpose, the one and only true god of the capitalist class.

With this surplus the capitalist pays the capitalist's "other expenses," and also pays political party campaign expenses, bribes city councils, state and national legislatures, courts, mayors, governors, and presidents—and precinct captains.

With this surplus the capitalist buys fine wine, beautiful automobiles, yachts, opera boxes, and homes—"and so forth."

With this surplus the capitalist pets and protects his parasitic favorites, male and female.

This sacred surplus.

Sweet and juicy surplus, bubbling, bubbling, ever bubbling up from the well-springs of capitalism—that is, from certain *"sacred" property rights,* the right to own PRIVATELY the industrial FOUNDATIONS OF SOCIETY.

Surplus—stolen life—by means of the *wage*-system legally pumped from the veins of the wage-paid toilers.

Surplus.

Let that word sink deep into your mind.

Fasten your eye upon that surplus.

Now, notice carefully:

First—Part of this surplus the capitalists at present consume personally;

Second—Part of this surplus the capitalists invest profitably;

Third—For a part of this surplus a *foreign* market must be found. Even tho' millions of honest workers whose labor produced this surplus, even tho' these and millions of their wives and children starve and shiver for the use of this surplus—still part of this surplus must be *shipped out of the country.* For the part of the surplus which the capitalist class do not consume personally and cannot invest profitably

—for that part of the surplus a *foreign* market must be had tho' millions suffer and sicken for higher WAGES WITH WHICH TO BUY that surplus which is being shipped abroad. Because your *wages* will not *permit you* to buy and enjoy even that part of the surplus, a *foreign* market must be found *and defended.*

And now we come to the *bayonet and the Gatling gun—* what they are for.

Commit to memory and *discuss with your fellow workers* the following:

Capitalists want soldiers, marines, militia, cossacks, Pinkertons, "coal-and-iron police," and so forth—chiefly for THREE general purposes:

FIRST: To HOLD DOWN the wage-earners and *force them to consent* to produce a surplus,—that is, more than their wages will buy;—or, in other words, to *force them to consent* to produce far more than they are permitted to consume. If the employer can't get a palavering, lying prostitute to wheedle the workers to consent—well, there's the bayonet. See that?

SECOND: To OPEN UP FOREIGN MARKETS for that part of the surplus which the workers are not permitted to consume and the capitalists do not consume personally or invest profitably;

THIRD: To DEFEND THE FOREIGN MARKETS for this part of the surplus.

Professor T. N. Carver (Department of Political Economy, Harvard University) states the case perfectly:*

"WHILE COMPETITION IS ABSENT, COMMERCE IS INDEED A BOND OF PEACE AND GOOD WILL BETWEEN THOSE WHO SELL IN RETURN. BUT THE MOMENT THAT TWO NATIONS EMBARK EXTENSIVELY IN THE SAME LINE OF INDUSTRY, THAT MOMENT COMMERCE BECOMES A SWORD, DIVIDING AND SETTING AT ENMITY THOSE WHO ARE RIVALS FOR THE SAME MARKETS. . . . THE PROSPERITY OF ONE IS THE OTHER'S DESTRUCTION.

---

* *Sociology and Social Progress*, p. 170. Emphasis mine.— G. R. K.

SUCH NATIONS STAND TO EACH OTHER AS TWO INDIAN TRIBES
WHERE THERE IS BUT GAME ENOUGH FOR ONE."

Thus commerce develops into militarism.

A PROTECTIVE TARIFF WALL IS EVIDENCE AND CONFESSION
OF THE EXISTENCE OF EMBARRASSING NATIONAL SURPLUSES OF
PRODUCTS.

The capitalist employer does not wish the wage-earners to
get such things into their minds.

"Don't say a word," caution the capitalists,—"the workers
can't see the point at all. Ha, ha,—all they want is a job.
How meek they are. How lamblike. . . . Just suppose they
should wake up. . . . Here! you flunkies, you bribed lecturers, orators and editors, keep *busy*. Keep right on talking
to the working people. Tell the working class to be satisfied
and humble and contented; preach to them that it will be all
right in the 'sweet bye and bye.' Oh, ha, ha, ha—all right
for the workers *'in the end.'* Don't tell them which end.
Tell the workers that *'something* will turn up, sometime—
sure.' Tell them to be 'patient and *hopeful,'* to 'hope for a
home *over there.'* (See Chapter Eleven.)

"It is a 'cinch.'

"If the workers go on strike to get a small thin slice of the
surplus—why, we CAPITALISTS have the militia, we *capitalists*
have police, we *capitalists* have the cossacks, we *capitalists*
have the mounted State guards, we *capitalists* have the regular
troops and marines, and we *capitalists* also have the injunction
courts and jails and 'bull-pens,'—we *capitalists* have all this
armed, bribed outfit to help us starve the workers back to
their jobs.

"We have a 'sure thing.'

"Lie low. Keep quiet.

*"Let no one speak to the workers about this matter of the
surplus.* The worker who sees that beautiful thing called
surplus, ceases to be a tame, blind thing, a humble lump, contented with only *part* of the product of his labor. . . . But
whatever happens—we business men control the powers of government—and that gives us the use of all the judges in gowns
and all the armed men in khaki we need to *defend our surplus*

game. A meek, satisfied, contented wage-earner is such a useful animal—just as satisfactory as a *chattel* slave. Like the slave, he's willing to produce a surplus. *When he objects we have him whipped and kicked*—with a policeman's club or a bayonet."

Discuss *with your fellow workers* this also:—

Armed men, MORE AND MORE ARMED MEN, must be had *at once* for a new and special reason. A new danger is now growing vast and dark,—like an increasing storm. The *army of the unemployed*—hungry, insulted and angry, not permitted to work, not permitted to produce, not permitted to enjoy, not even permitted to beg,—this army of eager, disgusted, angry men and women are looking through the masters' palace windows, where the masters and their pets feast on good things and sneer at the unemployed. With *modern* machinery, *modern* methods, *modern* knowledge, and *modern* skill the workers can produce *vast* surpluses *so rapidly* that the capitalists *can't dispose of it all promptly either in home markets or foreign markets;* and thus cannot—dare not —employ all the workers all the time all the workers are willing to work. Thus some factories are run part time, some are run reduced force, and thus millions of willing workers are snubbed at the mill, snubbed at the mine, and snubbed at the factory door where they *coax for permission to serve society* by producing useful things. Millions in danger of losing their jobs, millions working part time, millions with wages reduced, millions out of work—millions—these millions are growing restless, fretful, *thoughtful;* the capitalist fears this meek fretfulness and thoughtfulness will GROW into a vast, *loud,* BOLD ROAR OF PROTEST-AND-DEMAND BY THE WORKING CLASS.

Therefore,

Capitalists want more military legislation—and get it.

Capitalists want the strongest, healthiest jobless men to join the militia and the army and be ready to crush the other jobless men, ready to thrust bayonets into the rag-covered breasts of their weaker brothers if they should become loudly desperate with hunger.

Therefore,

Congress in 1907-08, legislating, as usual, in the service of the capitalist class, logically, naturally, obediently, *still further developed* the armed guard—the militia, the army and the navy—the *fighting machine,* the fist of the capitalist class. In March, 1908, the United States Government suddenly opened up many extra recruiting stations in New York City— in the open air in the public parks, where tens of thousands of jobless, discouraged, hungry men were to be found. The recruiting officers' chief argument was "plenty of good food and clothing and not much to do."*

Capitalists want working class militiamen and soldiers, in order also to keep them so flattered and excited about "protecting property" that they won't notice the fact that the armed defenders of property have no property of their own to protect.

It is so simple and easy.

Capitalists do indeed want war and military servants— but the capitalists are too shrewd, too self-respecting, too proud to expose their own well-fed glossy bodies to the modern butchering machinery. In time of war or "labor troubles" these "prominent citizens" stay at home, eat fine food, wear good clothes, sleep in warm dreamy beds—and secretly laugh at the poor hoodwinked fellows on the firing line eating "hard-tack";—they stay at home and plan for more profits— ever more profits from the increasing surplus.

Capitalists band together and stand together. Capitalists are CLASS loyal. The capitalist class even hire working-class men to defend the capitalist class with rifles; shrewdly the employers confuse and hire the working class to get "behind the gun" to murder the working class in front of the gun.

(B)—THE POLITICIANS DECLARE WAR:

Because the capitalists want war.

The politicians are either capitalists themselves or the political lackeys of the capitalists; and these ignoble flunkies take their pay in offices and opportunities to get graft. The

---

* See Index: "Recruiting."

capitalists pay the campaign expenses of their political flunkies, and, of course, whenever the capitalists *want* war their political flunkey prostitutes *declare* war.* After the war, on great public occasions, the politicians serve up some oratorically noisy nonsense to the widows and orphans and the poor old broken-down veterans about the "glory" of the war— about the grandeur of slaughtering and being slaughtered. Right here is where the fun comes in for the politicians, and sometimes for *some* ministers,—in seeing an opera-houseful or a groveful of working men clap their hands together and yell when the politicians, or some ministers, sometimes, whoop and yawp and tell the working class all about the glory and grandeur of war. No wonder the politicians secretly laugh. How stupidly ridiculous!

The glory of brothers butchering and being butchered—by themselves!

To "declare war" makes statesmen and rulers popular. In our own country "war" presidents, "war" governors, "war" congressmen, *are almost invariably re-elected.*

"The temptations of party politicians are of many kinds. . . . The worst is the temptation to war. . . . Many wars have been begun or have been prolonged in order to consolidate a dynasty or a party; in order to give it popularity or at least to save it from unpopularity; in order to divert the minds of men from internal questions which have become embarrassing, or to efface the memory of past quarrels, mistakes or crimes. Experience unfortunately shows only too clearly how the combative passion can be aroused and how much popularity can be gained from a successful war."†

Politicians do not join the militia and the army for actual service on the firing line—oh, no! No, thank you. They pass laws "to make the service attractive"—but they are so very careful not to let the attractions attract them.

The fact is, my friend, the "cold shoulder" from superior officers, and cold victuals, cold tents, cold lead, cold steel, and a puny fifteen or twenty dollars per month for murdering and being murdered—and the cold, cold ground for their

---

* For excellent example, see Chapter VI: "Tricked to the Trenches—Then Snubbed," Fifth Illustration.

† W. E. Lecky: *The Map of Life,* pp. 153-54.

own cold corpses—with infinite heartache, sighs, sobs, tears, and loneliness for their own dear ones—these things have *no* attraction for the shrewd men who profit by war and the crafty men who declare war.

Capitalist statesmen—that is, small men with big manners —politicians of the capitalist class, politicians financed by and for the capitalist class—these all band together, stand together. The capitalist *"reformer"* always stands for CAPITALISM—tho' he is willing to spray it heavily with perfume. These are CLASS loyal. They manipulate all the powers of government—including the department of war—in defence of the capitalist CLASS. They even hire working men —with rifles.

(C)—THE WORKING MEN FIGHT THE WAR:

Because they are meek and modest and humble and docile, and are always gullibly ready to obediently do whatever their crafty political and industrial masters order them to do. So, whenever the capitalists want war and the politicians declare war, the flimflammed, bamboozled *working* man straps on a knapsack, shoulders a rifle (or takes a policeman's club), kisses his wife and children good-bye, and marches away to fight a war *he* didn't want, a war *he* didn't declare, a war that belittles and wrongs *him* by injuring *his class,*—and marches away to butcher *other* working men whom he *doesn't know* and against whom he *has no quarrel.* He yells, kills, and slaughters— because—simply because—because—some crafty crooks, called "prominent people," *tell* him to do so. He screams and gets slain, he yells and gets slaughtered—simply because he *does not understand* the sly, devilish trick that is thus being played upon him and his class. Young working men are shrewdly flattered into joining the militia and the army in order to help the capitalist class *force the working class to keep still and starve;* or accept *cheap* food, *cheap* clothing, *cheap* shelter and *cheap* furniture as *all* of their share for *all* their work for *all* their lives.

Suppose the working man has a son in the local militia company, and suppose Mr. Workingman goes out on strike for two or three more nickels per day with which to *buy better food for the young militiaman's own mother and his little brothers and sisters.*   This young man in the militia company can be ordered to shoot or bayonet his own father who, on strike, is struggling for a few cents more with which to buy better food for the humble mother and hungry little brothers and sisters—if the father *on strike* doesn't *keep quiet and remain docile* while the local industrial masters starve him back to his old job at his old wages.   The capitalist holds the whip of hunger over the working class father's back, and the working class son holds a rifle at his own father's breast. The father must surrender.   Thus the young militiaman wrongs his own class, outrages his own father, helps humble his own little brothers and sisters, and spits in his own mother's face.

The war is the *class* war.

The militiamen and policemen are *local soldiers* ready for orders to shoot their neighbors, friends and relatives in the struggle for existence.   In the industrial civil war the capitalist class starve, seduce and bribe the working class to fight BOTH SIDES OF THE BATTLES.

The rulers rule.   They think—and win BY THINKING.

Think it over, young man.   Be loyal to your own father and mother and your own brothers and sisters—and your own class.   Be class loyal.

The *working* class *themselves* must save the *working* class.

Read Chapter Ten: "Now, What Shall We Do About It?"

NOTE: It is of the greatest importance that the working class reader should learn what his employer does not wish to have him learn concerning value, surplus value, rate of surplus value, profit, rate of profit, profit to capitalist class, profit to individual capitalist employer, division of the spoils of exploitation among capitalists, etc., etc.   Mr. Joseph E. Cohen's small book, *Socialism for Students*, is a model of clearness for the reader who is too busy to read big books and yet wishes to inform himself accurately on the secrets of this legalized robbery.   This book (published by Charles H. Kerr and Company, Chicago) is just what a busy worker needs in making a beginning in those economic and sociological studies which will give him a large outlook upon the world and a deep inlook into the mainsprings of human society.

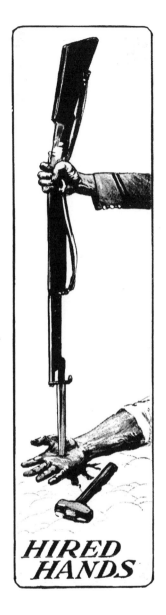

HIRED HANDS

Soldiers and militiamen are to the capitalist class what beaks are to eagles and tusks are to tigers.

CHAPTER FOUR.

The Cost of War—In Blood and In Cash.

SECTION I: THE COST IN BLOOD.

"Ez fer war—I call it murder."—James Russell Lowell.*

"The hero is a species of assassin."—Victor Hugo.†

Human blood, human life, under the present industrial form of society, is so cheap that even a sweet child's life, as a *wage*-earner, in the factory, can be bought for a few cents a day—almost a drug on the market, the "labor market." So cheap indeed is the life of the wage-working class that the blood cost of war is regarded as comparatively unimportant— considered unimportant by all except those who are sneeringly referred to as "sentimental people." These "sentimental people" presume to assert that the superiority of a nation's civilization is more convincingly indicated by its sacred regard for the purity and dignity of human blood than by its cheap and swaggering boasts about big battleships, "blooded" cattle, "blooded" horses, and "young men not only willing but *anxious* to fight,"‡ or by the nation's strutting announcement of our "readiness" to spill the toilers' blood at the factory door and on the battlefield.

Cheaply spilt human blood surely indicates a civilization fundamentally coarse and cheap.

Until human blood, human life, becomes too sacred to be sold for cash to escape starvation or bought for cash to win a profit on the bartered labor power—too sacred to be thus placed on sale, exchanged in the "labor market" as horses and

---

* Biglow Papers.

† Lecture on Voltaire.

‡ "I want for soldiers young men not only willing but *anxious* to fight,"—that foul and savage saying is one of the choice mouthings of Theodore Roosevelt, in a public address in which that cheap, distinguished and much flattered Noise disgraced the office of President of the American "Republic."

sheep are bought and sold in the "live-stock market,"—until then it will simply be impossible to realize the hideousness of the blood cost of war, impossible to compute and realize the vastness of the red crime committed against the working class, —against

"The poor souls for whom this hungry war opens its vast jaws."

The blood cost of war?

War spills the blood of slain soldiers.

War spills the blood of non-combatants.

War weakens the blood of soldiers who are smitten with befouling fevers and whose wounds and sores fester unattended on the battlefield or are ill-attended in rude military hospitals. Disease, in war, strikes with death four times as many soldiers as are killed with lead and steel.*

War weakens the national blood by selecting the strong-blooded for slaughter, thus reversing nature's method of selecting the weaker blooded for destruction.

War tends to open opportunity in the struggle for existence for the relatively weaker blooded to multiply in disproportionate degree.

War, it is estimated,† prevents, on the average, the birth of one child per soldier slaughtered on the battlefield, or serving three years or more in peace or war.

War weakens the blood of the nation by worse than wasting enormous supplies of food material and thus underfeeding those who toil.

War weakens the national blood by tainting the blood of great numbers of soldiers and through these tainting the blood of women and children—with venereal diseases contracted in unusual degree near the barracks and during war, and immediately following war. President William H. Taft, as Secretary of War, has said :‡

"Venereal diseases were again by far the most important diseases affecting the efficiency of the Army during the year. There were

---

* See Chapter Five, Section Two; Chapter Eight, Section 11; also Index: "Disease in the Army."

† Chatterton-Hill: *Heredity and Selection in Sociology*, pp. 320-22.

‡ Annual Report of the Secretary of War, 1907, p. 17.

constantly on sick report for this class of affections 739 men, equal to the loss for the entire year of the service of about eleven full companies of infantry. . . . As a cause for discharge venereal diseases were second."

Still more recently the Secretary of War, Mr. J. M. Dickinson, reports thus on the befouling of the blood of soldiers:*

"The diseases causing the greatest non-effective rate are in the order of importance: venereal diseases, tuberculosis, malaria, rheumatism, tonsilitis, dysentery, diarrhea, bronchitis, measles, typhoid fever.

"VENEREAL DISEASES CAUSE A GREATER SICK RATE THAN ALL THE OTHERS ADDED TOGETHER."

One of the best known publicists in the world, Mr. William T. Stead, puts the matter thus:

"Four out of five of all English soldiers who serve two years or more are tainted with venereal diseases."†

In the present chapter, devoted to the cost of war in blood and in cash, there is for the "blood cost" space for but little more than some statistics sufficient to indicate, for illustrative purposes, the amount of blood *actually spilt* in war during the last three generations. The authority for the statistical matter following is, chiefly, Chatterton-Hill's *Heredity and Selection in Sociology;* G. de Lapouge's *Les Selections Sociales;* and J. Bloch's *The Future of War.* ‡

The hot, red flood gushing from the torn veins of the working class, seduced or forced to attend "Death's feast" to slaughter and be slaughtered in little more than one brief hundred recent years, may be measured thus:

In the French Wars of the Revolution, 1789-1795—
Frenchmen 1,800,000
Other Europeans 2,500,000

---

* Annual Report of the Secretary of War, 1909, p. 17. Emphasis mine. G. R. K.

† Quoted by Elbert Hubbard in *Health and Wealth.* See *New Age,* Aug. 5, 1909.

‡ See also President D. S. Jordan's brilliant sociological studies of war, references in Chapter XII. of present volume. Of some interest are Victor Hugo's estimates in *William Shakespeare,* Part Third, Book III., Chapter I.

Wars of the Empire, 1795-1815—
 Frenchmen 2,600,000
 Other Europeans 3,500,000
In European and American wars since 1815—
 According to Lapouge's estimate....9,450,000
 Grand (Extremely Grand) Total..19,850,000 *

This total does not show the spilt blood of perhaps one hundred million men wounded, in battle, but *not killed.*

It is specially important to consider also that this enormous total of twenty million—in round numbers—does not include many millions of *non-combatants* who in one way and another were destroyed during the wars *and in consequence of the wars,* nor the immense number of non-combatants *wounded* but not *destroyed,* nor the vast amount of blood befouled and weakened with disease.

The number of men destroyed as combatants in the Franco-German War was 215,000. Lapouge estimates that for the brief Franco-German War the number of deaths among the non-combatants *above* the number that *would have died at the normal death rate* within the period consumed by the war *if there had been peace,* was 450,000. That is to say, during that short war of 1870-71 the number of non-combatants whose death was due to the war was *more than double* the number destroyed directly in the war. Now if this extra death-harvest rate among the non-combatants be calculated as being somewhat less than *half* true for all the wars of the civilized world for about one hundred years following 1789, we can safely *add* to the twenty millions slaughtered on the battlefield and in the military hospitals—to these, I say, we can add twenty millions more, who, like the four hundred and fifty thousand non-combatants in 1870-71, were smitten with the death-breath of war.

This gives us a "grand" total of forty millions (40,000,-000) men, women, and children actually slaughtered or otherwise destroyed as a result of *one hundred* years of "splendid"

---

* Chatterton-Hill in *Heredity and Selection in Sociology* makes the total 21,000,000.

WORN-OUT BOXING GLOVES OF THE RULING CLASS

and "glorious" and, "grand" and "Christianized" war;—
and (blessed be the *"mysterious* will of God who reigns" but
doesn't rule under capitalism) these forty million lives were
mostly WORKING CLASS LIVES.

Forty million lives in one brief century slashed down by
Mars, the "glorious" god of battles.

One Christian century—a festival of fiends, a loud ha, ha
from Hell.

One Christian century—a gash in the breast of the working class.

One Christian century—Mars and Caesar spitting in the
face of the nobly peaceful Christ.

One Christian century—a sea of blood.

One Christian century—an ocean of tears.

One Christian century—the butchering of brothers by
brothers.

One Christian century—a groan, a sigh, a sob.

Mars, god of war, devourer of men, scourge of women and
curse of little children; Mars, "strife and slaughter . . . the
condition of his existence," rushing in "without question as
to which side is right, . . . on his head the gleaming helmet
and floating plume"; Mars, "well-favored, stately, swift, un-
wearied, puissant, gigantic . . . foe of wisdom and scourge
of mortals"; Mars whose "emblems are the spear and the
burning torch, his chosen animals the vulture and the dog";*
Mars, butcher of mankind; Mars fiendishly drunk on the
tears of women and children; Mars, the mock of mothers,—
this race-cursing god, hour after hour, *day and night,* through
a whole hundred recent years, has devoured one human being,
has drunk more than two gallons of human blood—every
twenty minutes.

A torrent of blood has gushed from the deep, damned
war-wound in the breast of the working class. And in this
the morning of the twentieth Christian century we *hear* the
mouthings of hypocrisy, but we see the strut and dare of
crowned and flattered brutes and buccaneers everywhere.

---

* See Galey: *Classic Myths of English Literature,* pp. 57-8.

THE HISTORY OF IGNORANCE OBEYING ORDERS

> "Base distrust, the red-eyed hound of hate,
> Rules in a world by phantom foes alarmed."

Everywhere we see the crowned and consecrated cut-throats preparing for war. Soon again the booming roar of "gun thunder" will terrify the world. Even now in Turkey, in Russia, in Spain and in Africa the blood of humble working class brothers is being splashed in the face of mankind.

Rouse, brothers, rouse!

Refuse! Refuse to paint this sad world red with the blood of the toilers fooled by the mocking flattery of gilded cowards.

Let us force Senators, Congressmen, and Presidents—let us force Tsars, Emperors, Kings, Lords, Dukes and the Industrial Masters also—let us force every one of these shrewd, proud cowards into the bloody mire of the firing line and compel them to stay there till by spilling their own blood they learn what war is—for the working class.

The capture of the powers of government by the working class for the working class—that is our first move.

The *working* class must defend the *working* class.

SECTION II: THE COST IN CASH.

Remember—always remember: All the expenses of all the wars in all the world in all time have been paid with the results of productive labor. Always—finally—the working class pay all the expenses of all wars.

In a war

 (1) Soldiers cease to produce wealth,

 (2) Soldiers continue to consume wealth,

 (3) Soldiers actively destroy wealth.

A war involves three general items of expense; namely,

 Expenses before the war:—preparation

 Expenses during the war:—direct expenses, destruction of property, loss of producing power, etc.

 Expenses after the war:—pensions, interest on bonds, etc.

"In determining the cost of a war," says one writer,* "the items to be considered may be set down as follows:

(1) Preparations for prospective wars
(2) Direct expenditures
(3) Indirect losses
    (a) Destruction and depreciation of property
    (b) Labor value wasted
    (c) Damage to trade
    (d) Displacement of capital
(4) Subsequent expenditures
    (a) Compensation for property destroyed
    (b) Pensions and relief for the distressed
    (c) Interest on debt incurred
(5) Deterioration of population
(6) Moral results and effects on the vanquished."

Now let us try to get an idea of the actual cash cost of war in general by studying, first, the cash cost of one war as a specimen. Let us take the American Civil War. In the statement here following, items (4b) and (5) are somewhat over-estimated; item (6) is greatly underestimated. It is to be noted also that the following on the Civil War does not include all the items of the actual cash cost of that war; for examples, the economic loss in the weakening of the *national* blood, and the loss of the producing power of the soldiers on both sides *during* the war, the latter loss being probably more than $2,000,000,000. Two other very heavy items omitted here are the more than $2,000,000,000 that must in future years be paid out as interest on Civil War bonds and as Civil War pensions; and the $600,000,000 paid out in Civil War pensions from 1906 to 1910. However, if the omissions are carefully noted, the itemized statement will be found helpful in realizing the cash cost of war.

The American Civil War—Its Cost in Cash:

    (1) Direct expenditures, South.... $5,000,000,000.00
    (2) Direct expenditures, North.... 5,000,000,000.00
    (3) Increase in National Debt.... 2,800,000,000.00

---

* Restelle: *Arena,* October, 1906.

    (4) Interest on National War
         Debt:
         (a) 1865 to 1898...........   2,562,619,835.00
         (b) 1898 to 1910 (estimated)   400,000,000.00
    (5) Pensions, total to June 30,1906 3,259,195,396.60
    (6) Lost labor-power:
         One million selected m e n,
         slaughtered in battle or de-
         stroyed during the war by
         disease;* or from wounds
         and disease rendered wholly
         or partially unproductive for
         an average term of twenty-
         five years *following* the war:
         —an average loss to society
         per man, thus killed or weak-
         ened, of $500 for twenty-five
         years for one million men.. 12,500,000,000.00

    Total ("Grand" Total)...........$31,521,815,231.60

This sum, more than thirty-one and a half billion dollars, *this* sum looks different from the "Cost of the Civil War" as it is commonly set forth in elementary school histories for deludable children.†

Here is a suggestion: Have your child or some child of your acquaintance discuss this matter in the public school. The child should be assisted in preparing an attack upon the misrepresentation in the ordinary common school "History of the United States."

This sum, thirty-one and a half billion dollars, is well worth consideration.

This sum would pay for a 1700-dollar home and also for

---

* "In round numbers . . . so that it is safe to say that more than 700,000 men were killed in the war."—Professor MacMaster: *School History of the United States*, p. 422. See Index: "Noncombatants."

† See quotation from Preface of Bloch's *Future of War* near close of present chapter.

400 dollars' worth of furniture for each home—for a total population of 90 million people, estimating six per family in each home; or,

This sum is equivalent to the total savings of two million farmers for thirty weary years, supposing each farmer to save $500 per year;—and sufficient besides to establish eighty agricultural colleges and ninety teachers' colleges, *each* of these one hundred and seventy institutions provided with four million dollars' worth of land, buildings and equipment, each institution also provided with four million dollars as endowment fund to pay running expenses;—with a balance sufficient to construct a double-track railway from New York City to San Francisco at a cost of more than $48,000 per mile; or,

This sum is more than equivalent to the total wheat crop worth $1.00 per bushel growing on twenty-five million acres of fine land averaging twenty bushels per acre for over sixty-three years; or,

This sum would pay all the salaries of twenty-five thousand school teachers at $625 per year from the birth of Christ to the year 1909, and leave sufficient to establish fifty universities, each institution provided with ten million dollars' worth of buildings and equipment and each institution provided also with a ten-million dollar endowment fund for running expenses; or,

This sum is equal to the total savings of five million wage-earners, each saving one dollar per day, three hundred days per year for twenty-one years.

And we are not yet through with our Civil War expenses and shall not be for a long time. Professor Albert S. Bolles calls attention to the fact that we are not even yet through with the expenses of our Revolutionary War of more than one hundred years ago. Professor Bolles also says of the Civil War:*

"A hundred years are likely to pass before the account books for suppressing the Rebellion will be closed."

This is a good place to remind the reader that, of course,

* *Financial History of the United States*, Vol. III., p. 241.

as soon as the soldiers got home from the Civil War they had
to go to work to help create the wealth to pay the principal
and the interest on the war bonds held by the bankers and
other leading citizens who were too shrewd to go to the war
themselves.   Professor John C. Ridpath wrote thus of the
war bond-leech:*

"To him (the capitalist) it is all one whether this world blooms
with gardens, ripens with oranges, smiles with harvest of wheat, or
whether it is trodden into mire and blood under the raging charges
of cavalry and the explosions of horrid shells; that is, it is all one
to him if his coupons are promptly paid and his bond is extended."

Now, my friend, when the Honorable Mr. Noisy from
Washington or your legislature or elsewhere, gets you and your
neighbors out in the woods next Thirtieth of May or Fourth
of July and proceeds to fill the forest full of cheap and stupid
noise about the grandeur and glory of war, you should promptly treat him with the contempt he deserves.   You should also
protect the young people of your family and community from
the savage and dangerous suggestions made by many speakers
on such occasions—protect them by having the "other side"
of war presented.   The literature of peace-born-of-justice
might well be distributed on such occasions.

The cash cost of war is easily made evident by an examination of our annual current national bill for militarism.   Indeed, the annual cash cost of prize-fighter statesmanship, the
annual cost of developing the national fist, the annual cash
cost of this hypocritical "preservation of peace" by preparing
for war, needs special attention.

The combined average annual expense of militarism, that
is, of the Department of War and the Department of the
Navy (the Departments of Murder), is, for the United States,
as follows:

The Army and the Navy...................$200,000,000
The loss of producing power, the worse than lost
    labor-power,   of   121,786   "picked"   men
    (83,286   in   the   Army   and   38,500   in   the
    Navy), estimated at $600 each per year....   73,071,600

---

* *Arena,* Jan., 1897.

Interest on Public Debt (chiefly an expense of
 militarism), at present.................. 22,000,000
Pensions (admittedly a war burden).......... 150,000,000
Depreciation of forts, arsenals, ships, weapons
 and other war equipments by decay, and
 from the necessary discarding of "outgrown"
 murdering machinery................... 5,000,000
  Total $450,071,600

Since none of the items here set down is over-estimated
and since several of them are much under-estimated, the
grand total of four hundred and fifty millions must be regarded as an extremely conservative estimate of the annual
cost (in times of peace) of keeping the national fist ready for
a fight.*

But four hundred and fifty million dollars means nothing sufficiently definite to the human mind until it is considered in units larger than single dollars and smaller than
a million dollars. The sum of money *"necessary"* to defray
a year's expenses of a *poor* man's son or daughter in a high-
grade Middle Western college or university—may be taken
as a convenient unit of expense in considering the cash cost
of war.

Many worthy young men and women in the United
States pay their total annual expenses in high-grade colleges
and universities with $250. This estimate is confirmed by
the author's personal observation and by a letter of recent
date from the President of the University of Iowa to the
author.

OUR ANNUAL NATIONAL EXPENSE OF MILITARISM, $450,-
000,000, WOULD PAY THE ANNUAL COLLEGE EXPENSES OF
1,800,000 YOUNG MEN AND WOMEN; THAT IS, OF NEARLY
TWELVE TIMES AS MANY AS THERE WERE IN THE YEAR END-
ING JUNE 30, 1908, IN THE FIVE HUNDRED AND SEVENTY-

* The appropriations for the Navy alone in 1910 are $134,000,-
000,—which amount is just ten times as great as in 1886. The
New York *World's* estimate (editorial, March, 1910) is $500,000,000
as the annual cost of militarism in the United States.

THREE COLLEGES, UNIVERSITIES AND TECHNOLOGICAL SCHOOLS
OF THE UNITED STATES.

Five per cent. interest on $450,000,000 for *six minutes*
would provide $250 for a year's college expenses.

Five per cent. interest on one year's expense of militarism
in the United States for *two weeks and three days* would keep
one full regiment (1,000) young men in college for *four
years.*

Less than seven per cent. interest on $450,000,000 for one
year would pay one year's college expenses for a total number
of young men and women equal to the total number of men
in both the Army and the Navy, officers, privates and all.

The total present-rate cost of militarism in the United
States for two and a half years is $1,125,000,000. *Three and
a half per cent. interest* for *one* year on this amount would be
$39,375,000. This interest would pay the college expenses of
the total number of young men and women in all the 573
colleges, universities and technological schools in the United
States for the one year ending June 30, 1908 (that is, for
150,187 students), estimating the average expense at $250
for the year,—with a balance remaining of almost $2,000,000
for extra expenses.

According to Mr. E. J. Dillon,* "The cost of each of the
new armored battleships planned for the French Navy is
estimated at more than $15,000,000."

"Chairman Tawney of the House Committee on Appropriations
in promising to fight against the new $18,000,000 battleships, pledges
himself to a worthy cause."†

Six and two-thirds per cent. interest for *one* year on the
cost of a $15,000,000 battleship would provide a *four-year*
college education for the 1,000 marines on board.

Six per cent. interest for *ten hours* on the cost of a $15,-
000,000 battleship would pay the total expenses of a young
man or woman while doing the *four years'* work for the degree
of Bachelor of Arts in the great University of Iowa.

---

* *The Contemporary Review*, August, 1909.

† New York *World*, March 1, 1910. See also *The World*, February 1, 1910.

ONE NEW-TYPE "DREADNOUGHT" OF THE SORT NOW BEING
CONSTRUCTED FOR THE BRITISH NAVY (WHICH IS TO BE PRAC-
TICALLY DUPLICATED BY ALL THE OTHER "GREAT POWERS")—
ONE OF THESE MONSTERS WILL COST THREE TIMES AS MUCH
AS ALL OF THE NOBLE BUILDINGS OF THE UNIVERSITY OF CHI-
CAGO ERECTED UP TO JUNE 30, 1905; THAT IS, THREE TIMES
AS MUCH AS ALL THE BEAUTIFUL HALLS CONSTRUCTED DURING
THE UNIVERSITY'S FIRST THIRTEEN YEARS OF UNPARALLELED
ACTIVITY IN BUILDING.

The total value of all gifts and bequests received by all the
higher institutions of learning in the United States in the
year ending June 30, 1908, was $14,820,955; that is, $179,000
less than the cost of one first class British battleship.*

If there are forty-five State Universities in the United
States with a total of 6,750 teachers (150 each) receiving an
average salary of $2,000, their combined salaries are less
than the cost of one "Dreadnought."

Five per cent. interest on the cost of one "Dreadnought"
would pay the combined salaries of 1,500 country school teachers at $500 per year; or, the combined salaries of 750 country
preachers at $1,000 per year. (The average salary of a minis-
ter in Massachusetts is less than $800.)

ONE PER CENT. INTEREST ON ONE "DREADNOUGHT" WOULD
PAY THE COMBINED SALARIES OF THE PRESIDENTS OF TWENTY-
FIVE OF THE GREATEST UNIVERSITIES IN THE UNITED STATES
—AT AN AVERAGE SALARY OF $6,000 PER YEAR.

It is to be remembered, too, that a battleship is out-classed,
out of date and useless within fifteen years after it first glides
proudly into the water. But education—the systematic development of the intellectual and social powers and tastes, the
ripening of the appetites for the deeper, higher, finer forms
of life, charging the soul with knowledge and power for pleasure and achievement—education, which is "to the human soul
what sculpture is to a block of marble,"—education, in its
glorious influences, is immortal.

---

* See Report of Commissioner of Education, 1908, Vol. II.,
p. 617.

Prize-fighter statesmanship sounds loud and is, therefore, great; looks attractive and is, therefore, splendid—in the judgment of the gullible.   Prize-fighter statesmanship rests upon the gullibility of ignorance.

Of special importance in this connection is the item of information, furnished in a personal letter to the author of the present volume, by Dr. William T. Harris, who was for many years preceding 1906 our National Commissioner of Education.   The information is: *That of all the children in the United States more than 76 in every 100 never enter even the first year of the high school or schools of the high-school grade.*

Think of this matter in still another way.

The total cost of militarism in the United States for the year 1907-8 was over *six and a half times as great* as the total income ($66,790,924) of all our 464 universities, colleges and technological schools *from all sources and for all purposes for that same year.**

THE TOTAL COST OF MILITARISM IN THE UNITED STATES FOR THE FIFTEEN AND A HALF MONTHS ENDING JUNE 30, 1909, WAS GREATER THAN THE TOTAL VALUE OF ALL THE BOOKS, LIBRARIES, LANDS, GROUNDS, BUILDINGS, FURNITURE, SCIENTIFIC APPARATUS, MACHINERY, AND ALL THE ENDOW-MENTS, ALL THE INVESTMENTS AND ALL "PRODUCTIVE FUNDS" OF ALL KINDS BELONGING TO ALL OUR 464 HIGHER INSTITU-TIONS OF LEARNING.

There are in the United States 464 colleges, universities and technological schools admitting men only and both men and women; these institutions have in their libraries a total of 12,636,656 volumes, having (according to our Commissioner of Education, in his Report for the year ending June 30, 1908, page 617) a total value of $16,262,027—which sum is almost equalled by the cost of one first-class modern murdering machine, one "Dreadnought."

One 14-inch cannon and equipment costs $170,000.   One

---

* See Report of Commissioner of Education for 1908, Vol. II., pp. 616-17.   These 464 admit men only, or both men and women.

target-practice shot costs as much as President John Adams's education at Harvard University.

> "Whether your shell hits the target or not,
> Your cost is six hundred dollars a shot.
> You thing of noise and flame and power,
> We feed you a hundred barrels of flour
> Each time you roar. Your flame is fed
> With twenty thousand loaves of bread.
> Silence!   A million hungry men
> Seek bread to fill their mouths again."*

One broadside from a modern "Dreadnought" costs almost $20,000.

"The fact that we are spending during this fiscal year 72 per cent. of our aggregate revenue in preparing for war and on account of past wars (pensions, interest and principal payments on war debts), leaving only 28 per cent. of our revenue available to meet all our other governmental expenditures, including internal improvements, the erection of public buildings, the improvement of rivers and harbors, and the conservation of our natural resources, is, to my mind, appalling."—Congressman J. A. Tawney.†

"For the fiscal year 1908-9 the ordinary income of the United States was $604,000,000. Of that sum . . . 70 per cent. was spent for past wars and preparations for war. . . ."‡

This same "civilized" savagery is rampant everywhere.

"The great countries are raising enormous revenues . . . it is equally true that one half of the national revenues of the great countries in Europe is being spent on what are, after all, preparations to kill each other."—Sir Edward Grey, Foreign Secretary, British Cabinet.§

G. de Molinari sums up thus:‖

"Two-thirds of their [European nations'] combined budgets are devoted to the service of this debt [war debt], and to the maintenance of their armed forces by sea and land."

* P. F. McCarthy in the New York *World*.

† Address delivered at the Peace Banquet, Chicago, May 4, 1909; quoted in *Unity*, June 3, 1909.

‡ New York *World*, April 4, 1910. See also New York *Times* editorial, February 19, 1910.

§ In the House of Commons, March 29, 1909.

‖ *The Society of To-Morrow*, p. 30.

The New York *World* speaks boldly thus:*

"The preparations for war bear with tremendous weight in times of peace. . . . Six million picked men in the flower of youth are in arms in Europe. They are all strong men, those who would be most useful in industry. Great Britain's war-costs [to-day, in times of peace] including national debt service, $444,000,000, . . . are now nearly six times as great as her elementary school costs. An even more bitter contest over a greater war deficit which must be met by increased taxation is going on in Germany. . . . Russia runs behind $200,000,000 a year in her national finances . . . and famine is perpetual."

All the great governments of the world are increasing their murdering equipment—to be "prepared for war";—that is, prepared to provoke and dare. The annual expenses for war in England have doubled within the last ten years, and still the stupidity grows. England has 52 battleships, 4 armored cruisers, 16 cruisers, 84 destroyers, 20 submarines, and to these are to be added at once 8 "Dreadnoughts" costing from $12,000,000 to $15,000,000 each, and also an "appropriate" number of auxiliaries—armored and unarmored cruisers, torpedo boats, etc., the *additions* to the present naval outfit to cost over $300,000,000. France has 21 battleships with an "appropriate" number of auxiliaries, and is building 8 more battleships with auxiliaries. In Germany militarism amounts to even greater madness. In 1872, immediately following a great war, the German Empire spent $73,750,000 as direct expense of militarism; in 1898, not including the loss in labor power, the cost of the departments of murder was $337,-500,000. Increases in German militarism since 1898 have been startling, and so furious is the spirit of militarism and so insanely is the government already burdened with "war charges," that in the year 1907-8 bonds were sold to the extent of $25,000,000, as part of a special effort to raise an extra fund with which to make additions to her murdering equipment.

And thus it is with all the other "great" nations.

Although Russia now staggers under a four-and-a-half

* Editorial, May 4, 1909.

billion dollar national debt, and in 1908 was forced to borrow $75,000,000 to meet current expenses (and did her best
to borrow $400,000,000); although millions of her citizens
face starvation and hundreds of thousands of them are forced
into trampdom—yet Russian statesmen and naval experts
are planning a billion-dollar navy.*

"Certain facts will surely, some day, burn themselves into the
consciousness of thinking men. . . . The extravagance of the militarists will bring about their ruin. They cry for battleships . . . and
Parliament or Congress votes them. But later on it is explained that
battleships are worthless without cruisers, cruisers are worthless
without torpedo boats, torpedo boats are worthless without torpedo destroyers, all these are worthless without colliers, ammunition
boats, hospital boats, repair boats; and these all together are worthless without deeper harbors, longer docks, more spacious navy yards.

"And what are all these worth without officers and men, upon
whose education millions of dollars have been lavished? When at
last the navy has been fairly launched, the officials of the army
come forward and demonstrate that a navy, after all, is worthless
unless it is supported by a colossal land force. Thus are the governments led on, step by step, into a treacherous morass, in which
they are at first entangled, and finally overwhelmed."†

J. H. Rose, in his *Development of European Nations,*
Vol. II., p. 336, surveying the chief events in the evolution of
Europe since 1870, writes:

"The individual is crushed by a sense of helplessness as he gazes
at the armed millions on all sides of him. Tho' a freeman in
the constitutional sense of the term, he has entered into a state of
military serfdom. There he is but a bondman, toiling to add his
few blocks to the colossal pyramid of war. . . . From that life there
can come no song . . . some malignant Fury masquerading in the
garb of Peace."

Nearly everywhere war debts are piled like mountains
upon the backs of the people. Twenty-three years ago (1887)
Professor H. C. Adams (University of Michigan, Department

---

* Reference for most of the phrasing of this paragraph has been
lost.

† C. E. Jefferson, in the *Atlantic Monthly*, quoted in *Public
Opinion* (address?), March 26, 1909.

of Finance) sounded the alarm and stated the case strikingly:*

"The civilized governments of the present day are resting under a burden of indebtedness computed at $27,000,000,000. This sum, which does not include local obligations of any sort, constitutes a mortgage of $722 [now about $950] upon each square mile of territory over which the burdened governments extend their jurisdiction, and shows a per capita indebtedness of $23 upon their subjects. The total amount of national obligations is equal to seven times the aggregate annual revenue of the indebted states. At the liberal estimate of $1.50 per day, the payment of the accruing interest, computed at five per cent., would demand the continuous labor of three million men. . . . Previous to the present [nineteenth] century, England and Holland were the only nations that had learned by experience the weight of national obligations; but at the present time the phenomenon of public debts is almost universal. . . .

"It is all the more difficult to understand this new method of financiering, because it has made its appearance while wealth has been rapidly increasing. The world is daily growing richer as nature yields her forces with ever increasing willingness to serve the purposes of men; yet, notwithstanding increased opulence, the governments of the world are plunging headlong into debt."

The reader should keep in mind that the burdens of debt discussed here by Dr. Adams are almost wholly war debts, and that they have, since 1887, increased heavily—to about $35,-000,000,000, *almost three times the total amount of cash in the entire world.*

"Reflect for an hour upon the appalling aggregate," wrote Professor Ridpath (De Pauw University),† "consider the pressure of this intolerable incubus; try to estimate the horror of this hell; weigh the woe and anguish of them who rest under it, and then—despair and die.

"Twenty thousand millions of dollars; statesmen, philanthropists, preachers, journalists, mouthpieces of civilization, one and all of you, how do you like the exhibit? Does it not suffice? Who is going to pay the account? The people. Who, without lifting a hand or turning in their downy beds, will gather this infamous harvest during all of the twentieth century? Plutocracy.

"It has been the immemorial policy of the Money Power to foment wars among the nations; to edge on the conflict until both parties pass under the impending bankruptcy; to buy up the pro-

---

* *Public Debts*, pp. 3, 4, 6.
† *Arena*, January, 1898.

digious debt of both with a pail full of gold; to raise the debt to par; to invent patriotic proclamations for preserving the National Honor; and finally to hire the presses and pulpits of two generations to glorify a crime."

Henry Ward Beecher put the matter thus:

"Most of the debts of Europe represent condensed drops of blood."

Reflect again:

"In one short eighteen months the [British] war party now sitting on our necks has dissipated [in the Boer War] more money than the working class managed to accumulate out of their wages during the whole reign of the late Queen Victoria." (That is, from 1837 to 1901.) "The patient savings of two generations were [in the Boer War] dissipated at one cruel swoop."*

The following table shows the proportion in which the "great" capitalist governments spend the outraged people's substance for education and for militarism—in prize-fighter statesmanship:†

	Education.	Militarism.
England	$1.00	$4.25
France	1.00	4.80
Germany	1.00	2.57
Austria	1.00	4.50
United States..............	1.00	1.25
Denmark	1.00	3.66
Greece	1.00	5.00
Sweden	1.00	2.25
Italy	1.00	9.00
Belgium	1.00	2.00
Switzerland	1.00	.54
Russia	1.00	12.00

An American educator has written thus of the civilized

---

* See *The Investor's Review*, London, April, 1901, and *National Review*, London, June, 1903, respectively; quoted by Walter Walsh: *Moral Damage of War*, pp. 416-17.

† See Bloch's *Future of War*, pp. 137-39; recent *Statesman's Year-Books*, "national expense" tables; also *Labor Leader* (London), Nov. 1, 1907.

savagery to be seen in these worse than wasted treasures of the people:*

"The national debts of Europe represent a series of colossal crimes against the people. They were incurred in the prosecution of unnecessary wars, and for the support of unnecessary standing armies. With relation to these debts the people are divided into *two* classes—one class *owns* them and the other *pays the interest* on them. This relation comprehends the future generations in perpetuity. Every child born in Europe inherits either an estate in these debts or an obligation to pay interest upon them. Thus the *fruits of a great crime have been transmitted into a vested right in one class of people, or a vested wrong in another class.*

"If the European standing armies and navies had not been raised and kept up, and if the revenue devoted to their support had been expended for schools, there would not now be an uneducated person in Europe. If these standing armies and navies were now disbanded, and the revenue at present expended for their support diverted to the support of schools, and so applied for half a century, there would not be, at the end of that period, an illiterate person in Europe."

The following paragraph by Helmuth v. Gerlach is worthy of the workingman's special consideration:†

"Of all the German political parties one, viz., the Social Democratic [the Socialist] Party, has always been a consistent opponent of militarism. It looks upon militarism as the strongest support of the capitalistic régime, and therefore attacks it theoretically and actually with equal vigor. Its watchword is: 'No men and no money.' "‡

But everywhere these senseless burdens grow more vast. The end is not yet. The insanity of vanity and greed increases alarmingly—everywhere; but worst of all, the people are unwarned by the all-powerful capitalist press. Fortunately there are exceptions; for example, the New York *World*. Boldly and powerfully the *World* has recently warned the people. On July 20, 1908, the *World* said editorially:

"No more effective peace sermon could be preached than the estimate of General Blume, published by the German General Staff, as to the probable cost of a modern European war. Putting the num-

---

* Kim: *Mind and Hand*, pp. 290-92. Italics mine. G. R. K.
† *The International*, July, 1908.
‡ See Index: "Socialist Party and War."

ber of troops that Germany could call to arms at 4,759,000, the
cost to Germany, he says, of a war with another European power
would be [*direct* expenses] $1,500,000,000 a year as long as the
war lasted. On the basis of the war between Russia and Japan,
in which the Japanese lost in killed and wounded 20 per cent. of
their armies, Germany would lose in the same length of time ap-
proximately 900,000 men. . . .

"The account in blood and money would be duplicated if Germany
were engaged with only one power. If three or four or even more
powers were involved, as seems probable in the light of existing
alliances, Europe would be 'bled white' and plunged in lasting
disaster.

"*This is the other side of the question which public men who talk
glibly about the war seek to have the people forget.* They do not dwell
on the immense debt of victorious Japan, and its practical impover-
ishment, nor do they recall to attention the appalling waste of Russia's resources, its rickety finances, its shrunken commerce and the
tens of millions of starving subjects of the Czar. It will be many
years before the public credit of Great Britain, proud of the national
wealth, recovers from the setback caused by the Boer War and the
government is able to face much-needed reforms at home without
misgivings about its income."*

Statesmanship!

"Defense of our foreign commerce" is one of the heaviest
arguments offered by capitalist statesmen in defense of the
vast cost of militarism—with insufferable ignorance neglecting the fact that the total annual cost of militarism for nineteen European countries and the United States and Japan
(eight billion dollars) is equal to more than 66 per cent. of
the total annual export trade of all the nations of all the
world.†

Statesmanship!

"Great" men guiding the "Ship of State"—to the rocks!

Thus the nations stagger round and round in a stupid
circle, the statesmen planning international wholesale butcherings, the working class blinded with blood and sweat and
tears. Greater armies, greater navies,—then still greater

---

* Italics mine. G. R. K.

† "The export trade of all nations combined amounts to less than
$12,000,000,000 per annum." Harold Bolce: *The New International-
ism*, p. 87.

armies and still greater navies,—and then still more powerful
armies and navies: then impossible taxation, intolerable burdens: then bankruptcy:—then wrath, rebellion and revolution,—this constitutes the near-future program for at least
eight "great" nations of the world, if they continue, as at
present, to surrender to the vanity of kings, tsars, presidents,
mikados, and give free rein to the profit-lusting capitalist
masters of the world. Militarism is the international political
whirlpool. The maelstrom opens—the chasm yawns, spreads
wide its huge jaws for the capitalist ship of state.

Be not deceived:

IT IS SINCERE, WELL-FOUNDED FEAR OF BANKRUPTCY (AND
IT IS NOT CONSCIENCE) THAT CHIEFLY INDUCES MANY CAPI-
TALIST STATESMEN TO CO-OPERATE, AT PRESENT, SO LOUDLY
(AND PIOUSLY) WITH INTERNATIONAL PEACE SOCIETIES.

Bankruptcy, rebellion, revolution—

It is time for Caesar to be pious and whine for "a limita-
tion on armaments."

THE STARVED SLAVE BEGINS TO ASK QUESTIONS OF THE
FAT STATESMAN.

The ship of state begins to rock in the growing storm.

Statesmanship!

Industrial democracy stands by to seize its opportunity.

The producers will be the successors to plutocracy.

Despotism is digging its own grave.

Anent this matter a truly great authority, Professor J. E.
Thorold Rogers, says:*

"Many parts of the earth were once occupied by rich and industrious peoples which are now wholly waste. Such a decline may
come from the effects of a destructive conquest, of long and ruinous
wars. But in *almost all cases, the ruin of a race* is the fault of its
government. . . . *Nations* will not ruin themselves, said Adam Smith,
but *governments* may ruin them. . . . I will not say that spectacles of
this kind will never be seen again, of nations perishing by the vices
of those who administer their affairs. . . . Governments may borrow
for the purpose of carrying on a war, or of defending themselves
against aggression. The government generally asserts that it is the

---

* *Economic Interpretation of History*, pp. 393-94. Italics mine.
G. R. K.

latter motive which influences it, when every one sees it is the former. Whether their subjects or citizens see it or not, governments generally, almost invariably, avow it so persistently or savagely that their subjects are brought to agree with them."

What is the significance of the present cost of militarism for the world annually? No human mind can discern or take in the vast meaning of the blood-and-profit-lust politics that holds and damns the world to-day.

$8,000,000,000—Eight Billion Dollars!

Tossed to Mars, the red-stained god of war!

While the human race festers in ignorance!

$8,000,000,000—to blind and blindfold the multitude with their own blood and rags while their lives are robbed and ravaged by the eminent and respectable profit-glutton parasites of mankind.

$8,000,000,000—this huge sum baffles comprehension. Pronounce it: "Eight Billion Dollars." That sum embarrasses not only the mind, but the lips and the tongue.

Think that sum for a moment.

Now consider the fact that in twenty-one countries, namely, those of Europe and also Japan and the United States, militarism costs more than eight billion dollars—every twelve months.

ONE ITEM ALONE IN THIS COST OF MILITARISM IS ALMOST FOUR BILLION DOLLARS PER YEAR. That single item is the wealth that is *not* produced, but *could be produced* if the six million five hundred thousand strong, carefully selected young men in the standing armies of these twenty-one countries *were* engaged in producing wealth with *modern* tools, *modern* machinery, and *modern* knowledge of production. It is to be noted that in this estimate all of South America, China and other large parts of the world are not included.

Eight Billion Dollars—$8,000,000,000.

Men and women shudder when the telegraph flashes over the world that a city has suffered a ten-million or a twenty-million dollar fire. Let us try to get an idea of the cost of wealth-wasting militarism by expressing it in terms of loss by the devourer, fire.

$8,000,000,000—Eight Billion Dollars:

This sum, this expense of bull-dog-and-tiger statesmanship, of militarism, in twenty-one "highly civilized" countries—for twelve months in times of peace—is equivalent to a continuous loss by fire, throughout the year, day and night, of more than $913,000 an hour; or, about $15,219 per minute.

This sum, worse than wasted annually to be "prepared"—to slaughter—is equal to a loss by fire, burning day and night throughout the year, devouring seven homes per minute, each home worth $1,700 and each home containing also $475 worth of furniture.

The average working class family contains about six members—two parents and four children; and the average working class family would consider itself in good fortune to have a home worth $1,700 and provided with $475 worth of furniture. Seven such homes would contain forty-two members.

Now imagine an unbroken stream of people—men, women, and little children, frightened, pale, shuddering, the children screaming, the women in tears—fleeing past you through the street, driven by fire from their ruined homes, forty-two people rushing by you every minute, day and night, year after year, on and on, an endless stream of humbled and saddened souls, plunged in misery, their happiness swallowed by pitiless fire; or,

Imagine a fire *rushing* faster than a strong man at a brisk walk—imagine a fire rushing forward more than *eight miles an hour, consuming fifty such homes per mile,* making each year *thirty-six round trips,* burning going and coming, from New York City to St. Louis, Missouri; or one such round trip every ten days—imagine these losses, these annual losses—and you will perhaps have some idea of what it costs these twenty-one countries to brag and strut and piously prepare to settle their disputes as tigers settle theirs—by force.

It is as if the fiends of hell were crazed and loose on the earth.

And this is statesmanship!

Eight billion dollars virtually tossed into the flames by the well-fed kings, emperors, tsars, presidents, and champagne-guzzlers in the national legislatures of twenty-one "highly civilized" countries—while tens of millions of the toilers in these same countries shiver and starve, meanly clothed, meanly housed, meanly fed, their children growing up in the dull ignorance that renders them the easy tools and fools for the firing line.

One year's cost of militarism in these twenty-one countries ($8,000,000,000) would keep thirty-two million students in college for one year—allowing $250 each.

The cost of militarism in these twenty-one countries for less than nine hours and a half would pay all the expenses of 4,500 students in Harvard University for four years, allowing each student $500 per year.

SIX PER CENT. INTEREST ON THIS $8,000,000,000 FOR ONE YEAR WOULD PROVIDE A FOUR-YEAR COLLEGE EDUCATION FOR 480,000 YOUNG MEN AND WOMEN, ALLOWING EACH STUDENT $250 PER YEAR.

$8,000,0000,000 annually—in time of peace!

Clap your hands in stupid glee, O, blind devotees of the blood god Mars!

Celebrate!

Scream "Hurrah! Hurrah!"—in idiotic glad madness.

Yell, fool, yell: "Hurrah for hell!"

For war!

War! War! War!

It is great!

Isn't it?

It must be great, for "*great* men" say it is so.

"*Great* men" never deceive humble, common working men. Never. Of course not.

When "great men" call: "Rally to the flag, boys!" will my toiling brothers become again the fools and tools for such as they who in Parliaments and Congresses vote for this red-dripping stupidity?

$8,000,000,000 every twelve months on war and preparations for war—and yet *not a single silk-hatted snob sleeps in the dingy barracks, or eats the cheap "grub" fed to the privates, or submits to humiliating insults from "superior" officers, or spills his blood on the firing line*—not one any-where in all the world.

$8,000,000,000—the annual cost of lust—war lust.

The annual cost of jungle statesmanship.

THE COST THE WORKING CLASS PAY FOR BEING MEEK, DOCILE, OBEDIENT—READY TO SLAUGHTER THEMSELVES, READY TO BUTCHER THEIR BROTHERS OF THE WORKING CLASS.

$8,000,000,000, the price the working class pay for being prejudiced, ignorant, unwilling to read;—and for cringing, for neglecting to place the *working* class in the *legislatures of the world*.

$8,000,000,000—this sum proves the moral bankruptcy, proves the colossal savagery—of capitalists who *want* war, and proves also the intellectual and moral bankruptcy, the brainless incapacity and unspeakable villainy of the gilt-edged crooks called statesmen who are always ready to *declare* wars and who perpetually bleed society by thus "preparing for wars" in which they themselves, like the "business men," are too proud and cunning to fight on the firing line.

This sum also shows that the working class, stripped and dulled to supply this annual sum, *ignorantly consenting to and blindly hurrahing for their own destruction,* are in the condition of *hypnotized children*—almost utterly helpless, their eyes blinded with tears, their ears stopped with blood, their souls numb and dumb in a living death.

This sum—all this cash cost—is, in its last analysis, slyly *subtracted from the lives of the producing class, the working class—sucked from the veins of the humble multitude of toilers,* and the workers are so meek and weak and bloodless and stunned and stunted—so constantly in a dull, prideless stupor—that they are unable to stand erect in holy indignation, seize the powers of government and sweep this hell's nightmare from the world.

War devours the welfare of the workers.

The *capitalist* class dare not *place all the facts frankly before the working class.* Everywhere it is: "Hush! Hush! The *working* class must not study the burdens of war."

The workers? "They must not *think*. They must not *think*. They must *obey*."

That is the word for the working class:

OBEY.

A very eminent authority on war* says:

"Only *once* in recent history do I remember *any attempt* on the part of a European government to calculate the economic consequences of war under *modern* conditions. It was when M. Burdeau was in the French Ministry. He appointed a committee of economists for the purpose of ascertaining how the social organism would continue to function in a time of war, how from day to day their bread would be given to the French population. But *no sooner had he begun his investigation than a strong objection was raised by the military authorities,* and out of deference to their protest the inquiry was *indefinitely postponed.* Hence we are going forward blindfold."

A real statesman, Senator Charles Sumner, has said:†

"All history is a vain word, and all experience is at fault, if large war preparations . . . have not been constant provocatives of war. Pretended protectors against war, they have been the real instigators of war. They have excited the evil against which they were to guard. The habit of wearing arms in private life exercised a kindred influence. . . . The Standing Army is to the nation what the sword was to the modern gentleman, the stiletto to the Italian, the knife to the Spaniard, the pistol to our slavemaster,—furnishing, like these, the means of death; and its possessor is not slow to use it."

"Were half the power that fills the world with terror,
    Were half the wealth bestowed on camps and courts,
Given to redeem the world from error,
    There would be no need of arsenals and forts."‡

"Workers of the world, unite!" Rouse. Think. Rise. Hurl this curse of war from the world.

On the battlefield of industry unite.

On the battlefield of politics unite.

Seize the powers of government.

Use these powers of government—in self-defense.

---

* Bloch: *The Future of War*, Preface, p. XLVIII. Italics mine. G. R. K.

† *Addresses on War*, p. 292.

‡ Henry W. Longfellow: "The Arsenal at Springfield."

Great working class multitude, great meek majority! Stand erect in your vast class might and become—authority.

The working class must themselves defend the working class.

"Do not expect your chains to forge themselves into the key of freedom."

Begin.

Begin now.

Begin a campaign to capture the brain of your working class neighbor for the grand new Movement for the Freedom of the Working Class.

Do something.

Be Somebody.

Help conquer in our day.

War costs.

Meekness costs—costs the working class its labor, its blood and tears, its happiness—its Life.

Let us defend ourselves—AS A CLASS.

CHAPTER FIVE.

Hell.

Ah, so you are on your way to the recruiting station, are you? Well, there will be plenty of time to enlist to-morrow, and there are also seven days of next week that have not been touched yet. Do not be in a hurry to sign your name. Wait a little—wait at least till you have read the first two sections of this chapter.

Perhaps you are feverish.

Cool off before you enlist.*

Go back to the 60's and read three or four lines of American Civil War history before you enlist. Here they are in the words of a distinguished authority, A. S. Bolles:†

"With the swift cooling of the war fever bounties became necessary to stimulate enlistment. . . . In 1861 the highways were filled with volunteers eagerly rushing to the front; but in 1865 they went with much slower pace and with a much better conception of the hazardous game of war."

The hateful method called drafting had to be vigorously applied by the Federal Government after the young men found out what war really meant—for them.

And Professor John B. McMaster (University of Pennsylvania) makes it clear that even the hot blood of the young men of the South also cooled down to an extremely rational temperature as the slaughter proceeded. He says:‡

"Quite as desperate were the shifts to which the South was put for soldiers. At first every young man was eager to rush to the front. But as time passed . . . it became necessary to force men into the ranks, to 'conscript' them. . . ."

---

* See Index: "Desertion," also "Suicide, startling increase of, in American Army."

† *Financial History of the United States*, Vol. III., p. 245.

‡ *School History of the United States*, p. 423.

In this connection read the words of a great Union soldier, General Sherman:

"I confess without shame that I am tired and sick of the war. Its glory is all moonshine. Even success the most brilliant is over dead and mangled bodies, the anguish and lamentations of distant families appealing to me for missing sons, husbands and fathers. It is only those who have not heard a shot nor heard the shrieks and groans of the wounded and lacerated that cry aloud for more blood, more vengeance, more desolation."*

It is especially important that before you enlist you should get a distinct idea of the horrible deadliness of modern butchering machinery. Since General Sherman made the comment just quoted on the American Civil War the killing machinery has been improved astonishingly.

IN THE RECENT RUSSIAN-JAPANESE WAR INDIVIDUAL SOLDIERS, AS SHOWN BY ACTUAL COUNT AND OFFICIAL REPORT, RECEIVED AS MANY AS SEVENTY BULLET WOUNDS,—THEY WERE RIDDLED—TORN TO PIECES—WITH LEAD AND STEEL FIRED FROM MODERN SLAUGHTERING MACHINES. IF YOU WILL READ ALL OF THE PRESENT AND THE FOLLOWING SECTIONS YOU WILL NO LONGER WONDER WHY THE "VERY BEST PEOPLE" DO NOT ENLIST FOR ACTUAL SERVICE—AT THE FRONT.

I would suggest and even urge, brothers, that, before you enlist, you visit your dear pastor and read with him all of the present section on "Hell," and then ask him whether he and his sons will probably enlist for actual firing-line-sword-rifle-and-bayonet service. Also have a heart-to-heart talk with your loving friend, your banker, who takes care of your money for you. Read these paragraphs to him and ask him whether he is eager to rush to the front and whether he is urging his sons and sons-in-law to be ready to rush with him to the front for real fighting into "the grasp of death," into "the hurricane's fiery breath," where sabres flash, bullets hiss, and cannon roar.

By the way, do you deposit much money in the bank? Do you often visit socially at the banker's home? Did you

---

* Quoted in Mead's *Patriotism and the New Internationalism*, pp. 18-19.

ever see a cheap, fifteen-dollar-a-month soldier courting the banker's or the big manufacturer's daughter?

Well, hardly.

Wake up, my working class brother.

These leading citizens strut before you and fill you full of fierce and splendid talk about becoming "brave boys behind the gun"; but at the same time they despise you socially. Don't foolishly get *behind* the gun or in *front* of the gun— not at least till you have studied the gun.

A high-grade modern rifle can be fired twenty-five times per minute. This gun will pierce 60 pine boards each one inch thick. It will kill a man at a distance of four miles. A bullet with sufficient force to pierce a one-inch pine board will kill a man or a horse. Actual tests show that the best modern rifles will force a bullet through a target made of the following combination:—fifteen folds of cow-hide, sixteen one-inch pine boards, and one and four-fifths inches of hard beech wood. Bullets fired from rifles used in the American Civil War would do little damage after passing into or through the bodies of soldiers in the front ranks. Men in the second and third ranks felt much protected by the bodies of men in front of them. ALL IS DIFFERENT NOW. The best modern rifles will force a bullet through five horses at 27 yards; four horses at 220 yards; two horses at 1,100 yards. Even as recently as the war of 1870-71 and the war of 1877-78, bullets from rifles then used in the German army would not pierce a human skull at a distance of 1,760 yards, one mile; but with the best modern rifles bullets can be fired through the thick bones of an ox at a range of 3,850 yards, about two and one-fifth miles. Experiments demonstrate that the best modern rifles will force a bullet through three human bodies at a range of 3,900 feet; and through five human bodies at 1,200 feet. In the American Civil War bullets for long range work had to be fired high, describing a long high arch, thus missing all objects on the battlefield between the gun and the object aimed at. A bullet from a modern rifle will fly straight across the field for hundreds of yards with no elevation, even half a mile and more with but little elevation,

sweeping the whole width of the field between the gun and
the target.*

The deadliness of the modern rifle can be made clear in
another way. Says Bloch:

"According to the data of the Prussian general Rohne one hundred sharpshooters will put a battery out of action, firing at a
distance of 88 yards in the course of two and two-fifths minutes,
1,100 yards in the course of four minutes, 1,320 yards in the course
of seven and a half minutes, 1,650 yards in the course of twenty-
two minutes."

"The new Springfield rifle," says Fitzmorris,† "has a range of five
miles, the bullet having a velocity of 2,300 feet per second leaving
the weapon, or sufficient to drive it through four and a half feet
of white pine."

The "attractiveness" of war increases, of course, with the
likelihood that the improving markmanship of the enemy will
increase one's chances for meeting an "attraction." The
accuracy of fire is being rapidly improved by tireless target
practice in all the great armies of the world. Says Mr.
Wright, ex-Secretary of War :‡

"The results from target practice for the year 1907 and 1908
show that the average battery-hitting capacity has been rapidly
increased. . . . About sixteen times as many hits were made in 1906
from the same gun in a given time at the same range as were
made in 1900."

Under no circumstances should the delicate flesh of a big
business man be exposed to well-aimed bullets fired from a
modern rifle. His flesh is, of course, specially sensitive and
precious. Moreover, it is wholly unnecessary, because he can
buy the flesh of a common working class man for bullet stop-
per purposes very, very cheap, as a substitute. That is a much
better arrangement, the big business man thinks, and, of

---

* See J. Bloch: *The Future of War*, a volume of great value,
packed with information concerning several different phases of war
under present conditions. Published by Ginn and Company, New
York.

† *The Making of America*, Vol. IX., Special Article, "Army and
Navy," p. 388.

‡ Report for 1908, p. 33.

course, the working men agree with the business men on this matter just as they do on nearly everything else.

The Danish "Rexer" rifle is another instrument ready for use in war and in pacifying hungry people on strike. The "Rexer" weighs only eighteen pounds, uses high-power, small-calibre ammunition, is easily and accurately operated from a handy, portable "rest," can be conveniently carried on horse-back, rushed up front for short distances by infantry, can be fired slowly or, if desired, by simply holding the trigger, 300 times per minute. Equipped with this rifle one full regiment of soldiers or militiamen, each firing only 75 shots per minute, could fire into the ranks of wildly hungry strikers or unemployed one million five hundred thousand prosperity slugs in twenty minutes. With this gun ten militiamen could "quiet" five thousand strikers with twenty-five thousand shots in ten minutes.*

With the improved murdering machine called the Maxim gun 700 bullets per minute can be fired, bullets that will kill a man at a range of one and a half miles, bullets that will pacify a striker at a range of two miles. The Gatling gun equipped with an electric motor will discharge 1,800 death-dealing bullets per minute.†

"The Gatling gun," says Morris,‡ ". . . . is now, in its perfected form, in use all over the world. This consists of a cluster of rifle-barrels arranged around a central shaft and rotated by a crank. The magazine contains a supply of cartridges, which drop down and are rammed home one after another as the barrels rotate. This, in the later improved forms, is done with such rapidity that the gun can discharge its balls at the rate of 3,000 per minute. . . . Machine guns were designed for service against bodies of men."

ONE MODERN GATLING GUN WILL TEAR A BOARD FENCE TO PIECES A MILE AWAY IN FOUR MINUTES, AND AT A RANGE OF ONE MILE IT WILL GNAW OFF A FOOT-THICK PINE POST IN SEVEN MINUTES.

Don't enlist till next week.

---

* See A. Williams: *Romance of Modern Mechanics*, Chapter 27.
† McLaren: *Put up Thy Sword*, p. 127.
‡ *The Nation's Navy*, p. 292.

No wonder the politicians and big business men are "too busy" to get in line on the firing-line—patriotically. And, of course, they do not want their sons and sons-in-law to get up close in front of a belching Gatling gun,—in front of a modern murdering machine—patriotically.

IF A BATTERY OF MODERN GATLING GUNS, CONCEALED, USING SMOKELESS POWDER, LOCATED OUT OF HEARING A MILE AWAY OR NEARER AND EQUIPPED WITH A MAXIM NOISELESS ATTACHMENT,—SHOULD BE TRAINED UPON A REGIMENT OF MEN, EACH GUN POURING ONE THOUSAND BULLETS PER MINUTE INTO AN EXPOSED REGIMENT, THE ONLY OBSERVABLE RESULT WOULD BE THIS: THE REGIMENT WOULD MELT, STRICKEN BY AN UNSEEN, UNHEARD BREATH OF DEATH.

General William P. Duval, of the United States Military Staff and War College, estimates that the Maxim noiseless attachment for fire-arms "would produce just as much of a revolution in the art of war as did the smokeless powder. Psychologically, this new gun would double the terror inspired by the enemy possessing it. . . . The fear of the enemy would . . . at least be doubled."

Ordering the working class to go to war with the present fire-arms is like ordering a working man to make a gun, load it, dig his own grave, crawl down into it, and there scream "Hurrah for death!" and then shoot himself.

Perhaps the best way, at least the safest way, to get an accurate idea of the effectiveness of the slaughtering machinery of our day is to read what these guns accomplish in actual operation on the battlefield, pouring showers, streams, storms of lead and steel into the ranks of men. The propaganda of peace is powerfully served by books giving distinct impressions of war as it may be seen (and felt) on the field where modern arms are used. Some specially excellent books for such use are: *Human Bullets,* by T. Sakurai, a Japanese soldier;* *Port Arthur: A Monster Heroism,* by Richard

* Published by Houghton, Mifflin and Company, Boston.

Barry;* *The Red Laugh,* by Leonid Andreief;† *The Downfall,* by Emile Zola;‡ *The Future of War,* by Jean Bloch.§

Here following are some paragraphs from a vigorous book of this type, *Human Bullets,* just noted, passim, which treats of the Russian-Japanese War:

"The dismal horror of it [battle] can best be observed when the actual struggle is over. The shadow of impartial Death visits friend and foe alike. When a shocking massacre is over, countless corpses covered with blood lie flat in the grass and between the stones. What a deep philosophy their cold faces tell! When we saw the dead at Nanshan, we could not help covering our eyes in horror and disgust. . . . Some were crushed in head and face. Their brains mixed with dust and earth. The intestines were torn out and blood was trickling from them. . . . Some had photographs of their wives and children in their bosoms, and these pictures were spattered with blood. . . . After this battle we captured some damaged machine-guns. This fire-arm was most dreaded by us. . . . It can be made to sprinkle its shots as roads are watered with a hose. It can cover a larger or smaller space, or fire to greater or less distance as the gunner wills. . . . If one becomes the target for this terrible engine of destruction, three or four shots may go through the same place making a wound very large. . . . And the sound it makes . . . is like a power-loom. It is a sickening horrible sound! The Russians regarded this machine as their best friend. And it certainly did very much as a means of defense. They were wonderfully clever in the use of this machine. They would wait till our men came very near them, four or five ken only, and just as we were ready to shout a triumphant 'Banzai!' this dreadful machine would begin to sweep over us the besom of destruction, the result being hills and mounds of dead. After this battle we discovered one soldier . . . who had no less than forty-seven shots in his body. . . . Another soldier of a neighboring regiment received more than seventy shots. These instances prove how destructive is the machine-gun. The surgeons could not locate so many wounds in one body, and they invented a new name [meaning] 'whole-body-honey-combed-with-gun-wounds.' . . . It was invariably this machine-gun that made us suffer most severely. . . . The bodies of the brave dead built hill upon hill, their blood made streams in the valley. Shattered bones, torn flesh, flowing blood, were mingled with broken

*Published by Moffat, Yard and Company, New York.
† Published by J. Fisher Unwin, London.
‡ Published by The Macmillan Company, New York.
§ Published by Ginn and Company, New York.

swords and split rifles. What could be more shocking than this scene! We jumped over or stepped on the heaped up corpses and went on holding our noses. What a grief it was to have to tread on the bodies of our heroic dead! . . . What a horrible sight! Their bodies were piled up two or three or even four deep. . . . A sad groaning came from the wounded who were buried under the dead. When this gallant assaulting column had pressed upon the enemy's forts, stepping over their dead comrades' bodies, the terrible and skilful fire of the machine-guns had killed them all, close by the forts, piling the dead upon the wounded. . . . After a while the shells . . . began to burst briskly above our heads. Percussion balls fell around us and hurled up smoke and blood together. Legs, hands and necks were cut into black fragments and scattered about. I shut my eyes. . . ."

In what unqualified contempt do the masters of the world hold the toilers whom they send into such blood-wasting hells. Shakespeare has expressed the masters' scorn for the common soldier's flesh and blood thus:

"Tut, tut; good enough to toss; food for powder; food for powder; they'll fill a pit as well as better."

Here is a glimpse of the battle of Sedan:*

"Let your readers fancy masses of colored rags glued together with blood and brains, pinned into strange shapes by fragments of bones. Let them conceive men's bodies without legs, and legs without bodies, heaps of human entrails attached to red and blue cloth, and disembowelled corpses in uniform, bodies lying about in all attitudes with skulls shattered, faces blown off, hips smashed, bones, flesh and gay clothing all pounded together as if brayed in a mortar, extending for miles, not very thick in any one place, but recurring perpetually for weary hours, and then they can not with the most vivid imagination come up to the sickening reality of that butchery [the battle of Sedan, 1870]."

IT IS RELIABLY ESTIMATED THAT MODERN ARTILLERY IS CAPABLE OF DOING ONE HUNDRED AND SIXTEEN TIMES MORE DAMAGE THAN THE ARTILLERY USED BY THE GERMAN ARMY IN 1870. Even the simple instrument known as the range-finder adds much to effectiveness,—it enables soldiers to find the range in three minutes and pour death-dealing missiles

---

* *Arbeiter in Council* (Anonymous), pp. 155-56; published by The Macmillan Company, New York. A valuable book.

into the human targets promptly. This instrument weighs
about sixty pounds and is being rapidly improved.* A single
battery of modern artillery can hurl 1,450 rounds upon ten
regiments of men while they march one mile and a half.
These 1,450 shells arranged with time fuses to burst at the
target would sweep these ten thousand men with 275,000
bullets and ragged iron scraps. Bloch says:†

"In 1870 an ordinary shell when it burst broke into from 19
to 30 pieces. To-day it bursts into 240 pieces. Shrapnel in 1870
scattered only 37 death-dealing missiles. Now it scatters 340. A
bomb weighing about 70 pounds, thirty years ago, would have burst
into 42 fragments. Today, when it is charged with peroxilene, it
breaks into 1,200 pieces, each of which is hurled with much greater
velocity than the larger lumps which were scattered by a gunpowder explosion. It is estimated that such a bomb would destroy
all life within a range of 200 metres [about 200 yards] of
the point of the explosion. . . . With the increase in the number
of bullets and fragments, and in the forces which disperse them, increases also the area which they affect. Splinters and bullets bring
death and destruction, not only as in 1870, to those in the vicinity
of the explosion, but at a distance of 220 yards away, and this
tho' fired from a distance of 3,300 yards [about two miles]. . . .
In a time when rifle and artillery fire were beyond comparison
weaker than they are now, those who were left unhelped on the
battlefield might hope for safety. But now, when the whole field
of battle is covered with an uninterrupted hail of bullets and fragments of shells [at night too, with a search-light equipment], there
is little place for such hope."

Surely you can easily see that a business man's soft, fat
flesh won't do for a bullet-stopper. Here is where the cheap,
meek, weak wage-slaves come in handy—the *very stuff for
bullet-stoppers.*

In connection with this subject, remember that a bullet
fired from a modern rifle or a Gatling gun rotates over 3,800
times per second. This rotary motion produces the effect of
an explosion when the bullet strikes the stomach, bladder,
or heart—where there are liquids. The effect is horrible; with

---

* See Bloch: *The Future of War;* also Morris: *The Nation's
Navy,* p. 289.

† *The Future of War, Preface,* p. XXV., also pp. 9 and 157.

terrible violence "the liquids are cast on all sides with the destructive effect of an explosion."—(Bloch.)

Of course, the business man knows that *his* flesh should never be torn with such a horrible thing. He has nothing to fear, however. He will not go to war. He will send a cheap man, a wage-slave substitute. He knows it doesn't make any difference in the case of a cheap wage-earner who is only a working-class slave.

Ah, my working-class reader, it *will* make a difference when the working class become proud enough and shrewd enough to defiantly declare that it *shall* be different. The business man is too proud and shrewd to stand up before these modern flesh-tearing machines.

Don't be in a hurry to enlist, brother. Wait a few more days. Two weeks after next will do. The "very *best* people" in your town are not hurrying to enlist. Can't you see the point? Before you enlist, or before you consent to have your son or younger brother enlist, be sure to read some books describing real war with improved murdering machinery. A brilliant war correspondent, Mr. Richard Barry, thus describes a modern war-storm in his book, descriptive of the Japanese-Russian War, *Port Arthur, A Monster Heroism,* passim :*

"Toward three o'clock a second advance is ordered . . . nearly 15,000 men close in . . . now they are through [the wire fence] . . . half naked, savage, yelling, even Japanese stoicism gone. Up to the very muzzles of the first entrenchments they surge, waver and break like the dash of angry waves against a rock-bound coast. . . . *Officers are picked off by sharp-shooters, as flies are flecked from a molasses jug.* . . . So up they go, for the tenth time. . . . Spottsylvania Court House was no more savage. . . . Thus hand to hand they grapple, sweat, bleed, shout, expire. The veneer of culture sloughed as a snake his cast-off skin; they spit and chew, claw and grip as their forefathers beyond the memory of man. . . . The cost! The fleeing ones left *five hundred corpses in four trenches.* The others paid *seven times that price*—killed and wounded—to turn across the page of the world's warfare that word Nanshan. . . . A hospital ship left every day for Japan carrying from 200 to 1,000. . . . I lay in the broiling sun watching the soldiers huddle against

* Published by Moffat, Yard and Company, New York. Italics mine. G. R. K. See pp. 82-83.

the barbed-wire, under the machine guns . . . only to melt away
like chaff before a wind. . . . The 'pioneers' met with the death-
sprinkle of the Maxim [guns] . . . a machine rattled and the shale
beyond spattered. I was carried back [in memory] to a boiler
factory and an automatic riveter. Of all war sounds that of the
machine gun is least poetic, is most deadly. . . . The regiment
under fire of the machine guns retreated precipitately, leaving *one-
half its number* on the slope. . . . Overwhelmed on all sides, tricked,
defeated, *two-thirds of its men killed or wounded* . . . for out of that
[another] brigade of 6,000 men there are . . . uninjured but 640.
. . . Moreover in throwing up their trenches . . . *corpses had to be
used to improvise the walls. . . . The dead were being used to more
quickly fill the embankments.* . . . Soon dawn came and with it hell.
The battle was on again. Within his sight were more than a
hundred dead and twice as many wounded. Groans welled up like
bubbles from a pot. Arms tossed feverishly. Backs writhed in
despair. . . . Almost crazed by thirst and hunger, he [a wounded
soldier unattended for days on the battlefield] at length severed the
arteries of one of his comrades newly dead, and lived on [that is,
sucked blood from a comrade's corpse?]. He found worms crawling
in the wounds of his legs. He tore up the shirt of a corpse and
bound them. . . . How like a living thing a shell snarls—as some
wild beast, in ferocious glee thrusting its cruel fangs in earth and
rock, rending livid flesh with its savage claws, and its fetid breath
of poison powder scorching in the autumn winds. . . . All the way
up the base of the hill. . . . they were almost unmolested. . . . This
made them confident. But the Russian general . . . had ordered
his men to reserve their fire till we got within close range, and
then to give it to us with machine guns. . . . The aim was so sure
and firing so heavy that *nearly two-thirds of the command was
mowed down at once.* . . . Then came the thud of a bullet. It was
a different thud from any we had heard up to that time, and
though I had never before heard bullet strike flesh, I could not
mistake the sound. It goes into the earth wholesome and angry,
into flesh ripping and sick with a splash like a hoof-beat of mud in
the face. . . . The parapets of four forts were alive with bursting
shrapnel. A hundred a minute were exploding on each (at fifteen
gold dollars apiece). The air above them was black with glycerine
gases of the motor shells, and the wind blowing . . . held huge
quantities of dust. . . . 'No, the truth about war can not be told.
It is too horrible. *The public will not listen.* A white bandage
about the forehead with a strawberry mark in the center—is the
picture they want of the wounded. *They won't let you tell them the
truth* and show bowels ripped out, brains spilled, eyes gouged away,
faces blanched with horror. . . . Archibald Forbes predicted twenty

years ago that the time would come when armies would no longer be able to take their wounded from the field of battle. That day has come. We are living in it. Wounded have existed—how, God knows—on that field out there without help for twelve days, while shells and bullets rained about them, and if a comrade had dared to come to their assistance, his would have been a useless suicide. The searchlight, enginery of scientific trenches, machine-guns, rifles point blank at 200 yards with a range of over 2,000—these things have helped to make war more terrible than ever before in history. Red Cross societies and scientific text-books—they sell well and look pretty, but as for "humane warfare"—was there ever put into words a mightier sarcasm!'"

Read all of Mr. Barry's thrilling book and thus learn why the haughty "very best people," who despise the workingmen, socially, don't go themselves, up close, to the foul and bloody hell called war.

In the Russian-Japanese war 275 officers and 1,349 men were treated in a single hospital for insanity. Says Dr. Awtokratow:

"As might be anticipated, in the acute insanities, particularly in neurasthenic and confusional cases, the influence of the war gave a characteristic color to the mental symptoms, phases of panic terror, with hallucinations of bursting shells, pursuing enemies, putrefying corpses, and so forth, being especially frequent."[*]

A special despatch in the New York *Times* of December 11, 1909, reads:

"A carload of insane soldiers from the Philippines passed through Pittsburgh [Pennsylvania] today in charge of Major J. M. Kennedy, who was taking them to Washington from the Pacific Coast."[†]

The soldiers of the American Civil War did not use—had not even heard of—the terrible explosives of our day. Melinite, dynamite, cordite, indurite, motorite, ecrasite, peroxilene and other explosive compounds vastly increase the effectiveness of modern arms and in other ways also multiply the dangers of the modern battlefield.

Mr. Charles Morris describes a dynamite gun as follows:[‡]

---

[*] See *Literary Digest*, Nov. 9, 1907.

[†] See Index: "Insanity in American Army."

[‡] *The Nation's Navy*, pp. 289-90.

"The dynamite gun, compressed air usually being employed, while forty feet long, has a barrel of three-eighth inch iron, with one-eighth inch brass tubing. The projectile is of brass, forty inches long, rotation being given it by spiral vanes fixed to its base. It has a conical cast-iron point, twelve inches long. At a trial in 1895 shells were thrown as far as two thousand five hundred yards, and one containing one hundred pounds of dynamite was thrown a distance of two miles. Great accuracy of aim was attained. This dangerous weapon is an object of dread by naval officers."

Writing of modern explosives, M. Bloch says, in substance: Such enormous energy is developed in firing cannon using some of these explosives that gun, gunners and horses have been dragged a considerable distance. In the case of a shell exploding by slight accident due to excitement the body of the gun was broken into twenty pieces, the carriage and wheels were reduced to a pile of shapeless steel and wooden splinters; single fragments of the destroyed gun "weighed 363 pounds and were hurled 99 yards forward and backward from the place where the gun was fired, and nearly 108 yards on either side." He calls special attention to the *dangers due to having such explosives on the field of battle.* He says:*

"Notwithstanding the distance between guns, *a single explosion might embrace several guns and all their ammunition.*

"Not far from the battery ammunition cases will be placed. If these be not exploded by the concussion of the atmosphere they may very easily be exploded by some of the heavy fragments which fall upon them."

Let us look for a moment at a new kind of storm—a possible dynamite storm.

A rifle bullet fired into a stick of dynamite will explode the dynamite. A bullet accidentally fired from a high-power rifle into a dynamite factory even a mile distant might easily destroy the entire factory and destroy at the same time all life in and within hundreds of yards of the factory, because of the highly explosive nature of the dynamite. The same is true of factories in which other terrible explosives are being prepared for use on the battlefield. Such explosive materials in chests on the field of battle create, of course, enormous dan-

---

* *The Future of War,* pp. 21 and 22. Italics mine. G. R. K.

ger that *thousands may be destroyed with their own ammuni-tion.* One steel bullet, or one shell, fired from a modern high-power gun into a chest of shells or bombs, loaded as they are with highly explosive material,—one such bullet or shell thus fired, might set off a chest of shells and carry death to all around, these shells, exploding other chests of shells, and these still others, creating a sort of *hell in all directions.* The possibilities thus created by modern highly explosive ammuni-tion materials are terrible, horrible to contemplate. Suppose ten thousand men on the battlefield, and suppose an explosion due to a single shell crashing into a chest of shells. A series of explosions might follow. The first explosion, caused by one shot, might be communicated from the first bursting shell to the next, and so on in succession with startling rapidity. The thundering explosions would cause a cyclone of flying splinters of wood and steel, scrap-iron, cannon barrels, wagon wheels, the torn carcasses, the mingled flesh, blood and bones of dismembered horses and men,—a storm of hopeless and hideous confusion, a harvest of death utterly indescribable. Thousands of brave young fellows from the farm, factories, mines and other industries would thus be practically annihi-lated with their own ammunition.

What a place this would be (up close) for "prominent citizens"—bankers, priests, preachers, bishops, senators, law-yers and "captains of industry"! A storm of blood and steel! No, brother, oh, no. No dynamite cyclone for these pul-monary patriots. Hardly. There is plenty of "common" flesh and "common" blood of the "plain people" which can be bought cheap, dirt cheap.

Reflect for a moment on the horrible possibilities of the airship carrying a light machine gun with a good supply of ammunition, or carrying 1,000 or 1,500 pounds of dynamite aloft over an army, a city, or a fleet. The airship, though still very new, is already sufficiently developed to make it practica-ble to work wholesale ruin in this way. In March, 1909, Count Zeppelin's dirigible airship, 445 feet long, 50 feet in diameter, carrying three motors, a searchlight, and twenty-five people, fifteen of them soldiers, made a hundred-and-fifty-mile trip at the rate of almost forty miles an hour. Hudson Maxim, the inventor and expert in high explosives, torpedo boat-destroyers, noiseless gun attachments, and the like, speaks thus of the airship as a fighting machine:*

"The great field for operations with high explosives carried in airships will be the raiders' outfit. Aerial raiders would be able to do wide destruction on unprotected inland cities and towns, destroying railroads, blowing up bridges, arsenals, public stores, powder magazines and powder mills, and in levying ransom on moneyed institutions. . . . In future wars, the fronts of battle will be skyline and opposing skyline, and over the stupendous arena missiles of death will shriek and roar, while sharp-shooters with silent rifles will make ambush in copse and every hedge and highway."

Now let us look for a moment at the greater cannon.

"A day will come," said Victor Hugo,† "when a cannon will be exhibited in the public museums, just as an instrument of torture is now, and people will be astonished how such thing could have been."

The new 14-inch gun fires a 1,600-pound projectile. Used at its maximum capacity it puts itself out of commission in six and one-half hours because of the frightful wear of the gun's heavy charges upon itself.‡ The 16-inch seacoast gun exhibited at the World's Fair in 1904 is officially described as having a "muzzle energy of projectile . . . 76,904 foot tons."

"The Masonic Temple in Chicago, until recently the largest office building in the world, weighs 30,000 tons. In firing a 14-inch gun, sufficient energy is developed to lift the Masonic Temple two feet in one second. The force behind a single eight-gun broadside from 14-inch guns would raise that building sixteen feet in a single second."§

The United States Government has a 16-inch cannon; it can throw a shot weighing 2,000 pounds to an extreme range of twenty-one miles, and has an effective range of twelve miles. It has been fired four times.

---

* Lecture, "The War of the Future," at Amherst College, Dec. 3, 1909.

† Quoted in Charles Sumner's *Addresses on War*, p. 138.

‡ See *Scientific American*, Sept. 21, 1907.

§ J. F. Haskins, New York *Globe and Commercial Advertiser*, Feb. 1, 1909.

And now think of a murdering machine 50 feet long, weighing 260,000 pounds, consuming 612 pounds of smokeless powder per charge, firing a projectile weighing 2,400 pounds through 23½ inches of Krupp steel armor, and having a range of almost nine miles—a monster butchering machine. The United States Government exhibited such a gun at the World's Fair, at St. Louis, in 1904,—exhibited this hell's masterpiece with pride, true, Christian, savage pride.

This huge gun was exhibited—shrewdly.

What for?

Many youths from Christian homes looked upon this mechanical monster and themselves became monsters—in their hearts—eager to butcher, "not only willing, but *anxious* to fight."

Human slaughter has become a science. The machines are perfect and ready, all ready, for the *working* class to use—on the working class.

SECTION TWO: THE SILENT DESTROYER—DISEASE.

The barking rifle, the snarling Gatling gun, and the booming cannon—these have also on the battlefield a foul and powerful confederate, Disease. Disease joins in to poison the blood the guns do not spill. On this important matter the reader will appreciate the expert testimony here offered.

"In every great campaign," says L. L. Seaman,* "an army faces two enemies: First, the armed force of the opposing foe with his various machines for human destruction, met at intervals in open battles; and, second, the hidden foe, always lurking in every camp, the spectre that gathers its victims while the soldier slumbers in the barracks or bivouacs, the greater silent foe—disease. Of these enemies, the history of warfare for centuries shows that in extended campaigns, the first or open enemy kills twenty per cent. of the total mortality; while the second, or silent, enemy kills eighty per cent. In other words, out of every hundred men who fall in war, twenty die from casualties of battle, while eighty perish from disease. . . . It is in these conditions that we find the true hell of war. . . . Health alone, however, is no guarantee against the in-

---

* *Appleton's Magazine*, April, 1908.

sidious attacks of the silent foe that lingers in every camp, and bivouac. It is this foe, as the records of war for the past two hundred years have proved, that is responsible for four times as many deaths as the guns of the enemy, to say nothing of the vast number temporarily invalided or discharged as unfit for duty. . . . In the Russo-Turkish war, the deaths from the battle casualties were 20,000, while those from disease were 80,000. In our great Civil conflict . . . 400,000 were sacrificed to disease to 100,000 from battle casualties. In a recent campaign of the French in Madagascar 14,000 were sent to the front, of whom 29 were killed in action, and over 7,000 perished from preventable diseases. In the Boer War in South Africa the English losses were ten times greater from disease than from the bullets of the enemy. In our recent war with Spain fourteen lives were needlessly sacrificed to ignorance and incompetency for every man who died on the firing line or from results of wounds.

"In our Spanish Army we had:

170,000 men,
156,000 hospital admissions in three months,
3,976 dead.

"The remainder were mustered out, most of them, in shrunken and shriveled condition which the reader probably remembers. Our Army of Invasion numbered 20,000; in 1908 there were 24,000 pensioners; of these 24,000, over 19,000 are invalids and survivors of the war; and there are over 18,000 claims pending."

Here is Theodore Roosevelt's testimony:[*]

"Our army [in Cuba] included the great majority of the regulars, and was, therefore, the flower of the American force. . . . Every officer other than myself except one was down with sickness at one time or another. . . . Very few of the men indeed retained their strength and energy . . . there were less than fifty per cent. who were fit for any kind of work."

Disease as a destroyer appears in the data furnished by C. Goltz, a few lines of which interesting facts run thus:[†]

"It is horrible to see trains packed full with sick soldiers sent away from the army. . . . The loss from sickness is almost incredible, and one example is sufficient to prove that these losses may put all success at stake. The sanitary conditions of the German army in France in 1870 was very favorable; there were no dangerous infectious diseases. Nevertheless, 400,000 men were entered at the hospitals during the campaign, in addition to those dangerously wounded."

---

[*] *The Rough Riders*, pp. 202, 209.
[†] *The Nation in Arms*, p. 376.

Anitchkow thus testifies:*

"In such a rich country as France, and in such a splendid climate, the army lost four times more from disease than from battles. [Franco-Prussian War, 1870-71.] It is evident that the force of modern arms . . . presents less danger than infectious diseases and other sicknesses inseparable from the rough life of large camps."†

An anonymous author, quoted on a preceding page, calls attention‡ to a matter of great importance in this connection, namely, the decreasing opportunity to carry the wounded off the battlefield and the consequent increasing terrors for the men who lie torn, feverish and unattended on the field lighted at night with searchlights and raked with machine guns, not only during the day, but also at night, making prompt rescue and surgical attention impossible. He writes:

"One of the most cruel features in future battles will be the contrast between the great improvement in medical service, and the increasing difficulty, despite the Red Cross, of giving aid to the wounded. . . . His conclusion [the conclusions of Dr. Bardeleben, who was Surgeon-General of the Prussian Army during the Franco-Prussian War] was that the whole system of carrying away the wounded on litters during the battle must be abandoned as altogether impracticable. This I believe has proved to be generally true. And now battles last a week or ten days! Something, of course, can be done under cover of the night—though the custom of fighting at night prevails more and more. . . . It is probable that, in spite of all improvements in medicine and ambulance, the sufferings of the wounded in the great battles in Manchuria and at the siege of Port Arthur have been as great as, if not greater than, those of any war of recent times."

Here it is to be emphasized by the young man who is thinking of joining the army that in spite of the loud outcry against the poor fellows of our army in the Cuban war in the way of criminally inefficient medical service, our great and extremely patriotic statesmen who love the common soldiers so dearly have in the twelve years since the war made no ade-

---

* *War and Labor*, p. 54.
† But see Professor Mayo-Smith's *Statistics and Sociology*.
‡ *Arbeiter in Council*, pp. 150-51.

quate preparation to prevent another such outrage. Let the following stand as evidence of this statement:*

> "*Under the existing organization it would be impossible to prevent a breakdown of the Medical Department* in case of a war involving the mobilization of the volunteer forces, nor would it be possible to spare the necessary Regular medical officers to apply in those voluntary forces the modern sanitary measures so vital to the health and efficiency of the troops, without which unnecessary suffering is produced and disaster is invited."

Thus also the New York *Times*:†

> "The admission rate into the hospitals for the American Army is [now in the time of peace] 1,250 per 1,000 each year. The *British Annual* notes that this enormous rate is well above that for the French, German and Austrian armies, while the hospital lists for the British Army show a rate of but 324 per thousand."

However, all this, so far as personal danger is concerned, is of *small importance to the leading citizens,* because *they*—these leaders—will never lead or be led to war. They have nothing to fear from hissing bullet, burning fever, and the death-grip of devouring diseases in war. The plain, cheap wage-slave, the industrial draft-horses, the common men forced to keep books for a poor little salary, the fifteen-dollar-a-week clerks, the blistered miners, the tanned railroad men, the grease-stained machinists, the soil-stained farm toilers, these, all these and many others must learn one thing distinctly, and that thing is this: Modern human butchering machinery has been so highly developed, and disease in war is so hideous, that "our best citizens," "our very *best* people," "our most successful men," politely (and intelligently) decline all "glorious opportunities" to have their smooth fat bodies exposed to the steel-belching machines, or have their health ruined on the battlefield and in the "dead-house" called a military hospital. The common earth must not drink up their rich aristocratic blood; no rough army surgeon shall carve and slice and saw the "leading citizens" and carelessly toss

---

* Annual Report of the Secretary of War (William H. Taft), 1907, p. 25. Italics mine. G. R. K.

† Editorial, Oct. 7, 1909.

their severed arms and legs into a bloody heap of flesh as a butcher tosses scraps and trimmings from steaks and chops from his cutting block. Why, *certainly* not. It should be remembered that such people as bankers, big manufacturers, mine-owners, Senators, Congressmen, great editors and the like, do not have much physical exercise and at the same time they eat daintier food. They are not strong in muscle, except for golf, horseback riding, swimming, hunting trips, mountain climbing. They are softer in flesh than the wage-earner. They belong to the "very *best* families," and hence their flesh is finer, their "blue" blood is richer and more sacred than the wage-earner's cheap red ooze. They are the social thorough-breds, and the thoroughbreds believe that the thoroughbreds should be kept well out of danger, while just the common social draft-horses are rushed to the front where the modern butchering machinery is ready to mow down men by the thousands and befouling disease is ready to rot the unspilt blood.

My working class brothers, mark it well: In the gilded, palatial homes of the industrial masters, in their club houses, in their elegant business offices, in the legislative halls where "statesmen" meet,—there the so-called best people, the still-fed, stall-fed snobs and Caesars of society never for one moment consider the matter of going themselves to the front, never for an instant plan to go themselves into the cyclones of lead and steel or into the death-grasp of disease in war.

Never!

To them the idea is so—well, so *unkind*—also ridiculous.

Their minds are made up.

They will not go.

But you, you brothers of the working class, you who toil on and on for cheap clothing, cheap shelter and cheap food— you whose very lives are bought and sold on the installment plan, for wages day by day—you who are forced to become the socially despised human oxen—you—you will be forced to the front, blinded with flattery and confused with gay-colored flags and booming drums—you will virtually be forced to cut your own throats—forced to blow out your own brains and

blood with these modern steel destroyers, and forced to expose your lives to the grim curse, Disease. You will groan
and scream and slowly rot and die in a dingy hospital tent
or shed far from those you love—laughed at (secretly) by
the *prominent* people who have *already* made up *their* minds
not to go to war.

How long, O brothers of the working class, how long can
you be seduced to slay yourselves?

Leading citizens will bring about and brag about the wars.

But you, my brothers, will fight the wars.

Grim Disease waits ready to give you her slimy embrace.

The cold steel machines are ready—ready for heated men.

Keep cool.

Beware of the "war fever."

NOTICE CAREFULLY :—Your wealthy employers are not enlisting for the firing line. *They are immune from the fool's
fever.*

Wait a little before you enlist. Think it over—till week
after next.

YOU ARE SAFE—(JUST THINK OF IT)—ABSOLUTELY SAFE
FROM DEATH IN THE NEXT WAR—IF YOU CAN KEEP OFF THE
FIRING LINE TILL THE "PROMINENT GENTLEMEN" OF YOUR
COMMUNITY HAVE BEEN ON THE FIRING-LINE FOR THIRTY
DAYS.

Once again, brother, admit this thought to your brain :—
The working class must be the protectors of their own class—
always.*

SECTION THREE : PEACEFUL SLAUGHTER—IN INDUSTRY.

Surely it is bad enough to have the workingmen slaughtered while on the battlefield where each is armed and has his
heart full of stupid hate for his fellow workingman of some
other country. But it is outrageous that men, women, and
little children should be killed and wounded by the hundreds
of thousands every year in our own country while they are

---

* See Index: "Another War."

engaged in the useful, peaceful pursuits of industry. Let us briefly consider this matter.

The owner of a *chattel*-slave worker is careful to PROTECT the chattel-slave from accident, from sickness and from death. The slave-owner buys the slave, buys his *whole* life, at *one* purchase; and he is interested, therefore, in having the slave alive and well and sound as long as possible in order to get out of the slave as much labor-power as possible.

But the capitalist employer of the WAGE-slave worker does not buy the wage-earner *for life;* he buys the wage-earner, the wage-slave, IN SECTIONS; that is, for a month, or a week or a day at a time—eight or ten hours' labor-power per day. Thus there is *no risk* for the capitalist if the wage-earner falls sick and dies; he is not responsible for the wage-earner's health. If the grinding toil ages or sickens the wage-earner it is nothing to the employer of the wage-slaves. There are *plenty more* wage-slaves eager to sell their labor-power if some get sick or wounded, or die.

Of course it costs the employer, it is expensive to him, it reduces the precious surplus,—it cuts down the profits on the labor-power he buys for wages—to ventilate his factory perfectly, to keep it clean of dust, foul odors and poisonous gases, to arrange safeguards about dangerous machinery in order to protect the wage-earners against accident and sickness. Railway companies, for example, are very slow to provide all possible safeguards to protect employees—simply because it is expensive, cuts down profits, reduces the surplus value. Human life, however, is very cheap under the wage-system. Of course a safety device, a ventilator, might save a human arm or a human life—of a wage-earner; but the life-saving arrangement costs quite a bit of money. A new human *arm,* another human *life* (another worker) can easily be found to take the place of the lost arm or the destroyed life—and *without extra expense to the capitalist employer.* There are plenty of wage-slaves waiting 'round anxious to be hired, and thus a WAGE-slave limb or life can be replaced as easily as a wooden plug or a broken wheel in a machine, and with no such loss as there would be if his workers were CHATTEL-slaves. Thus the wage-slave plan is cheaper—more *profitable* —and surely more *convenient.*

You can see that—can't you?

Of course "it is cruel"—there is no sentiment in such a procedure. But that does not matter, under capitalism: "Business is *business"*—and *"there is no sentiment in business,"* we are assured of that by leading Christian business men.

Hence everywhere there is vicious neglect by the capitalist employers in the matter of protecting the health, limb and life of the WAGE-workers, the WAGE-slaves. The wage-system is in this respect far more cruel and murderous than the chattel-slave system. Of course it seems impossible that capitalism is more inhumanly scornful of human life than was chattel slavery. But here following is some evidence to show how the greed for profits under the wage-system results in the slaughter of men, women and children—far worse than under the chattel-slave system, even far heavier slaughter than in actual war, real war in which even wholesale butchery with sword, rifle and cannon means magnificent success.

"It is the common consensus of opinion," says The New York *Independent,*[*] "among investigators that industrial casualties in this nation number more than 500,000 yearly. Dr. Josiah Strong estimates the number at 564,000. As there are 525,600 minutes in a year, it may readily be seen that *every minute (day and night) our industrial system sends to the grave-yard or to the hospital a human being, the victim of some accident inseparable from his toil.* We cry out against the horrors of war. . . . But the ravages . . . of Industrial warfare are far greater than those of armed conflict. The number of killed or mortally wounded (including deaths from accidents, suicides and murders, but excluding deaths from disease) in the Philippine War from February 4, 1899, to April 30, 1902, was 1,573. These fatal casualties were spread over a period of three years and three months. But one coal mine alone in one year furnished a mortality more than 38 per cent. in excess of this.

"The Japanese war is commonly looked upon as the bloodiest of modern wars. According to the official statement of the Japanese

[*] March 14, 1907. Italics mine. G. R. K.

Government, 46,180 Japanese were killed, and 10,970 died of wounds. Our industrial war shows a greater mortality year by year.

"But we are all of us more familiar with the Civil War, and we know what frightful devastation it caused in households North and South. It was, however, but a tame conflict compared with that which rages today, and which we call 'peace.' The slaughter of its greatest battles are thrown in the shade by the slaughter which particular industries inflict today. Ask any schoolboy to name three of the bloodiest battles of that war, and he will probably name Gettysburg, Chancellorsville and Chickamauga. The loss on both sides was:

	Killed.	Wounded.
"Gettysburg	5,662	27,203
Chancellorsville,	3,271	18,843
Chickamauga	3,924	23,362
Total . ,	12,857	69,408

"But our railroads, state and interstate, and our trolleys in one year equal this record in the number of killings and double it in the number of woundings. . . .

"But whose interest is it that the lives of the workers shall be . . . guarded? *The employer class has no material interest* in the matter. The worker is 'free,' *legally,* to refuse to work under dangerous conditions. If, *economically,* he must accept work under these conditions [or starve], that is another matter."

Another witness* sets forth the murderous carelessness of the lives of the workers in modern industry thus:

"In Allegheny County, Pa., including Pittsburgh, 17,700 persons were killed or injured last year in the mills and on the railroads or in some of the workshops of that interesting Inferno. This number has been recorded and reported, and there were, of course, others whose deaths or injuries were not reported. . . . Life and limb are needlessly sacrificed—hundreds of thousands of lives every decade. This is one of the penalties that we pay for quick industrial success."

"Quick industrial success" is good, a fine phrase indeed— in the mining industry, for example, in which in the United States from 1889 to 1909 over 30,000 men were killed.† If a war were on in the Philippines and 1500 of our men

---

* *World's Work,* March, 1906.

† Museum of Safety and Sanitation, Bulletin, issued December, 1909.

were being slaughtered every year the generals and captains in charge of our forces would be regarded as failures. Yet the captains of industry, in the capitalist administration of the mining industry alone, in the United States sacrifice more than 1500 brave men of the great industrial army every year.

That the modern industry, inspired by insane lust for *profits-for part of the people* rather than by *welfare for all the people*—that this modern industry is far more deadly than real war on a large scale—this seems impossible. Yet it is not at all an impossibility; it is reality; it is experience; it is fact; it is the savagery of capitalist civilization.

ALL THE PROFIT-MONGERS' PROUD AND STUPID BOASTING OF THE NOBLE TRIUMPHS OF CAPITALIST "PHILANTHROPY" CAN NOT HUSH THE LOUD-SHOUTING FACT THAT THE SICKLE OF DEATH CUTS DOWN THE TOILERS FAR MORE RAPIDLY WHILE PEACEFULLY ON DUTY IN THE INDUSTRIES THAN IT SLASHES DOWN IN TIME OF WAR ON THE FIRING-LINE AND IN THE MILITARY HOSPITAL—FAR MORE THAN THE RIFLE, SWORD, BAYONET, AND DISEASE COMBINED.

This is true, horrible and important. And because it is true, horrible and important, all doubt concerning the matter should, as far as possible, be dispelled. And, therefore, still more evidence is here offered to make the matter clear.

The eminent publicist, Dr. Josiah Strong, testifies:*

"We might carry on a half dozen Philippine wars for three-quarters of a century with no larger number of total casualties than take place yearly in our peaceful industries.

"TAKING THE LOWEST OF OUR THREE ESTIMATES OF INDUSTRIAL ACCIDENTS, THE TOTAL NUMBER OF CASUALTIES SUFFERED BY OUR INDUSTRIAL ARMY IN ONE YEAR IS EQUAL TO THE AVERAGE ANNUAL CASUALTIES OF OUR CIVIL WAR, PLUS THOSE OF THE PHILIPPINE WAR, PLUS THOSE OF THE RUSSIAN-JAPANESE WAR.

"Think of carrying on three such wars at the same time, world without end."

Losses from sickness in war and from sickness contracted

* *North American Review*, Nov., 1906. Emphasis mine. G. R. K.

in industry are, it should be remembered, not included in Dr. Strong's calculations.

President Roosevelt in his Annual Message of 1907 bluntly stated the facts as follows:

"INDUSTRY IN THE UNITED STATES NOW EXACTS . . . A FAR HEAVIER TOLL OF DEATH THAN ALL OF OUR WARS PUT TOGETHER. . . . THE NUMBER OF DEATHS IN BATTLE IN ALL THE FOREIGN WARS PUT TOGETHER FOR THE LAST CENTURY AND A QUARTER, AGGREGATE CONSIDERABLY LESS THAN ONE YEAR'S DEATH RECORD FOR OUR INDUSTRIES."

It is inevitable that this slaughter of the toilers both in industry and in war will work rapidly and disastrously against the general blood-vigor of society. Serious and conservative students of the blood-letting and blood-weakening tendencies of capitalistic society are beginning to sound the alarm. The startlingly visible results in British society serve as excellent illustrative material. For more than two hundred years vast numbers of the soundest, strongest British workingmen have been slaughtered or weakened in war; and for more than a hundred years (the era of intense machine production) the British workingmen, women, and children have been cruelly overworked, underfed and ill-clad in the struggle for existence—*in the industrial civil war called capitalism.* And here are some of the results:

"In Manchester," says Thomas Burke,* "out of 12,000 would-be recruits [for the South African War], 8,000 were rejected as virtually invalids, and only 1,200 could be regarded as fit in all respects. . . . General Sir Frederick Maurice declared that, according to the best evidence he could obtain, it was the fact that for many years out of every five recruits only two were found to be physically fit after two years' service. . . . It was, indeed, a startling fact that 60 per cent. of the men offering themselves for active service were physically unfit."

Thus the well-known preacher and lecturer, Dr. Newell Dwight Hillis, of Brooklyn, New York:†

"Many forms of public charity, from a scientific viewpoint,

---

* *The Forum,* Jan., 1905.
† Brooklyn *Daily Eagle,* Feb. 13, 1907.

seem a curse, while wars and many industries seem the enemies of the blood of the nation. . . . The national physique has suffered an incalculable loss. In one factory town [in England] the military commission, examining young men for the South African War, rejected nineteen out of twenty, because of some defect in the eyes or lungs or legs."

It is to be remembered that many thousands of men who report for examination as candidates for military service are so evidently defective that no formal examination is necessary for their prompt rejection. It is also important to consider the fact that there are many thousands of men who would gladly join the army, but make no application, knowing well, in advance, that they would be rejected as unfit. Thus the statistics showing that a large per cent. of those reporting to the military department as candidates for the service are "rejected on examination," even these statistics do not fully reveal the unfortunate condition of affairs. In ten of the largest cities of England and Scotland in the year ending September 30, 1907, there were 34,808 applicants for admission to the army. Forty-seven per cent. of these applicants were rejected as physically unfit.* Of course, the percentage of rejections would have been far heavier if all had applied who would have been glad to join the army.

The next generation of English working-class people will probably be far more physically defective than the present generation.

In Westham public school (London) it was recently found:

". . . That 87 per cent. of the infants and 70 per cent. of the older children were below the normal physique. These were all children of the dockers.

"Neglecting the kindly and assuageable problem of rural poverty, we seem driven to the conclusion that some seven and a half millions of people are at the present moment in England living below the poverty line—a problem which if only definitely realized in its squalid immensity is surely enough to stagger humanity."†

In England, because of the physical decline of the working class, the Government has so much difficulty in finding a

---

* *Labor Leader*, London, July 17, 1908.

† C. F. G. Masterman: *Contemporary Review*, Jan., 1902.

sufficient number of sound men to fill the ranks that it has been necessary, since the Battle of Waterloo, to repeatedly lower the physical requirements for enlistment.

Thus do our brothers and sisters of the working class decay—driven to death—in the mills and mines and other industries. And in many parts of the world the fleshless skulls of the toilers slaughtered on the battlefield stare and grin at the present generation of workers decaying, dying in the capitalist industrial warfare. The president of Stanford University, Dr. David Starr Jordan, writes:*

"It is claimed on authority . . . that the French soldier of today is nearly two inches shorter than the soldier of a century ago. . . . There [in Novara, Italy] the farmers have ploughed up skulls of men till they have piled up a pyramid ten to twelve feet high. . . . These were the skulls of the young men of Savoy, Sardinia, and Austria,—men of eighteen to thirty-five, without physical blemish so far as may be. . . . You know the color that we call magenta, the hue of the blood that flowed out over the olive trees. . . . Go over Italy as you will, there is scarcely a spot not crimsoned with the blood of France, scarcely a railway station without its pile of French skulls. You can trace them across to Egypt, to the foot of the Pyramids. You will find them in Germany, at Jena and Leipzig, at Lützen and Bautzen and Austerlitz. You will find them in Russia, at Moscow; in Belgium, at Waterloo. 'A boy can stop a bullet as well as a man,' said Napoleon; and with the rest are the skulls of boys . . . 'born to be food for powder,' was the grim epigram of the day."

This vast crime, this phase of hell for the working class, is well stated by J. H. Rose:†

"Amidst the ever deepening misery they [Napoleon's army] struggled on, until the 600,000 who had proudly crossed the Niemen for the conquest of Russia, only 20,000 famished, frost-bitten, unarmed spectres staggered [back] across the bridge of Lorno in the middle of December. . . . Despite the loss of the most splendid army ever marshalled by man, Napoleon . . . strained every effort to call the youth of the empire to arms. . . . THE MIGHTY SWIRL OF THE MOSKOW CAMPAIGN SUCKED IN 150,000 LADS UNDER TWENTY

* *The Blood of the Nation,* pp. 45-47.
† *The History of Napoleon.* Emphasis mine. G. R. K.

YEARS OF AGE INTO THE VORTEX. . . . The peasants gave up their sons as food for cannon. . . . In less than half a year after the loss of half a million men a new army nearly as large was marshalled. . . . But the majority were young. . . . Soldiers were wanting, youths were dragged forth."

President Jordan, quoting Mr. Otto Seek, said:*

"Napoleon in a series of years seized all the youth of high stature and left them scattered over many battlefields, so that the French people who followed them are mostly men of smaller stature. More than once in France since Napoleon's time has the [physical] limit been lowered."

The ancient Romans, a large robust people, spilt so much of the best blood of the best men in their "glorious" wars that their modern descendants, the Italians, are conspicuously inferior, physically, to their ancient ancestors; comparatively they are stunted. The "glorious" victories of Caesar alone cost more than a million picked men on the battlefield.†

These vast, incalculable wrongs thrust into the lives of the working class—will they ever be righted?

Day dawns even now.

The lust for blood and profits will yet be cheated of its victories and victims—in the hastening future.

Our working class brothers in Europe are already rousing and shaking off the cruel spell of the gilt-braided butchers and silk-hatted capitalist statesmen and industrial Neros; *the toilers in Europe are learning to seize the powers of government in self-defense,—quietly and legally, of course, but—* DEFIANTLY.‡

We—driven, robbed and despised in the factory; betrayed, buncoed and slaughtered on the battlefield; voiceless in the control of industry, voiceless in the capitalist political party conventions, voiceless in the judiciary, voiceless in state and national legislatures, voiceless in the state and national executive councils, ridiculed by "high society," scorned everywhere

* In an address, "The Biology of War," May 3, 1909, Chicago.
† Reference for substance and part of phrasing of this paragraph has been lost.
‡ See Index: "Four Historic Events."

—we also must learn to defend ourselves. We must seize the powers of government and defend our class—everywhere.

Brothers, my American brothers, brothers of all the world, —if you have minds exercise them—for your own class; if you have pride, show it—for your class; if you have loyalty, prove it—for your class; if you have power, use it—use it in self-defense—for your class; if you can climb, why, climb, united with your class altogether—climb out of hell, the hell of capitalism.

Divided, your masters despise you.

United, your masters dread you.

Get together, brothers, and get up off your knees.

Refuse to go to hell—the hell of war.

Refuse to stay in hell—the hell of capitalist industry.

Unite! For peace and freedom—unite!

Form, toilers, form!

Organize!

A solid front on the battlefield—of industry.

A solid front on the battlefield—of politics.

A suggestion: Let each one of a hundred thousand men and women patiently and repeatedly bear light to the brain of one new man or woman each month for two years, and *teach each new man to become a teacher of other men and women.* Get some good book, a book that burns, a book that kindles a passion for freedom and justice; and lend that book to a new person each month *till the book is worn out.**

Light a lamp in your neighbor's brain.

Strike a fire in your neighbor's heart.

Revolutionize him.

Dare.

To-day.

Society is, and always will be—as free as the majority have sense enough and pride enough to make it; or as tyrannical as the majority are meek enough to permit it to be.

Conditions always express the will or lack of will of the majority.

---

* See "What to Read," Chapter Twelve.

CHAPTER SIX.

Tricked to the Trenches—Then Snubbed.

"On the whole, the patriotism of the average citizen rises and falls inversely with the Income Tax; . . ."*

Imagine J. P. Morgan, rifle in hand, doing picket duty on a dark, sleet-drizzling night. Imagine J. Ogden Armour, George Gould and Thomas F. Ryan with heavy shovels digging trenches, stopping at noon to eat some salt pork, embalmed beef and stale crackers. Imagine Reggie Vanderbilt as a freighter hurrying rations to the front and taking care of six mud-covered horses at night. Imagine the strong younger John D. Rockefeller on the firing line with his breast exposed to the hellish rain of lead from a Gatling gun. Yes, indeed,—just imagine a whole regiment of big bankers and manufacturers dressed in khaki, breakfasting on beans and bacon, then rushing sword in hand to storm a cannon-bristled fort belching fire and lead and steel into their smooth, smug faces—for fifty cents a day.

Brother, when you are ordered to the front just glance around and notice the noisily patriotic gentlemen who keep to the rear—at home where it is safe and delightfully quiet. These patriots in the rear will sweetly say, "See you later!" If you ever get back from the war, they will see you when they flatteringly give you a "welcome home." Mark you: When war breaks out these "best people" do not say, "*Come on,* boys, come on—follow us." Hardly. It is "*Go* on, boys, go *ahead,* go right on. We will be with you." That is, they will be with you as far as the railway station, and after that these "prominent people" will give the "brave boys" absent treatment.

The man in the factory and in the mine is the "hand," the "hired hand," of capitalist society; and when he shoulders

---

* J. H. Rose: *The Development of the European Nations*, 1870-1900, Vol. II., p. 328.

a rifle for military service he becomes the steel-toothed jaw
of capitalist society. SOLDIERS ARE TO THE CAPITALIST CLASS
WHAT TEETH ARE TO TIGERS AND BEAKS ARE TO EAGLES.
Soldiers are often called the "dogs of war"; and they are,
indeed, the watchdogs of capitalism—with barracks, armories
and tents for kennels. Bankers, manufacturers, mine owners
and the like despise the very thought of living themselves in
the military "war-dog" kennels. Such men can not be tricked
to the tents and trenches.

In wheedling young men to join the army and the navy
the National Government is hard put to it; must even make
fun of the poverty and ignorance of the humble toilers in the
industries—and openly sneers at them. Here is a sample of
the vile means used by the Government to shame green young
fellows into the army and the navy.*

"WANTED—for the United States Marine Corps—Able-bodied
men who wish to see the world. . . .

    "Regular pay $12.80
    "Post Mechanics, fifty cents per day.............. 13.00

    "Total $25.80

"Which is better for a young man *who can never hope to travel
on his own account:* to enlist in the Marine Corps for four years
. . . where he will be able to see a great portion of the world and
perform a loyal duty to his country,—or, to *drudge away on the
farm, in the shop and various other places, for from ten to fifteen
hours per day in all kinds of weather,* and at the end of the month
or better still, of four years, not have as much clear cash to show
for all his hard and wearisome labor as he would have, had he
enlisted? . . . he [the enlisted man] is always *clean.*"

There you have it, young farmer, young mechanic: the
Government throws it right into your teeth—the sneer that
as a *wage*-earner in the shop and mine and on the farm, you
are cornered; that with all your toiling and sweating you
will always be a "dirty-faced tender-foot" living humbly

---

* Copied from a Government advertisement in front of recruiting headquarters in Allegheny, Pennsylvania, September 7, 1907.
Italics mine. G. R. K. This same form of advertisement has also
been used in many other cities.

around the old home place, never having opportunity to see
the world you live in; that you can not even hope to travel
on your own account, simply because as a *wage*-earner you
don't *own* enough of "your" country—you can not get ahead
far enough financially—to enable you to do so. If you want
to see the world you will have to join the butchers in the
service of the rulers. In its effort to tease and trick you
aboard its great warships, into the "armed guard" work, your
own Government makes fun of your humble income and
taunts you for always staying around home like a "sissy boy."
The Government also tells you that your face is dirty and
that a military man's face "is always clean." The Government's advertisement just quoted is like the sneer at the
soldier's poverty by that elegant aristocrat, Ralph Waldo
Emerson :*

"Where there is no property the people will put on the knapsack for bread."

Think of ten million five hundred thousand trained strong
men in five European countries ready to leap into the
trenches at the word of command. 'In a war between the
Dual Alliance and the Triple Alliance there would be over
ten million men under arms, thus :†

Germany	2,500,000
Austria	1,300,000
Italy	1,300,000
France	2,500,000
Russia	2,800,000
Total	10,400,000'

These would not so much be tricked to the trenches as
they would be forced to the trenches. Emperor William of
Germany at Potsdam, in November, 1891, addressed the
young men who had just been compelled to take the military
oath. He said:

"You are now my soldiers, you have given yourselves to me

---

* "Lecture on War."
† See Bloch: *Future of War,* Preface XXXII.

body and soul. There is but one enemy for you, and that is my
enemy. . . . It may happen that I shall order you to fire on your
brothers and fathers. . . . But in such case you are bound to obey
me without a murmur."*

Think of ten or fifteen million men ready to be forced or
tricked to war to *do the bidding of rulers* whom these *big
strong men outnumber ten thousand to one;* ready to do the
bidding of a coterie of parasitic cowards; ready—cheap, weak,
humble and contemptible—ready to scramble to the trenches
and obey the murderers' orders: "Kill! Kill! Kill! Kill!
Slay! Slaughter! Butcher!"

That millions of strong men should, like whipped dogs,
grovel on the ground before their masters and fight at the
word of command—this, of course, is ridiculous; and naturally these millions of meek, weak, prideless, grovelling common soldiers—all over Europe—all over the world—are held
socially in supreme contempt by the political and industrial
masters of society. But whether the soldier is conscripted,
"drafted," or volunteers to serve, the masters' contempt is
complete.

The soldiers during a war, the workers who support a
war, and both the soldiers and the toilers after a war—are
held in contempt even by those who praise them most. It
will help somewhat in realizing this to make a short study of
several actual cases as illustrations. The examples following
are, most of them, from English and from American history.
In all the illustrations the mocking insincerity of the profit-
lusting, long-distance patriot is easily seen.

First Illustration: The English in the Napoleonic
Wars, and in the Boer War.

Never in modern times did a nation of toilers longer or
more loyally support a war than did the working class of
England support the British Government in the Napoleonic
Wars—a fifth of a century of continuous blood-letting. Never
before or since did the working class of a nation longer or

---

* See Charles Seignobos: *The Political History of Europe
Since 1815*, p. 504.

more gladly give up its choicest men to butcher and be butchered than did the English working class for the Napoleonic Wars. Never did men serve more loyally or longer or fight more bravely. This long storm of death closed with the awful Battle of Waterloo in 1815.

After such service we might expect the patriotic capitalists of England to be most thoughtfully and finely kind to the toilers who supported the wars and to the veterans who fought the wars.

But what happened?

After the Battle of Waterloo, leaving tens of thousands of their comrades on the skull-strewn plains of the Continent, the hypnotized veterans—scarred, ragged and proud—returned home—home from hell—returned to England with glad hearts ignorantly and gullibly expecting a joyous "welcome home" by the masters who had flattered, brutalized, ruled, and used them. Welcome home! The cruel mockery of it! The hideous irony of the masters' prompt treatment of them! Promptly these brave and ignorant men from the battlefields were openly scorned and threatened by the industrial masters of England. Never were masters more cruel toward deluded veteran patriots. Never were masters more heartless toward millions of half-starved toilers—than were the British masters toward the half-starved ragged British workers whose labor had supported the army in the field for twenty years.

Promptly at the close of the Napoleonic wars a movement was made in the British Parliament to relieve the *leisure class* of one-half the income tax, but none was made to ease the burdens of the starving working class. There was biting irony in the fact that

"One of the first parliamentary struggles [following the war] was the proposal of the government to reduce the income tax from 10 to 5 per cent., and to apply this half [the unremitted half] of it, producing about $37,500,000, toward the expense of maintaining a standing army of 150,000 men."*

---

* See Brodrick and Frotheringham: *The Political History of England*, Vol. XI., p. 172, et seq.

Of course *the purpose* of this to-be-increased army was to have an *armed guard ready to crush the "hobo" heroes home from the war and unemployed, ready also to hold down the great multitude of poorly paid or unemployed toilers—all* now loudly complaining against the increasing misery thrust into their lives.

The landlords at once advanced the land rents and the house rents so outrageously that many thousands of feeble working class veterans were forced into trampdom, and were then brutally abused for vagrancy. The huge and hungry army of the unemployed actually found that in some ways peace was, at that time, even worse than war—for the working class.

This outrageous treatment, this brutal contempt for the workers from their pretentiously patriotic rulers may seem to the reader impossible. The case, however, is so typical as to be worth space for evidence. And here is some testimony from witnesses not prejudiced, perhaps, in favor of the workers. Professor J. E. Thorold Rogers writes thus of the matter:*

"In point of fact, the sufferings of the working classes (in England) during this dismal period [the first twenty years of the nineteenth century] . . . were certainly intensified by the harsh partiality of the law; but they were due in the main to deeper causes. Thousands of homes were starved in order to find means to support the great war, the cost of which was really supported by the labor of those who toiled on and earned the wealth which was lavished freely, and at a good rate of interest for the lenders, by the government. The enormous taxation and the gigantic loans came from the store of accumulated capital, which the employers wrung from the poor wages of labor, or the landlords extracted from the growing grains of their tenants. To outward appearance, the strife was waged by armies and generals; but in reality the resources on which the struggle was based were the stint and starvation of labor, the over-taxed and under-fed toils of childhood, the underpaid and uncertain employment of men. Wages were mulcted in order to provide the waste of war, and the profits of commerce and manufacture."

---

* *Work and Wages*, p. 507.

The case is summed up by another authority:*

"Distress instead of plenty, misery instead of comfort—these were the first results of peace."

The English historian, J. R. Green, is thus frank:†

"The war enriched the landowner, the farmer, the merchant, the manufacturer; but it impoverished the poor. It is indeed from these fatal years that we must date that war of the classes, that social severance between employers and employed, which still forms the main difficulty of English politics."

S. R. Gardiner furnishes this testimony:‡

"Towards the end of 1816 riots broke out in many places, which were put down. . . . The government ignored the part which physical distress played in promoting the disturbances. . . . The Manchester Massacre . . . a vast meeting of at least 50,000 gathered on August 16, 1816, in St. Peter's Field, Manchester. . . . The Hussars charged, and the weight of disciplined soldiery drove the crowd into a huddled mass of shrieking fugitives, pressed together by their efforts to escape. When at last the ground was cleared many victims were piled one upon another."

The people who had fed and clothed and armed the soldiers, were now cut down and trampled down in heaps by mounted soldiers. The historians Brodrick and Frotheringham summarize the matter as follows:§

"Four troops of Hussars then made a dashing charge . . . the people fled in wild confusion before them; some were cut down, more were trampled down; an eye-witness describes 'several mounds of human beings lying where they had fallen.'"

Justin McCarthy's statement of the case is instructive:‖

"There was wide-spread distress [in 1816]. There were riots in the counties of England arising out of the distress. There were riots in various parts of London. . . . The Habeas Corpus Act was suspended. . . . A large number of working men conceived the idea

---

* Jephson: *The Platform—Its Rise and Progress*, Vol. I., p. 283·
† *History of the English People*, Vol. IV., p. 377.
‡ *A Student's History of England*, pp. 877-80.
§ *The Political History of England*, Vol. XI., Ch. 8.
‖ *Sir Robert Peel*, Ch. 3.

of walking to London to lay an account of their distress before
the heads of government [Perfectly reasonable?]. . . . The nickname
of Blanketeers was given to them because of their portable sleeping arrangements. (Every man carried a blanket.) . . . The 'Massacre of Peterloo' . . . took place not long after. . . . It was a vast
meeting—some 80,000 men and women are stated to have been present. . . . The yeomanry, a mounted militia force, . . . dashed in upon
the crowd, spurring their horses and flourishing their sabres.
Eleven persons were killed and several hundred were wounded. The
government brought in . . . the famous Six Acts. These Acts were
simply measures to render it more easy to put down and disperse
meetings . . . and to suppress any manner of publication which they
chose to call seditious. . . . It was the conviction of the ruling class
that the poor and the working classes of England were preparing
a revolution. . . . In 1818, a motion for annual parliaments and
universal suffrage was lost by a majority of 106 to nobody."

Says Professor Jesse Macy:*

"By a series of repressive measures popular agitation was arrested. . . . *Popular agitation was brought to an end by force.* So
complete was the repression that there occurred no great political
consequences until the movement which carried the Reform Bill
[1832]."

"Silence!" is *always* the order of despotism when the
"bruised lips" of starving slaves speak loud for freedom.

Thus did the proud, "patriotic" masters of England spit
in the faces of the starving working class who supported the
war and laugh to scorn the old working class soldiers who had
fought the long and horrible war. Thus were the battle-
scarred heroes—and their families—sabred and bayoneted.
Thus were some of the rights they already had, torn from their
hands. Thus were they denied a voice in the government they
served. Thus were the toilers and veterans outraged—duped,
despised, snubbed—during and after the "glorious" Napoleonic wars.

The shameless Caesars who constituted the English government of the time heaped wrong upon wrong by sending
police spies into the great public meetings of the ragged veterans of war and industry *to stir them up to violence, thus*

---

* *The English Constitution*, p. 423. Italics mine. G. R. K.

furnishing the government excuse for its brutalities and repressive legislation.*

An anonymous author furnishes interesting fact and comment :†

"The world will have to revise its notions of patriotism in the light of modern commerce. . . . Look at the strength of the interests. Where is the Government that would dare prohibit Birmingham firms from executing [filling] orders for a foreign Government? Even in our small frontier wars [British] soldiers must expect to be shot at with British rifles."

At one time in the Napoleonic wars English manufacturers, "*patriotic* business men," of course, filled one order for 16,000 military coats, 37,000 jackets, and 200,000 pairs of shoes to be used, as the commercial patriots knew, by the French army while slaughtering English soldiers.‡ That was about a hundred years ago. But the silk-hat patriot is still the same hypocrite, talking loudly about "honoring the hero" whom he despises both socially and industrially. British veterans of the Boer War of recent years—tens of thousands of them—have cursed the day they enlisted, with the patriotism of ignorance, to serve in South Africa. The Government broke its promises with them shamelessly and wholesale; and many of these veterans, on returning from the war, were scorned at the English factory door, turned down at the shops and mines, and had to beg on the streets of London and other cities. It is the old story: duped, tricked, teased to the trenches—then snubbed, as usual.

When the soldier boys got back to England from the Boer war they were weak, poor, ragged and very weary, many hundreds of them scarcely able to walk. But no matter: they

---

* See, for example, J. F. Bright: *A History of England,* Period III., p. 1352.

† *Arbeiter in Council,* p. 501.

‡ Bourienne's *Memoirs,* Vol. VII., c. 20. Reference in *Arbeiter in Council,* p. 499. For cases equally monstrous in the American Civil War history, see Myers' *History of Great American Fortunes,* Vol. II., pp. 127-38, 291-301; Chapters 11 and 12; Vol. III., pp. 160-176.

were at once driven from the ships like cattle, forced to fall into line, and march wavering and staggering from weakness and weariness—forced to march past the Queen's reviewing stand, to be smiled at and flattered by a bunch of royal and noble parasites and thus be "honored" while they starved, "honored" as they staggered past in their rags, gazed at by shining gluttons and fat-headed lords who were too shrewd and cowardly to go themselves to South Africa to slaughter the Boers, steal gold and diamond mines and otherwise defend their own capitalist interests.

On this cruel reviewing march of many weary miles past the Queen of the home-coming butchers a great number of the men fainted in their famished weakness. Many eye-witnesses to this outrage were in tears. . . .

The march ended.

The guns were put away with pride.

The blood of Dutch workingmen was wiped from the English swords—with British pride.

Blood-stained banners were piously placed in libraries, museums, and churches—with true Christian pride.

The war was over.

The butchers had come back to *"their"* dear country—and washed their hands.

Then—then what?

Then these cheap and stupid assassins of their class went to *look for a job*—teased the lordly parasites of England for whom they had been fighting—teased them for a job, whined like spaniels at the feet of the industrial masters of England, begged for a job.

And received insults.

A JOB IS NOT GUARANTEED BY ANY CAPITALIST CONSTITUTION ON ALL THE EARTH, EVEN THO' A JOB MAY MEAN SALVATION FROM STARVATION.

A hunting dog, having found the shot-mangled bird in the grass and briars, brings the game to his master confident of substantial favors—and gets the favors.

These English human hunting dogs had obediently hunted

human game in South Africa, and they returned to their masters, their faces shining with the expectancy (and, almost, with the intelligence) of a retriever with a bleeding bird in his mouth.

And they were slapped in the face at the factory door with "Not wanted!"

Snubbed.

"Honored." "Reviewed." Reviewed? Certainly. That is part rule-by-wind trick.

Flattered—then kicked in the face when they asked for permission to work and by work save their own lives from the wolves of poverty.

"A nod from a lord is a breakfast—*for a fool.*"

SECOND ILLUSTRATION: THE AMERICAN WORKING CLASS REVOLUTIONISTS:

The American working class soldiers a hundred and twenty-five years ago were also equally despised by the industrial and political masters of that time. The poor men, the working class men, in Washington's army after fighting for years, half starved, always in rags, sleeping in wind-swept tents at night, oftentimes shoeless, making bloody tracks in the snow and on the ice as they marched,—these battle-scarred veterans of the working class, after fighting for years in the "great Revolutionary War for freedom,"—these were not permitted to vote for many years after the war. It was not, indeed, till many years after the adoption of the "great" new Federal Constitution of the "free" people that these humble working class veterans were permitted to take part as voters in the government.

This was contempt supreme. Tricked to the "war for freedom"—then, after "glorious victory," snubbed, as usual.

Of course, this page of "splendid" Revolutionary War history, this bright particular page of unqualified contempt of the so-called "great leaders" for the working class soldiers after the fighting was all over—this page is shrewdly hidden from the working class children in the common schools, the grammar schools and high schools of the United States,— this page is practically suppressed. The working class child in the public school is wheedled into being a blind devotee of the "great" Constitution and an ignorant worshipper of the "great men" who so cordially despised the men of the class to which the child belongs. There is plenty of evidence, however, that these "prominent" and "very *best* people" of American Revolutionary War times had nothing but political contempt for the working class veterans. President Woodrow Wilson (Princeton University) writes:*

"There were probably not more than 120,000 men who had a right to vote out of all the 4,000,000 inhabitants enumerated at the first census [1790]."

The political and social contempt felt for the poor men of the times of George Washington is made clear by Professor F. N. Thorpe (University of Pennsylvania) thus:†

"An unparalleled political enfranchisement [from 1800 to 1900] extended the right to vote, which in 1796 reposed in only one-twentieth of the population, but a century later in one-sixth of it— the nearest approach to universal suffrage in history."

This same scorn for the thirteen-dollar-a-month men, who do the actual fighting, is seen in one form or another in the more recent American wars. The purse-proud rulers of the present day are so blatant in their expressions of patriotic admiration for the "brave boys" that the following illustrations are deemed worthy of the space required for their presentation—in order that the working class reader may not fail to recognize the mocking hypocrite in the gold-lust patriotic shouters who now decorate their palaces on holidays with "Old Glory."

THIRD ILLUSTRATION: THE AMERICAN CIVIL WAR—THE BANKERS AND "PROMOTERS"—AND THE BOYS IN BLUE:

Thousands of Union veterans have declared: "The American Civil War was a rich man's war and a poor man's fight.

---

* *History of the American People,* Vol. III., p. 120.
† *A History of the American People,* p. 556.

We were duped. But we shall never be duped again." (See Chapter VII., Sections 14 to 16.)

The volunteer Union soldiers who, at Lincoln's first call, hurried to enlist for the war, understood distinctly that the government would pay them *"in gold or its equivalent."* But the soldiers were forced to accept even their puny 43 cents a day in greenbacks containing the famous "exception clause," which clause destroyed from 20 to more than 65 per cent. of the purchasing power of the money during the war and for years following the war. But the silk-hatted patriots, the "leading citizen" manufacturers, the bankers and the heroic sharks in Congress at the time, these who issued greenbacks and bought Government bonds, *these* noble gentlemen not only *despised the very money they forced the soldiers to take for fighting,* but, at the same time, arranged, virtually, for an iron-clad agreement that not only the principal of, but also the interest on, the Government bonds they "patriotically" bought, must be paid in gold.* Gold for the patriot in business—"rag money" for the patriots in the trenches. At one time, owing to the "exception clause" on the paper money forced upon the soldiers, one gold dollar would buy as much as two dollars and eighty-five cents of paper money. Of course, the soldiers and the "common people" complained loudly. Says a high authority :†

"Much opposition was caused by the clause inserted by the Senate, which provided for payment of interest on bonds in coin, which practically meant discrimination in favor of one class of creditors, and, as Stevens said, 'depreciated at once the money which the bill created.'"

---

* "Apart from the phraseology of the statutes it appears during the early years of the War the possibility of the payment of the bonds in other than coin was hardly raised. According to the explicit statement of Garfield in 1868, when the original five-twenty bond bill was before the House in 1862, all who referred to the subject stated that the principal of these bonds was payable in gold, and coin payment was the understanding of every member of the committee of ways and means. . . . It thus became practically an unwritten law to pay the obligations of the United States in coin." —Dewey: *Financial History of the United States,* paragraph 148.

† Hepburn: *The Contest for Sound Money,* p. 188.

The Wall Street patriots never miss an opportunity to remind us with great show of pride that they "furnished the money with which to carry on the Civil War." They did furnish a good deal of money, and like true patriotic Shylocks they took blood-sealed, interest-bearing bonds in exchange for their cash. On every possible occasion the bonds were *bought at such a sacrifice price as to almost bleed the nation to death in the presence of its enemies.* Dr. H. C. Adams (University of Michigan, Department of Finance) says:* That, "estimated on the average price of gold," the Federal Government, "for the forty-five months of the Civil War" realized from public obligations of all sorts less than 67 per cent. That is to say, certain bloodless patriots' lack of faith and their desire also to "push a good thing" and take at least a "full pound of flesh"—resulted in their dear Government's loss of blood in its financial transactions to the extent of more than 33 per cent.

This disastrous shrinkage was due unquestionably in a very large measure to the bankers' manipulation of the Government's financial affairs for their own private benefit. These glittering Shylocks were beautifully, even prayerfully, enthusiastic in their hand-clapping for their dear country's welfare; and yet they showed almost perfect emotional self-control. Mr. Lincoln hated their gold-lust "patriotism," but he was compelled to bow low before their power. The lovingly patriotic embrace which our country received from the bond-leech capitalists during the Civil War clearly revealed their amiable intention to bleed their country just as nearly to death as possible—and yet not *kill* it lest the precious goose should cease to lay such interesting eggs.

Your "patriotic" war-bond buyer is a temperamentally calm person.

Some citizens bleed for their country, others bleed their country.

"Guard against the impostures of patriotism."—George Washington.†

---

* *Finance*, p. 540, also *Public Debts*, p. 131.

† Rice: *The Father of His Country—Year Book.*

Professor J. E. Thorold Rogers* states as follows the spirit of much of the argument in the British Parliament, even by many conservatives, concerning the bond-leech patriots who purchased British Napoleonic War bonds:

"But we have to endure, in addition to our misfortunes, the sight of the stock-jobbers and fund-holders, who have *fattened on our misery*, and are now receiving more than half our taxes. And for what? We have put down the Corsican usurper, and restored peace to Europe, legitimacy to its thrones. These people [the bond-holders] not only get under our funding system at par, stock, with a number of incidental advantages, in exchange for some £50 or less, but they paid [even] this inadequate quota in notes which were constantly at a discount of 30 per cent. *It is intolerable, it is unjust, that we should redeem such stock under the terms of so monstrous and one-sided a bargain.*"

Perhaps, reader, you are one of the old gray men who "fought under Grant and are proud of it." I do not criticize you, gray old man. I am offering you and younger men things to think about. A distinguished historian assures us that there were at one time during the War one hundred and fifty bankers in Congress. Inside and outside of Congress these, and other leading-citizen Mammonites, connived to bleed you and bleed the nation—utterly without shame. They alarmed President Lincoln repeatedly. They never let up in their swinish scramble for gold during the War. And after the War they continued their unholy manoeuvring—patriotically. For example, at one time following the War, after you soldiers had elected your General to the Presidency, these blushless blood-suckers sought to corner the gold market and thus scoop up a barrel of profits. To accomplish this it was necessary to have the President out of the way for a short time in order to render it impossible for him to rush to the rescue with the Federal Treasury. Read their plan to "turn the trick" in the words of a Wall Streeter himself, Mr. Henry Clews :†

* *The Economic Interpretation of History,* p. 454. Italics mine. G. R. K.

† *Twenty-Eight Years* (new edition *Fifty Years*) *of Wall Street,* p. 194.

"He [Grant] was prevailed upon to go to a then obscure town in Pennsylvania, named Little Washington. The thing was so arranged that his feelings were worked upon to visit that place for the purpose of seeing an old friend who resided there. The town was cut off from telegraphic communication, and other means of access were not very convenient. There the President was ensconced, to remain for a week or so about the time the Cabal was fully prepared for action."

Mr. Henry Clews' own case is so finely typical of the banker-buncombe-patriot that a few lines may profitably be given here to him to illustrate his class.

This glittering patriot, Mr. Clews, was a young man when the Civil War broke out. His young heart—just as a banker's heart should be, for business purposes—was warm with the holy fervor of a patriot. He loved the flag—tenderly, of course, just as a banker always loves an "attractive proposition." The war was an opportunity—a splendid opportunity—to *"make money"* or to *"fight for the flag."* After much patriotic (and no doubt prayerful) meditation he reached the conclusion (his first fear was confirmed) that if *he* went to the war he might unkindly be crowding out some other young fellow who also wanted to "fight for the flag." So, just as a banker patriot would naturally do, he modestly decided to stay at home and humbly take the opportunity to "make money." He at once organized a bond-buying, gold-lust syndicate, and as its organizer he went to Washington to buy bonds—at a *discount* (as he confesses), *tho' believing there was to be only a mere flurry* (as he confesses), and especially to examine *carefully* (as he confesses) into the *precise degree* of risk assumed in buying the Government's bonds.

Patriots in the trenches risk all. Patriots in the bond-buying business are not that kind; and they study the risk with great care, and coolly avoid not only the blood risk, but also the money risk—with skill, also with patriotism.

Calmly.

It seems that Mr. Clews went to Washington on a night train. He relates that when he awoke in the morning he

raised the car window-shade and cautiously peeped out.* He
saw a long line of cars loaded with cannon. He was *astonished*—he confesses. Naturally, a banker is afraid of a cannon. "As I went around collecting information," he says,
"the sight of those cannon that at first had made such an
indescribable impression upon me continued to haunt my
vision wherever I went. . . . I felt that the contest would
be a long and bloody one. . . . I was convinced that war to
the knife was imminent, and that Government bonds must
have a serious fall in consequence." He telegraphed his syndicate to "sell out" and "clear the decks," "to unload."†

Note that as soon as these far-from-the-firing-line patriots
sniffed danger for their gold they were, as Mr. Clews virtually
confesses, ready to leave the Government in the lurch and
let the boys in the trenches starve till the bonds could be
bought at a strangle-hold advantage in the way of discounts.
Mr. Clews relates, with unmanageable pride, that the Secretary of the Treasury received him with great courtesy and
supplied him with a large amount of useful information—
information of the "inner" "ground-floor" sort so extremely
helpful to the organizer of a bond-buying syndicate; also that
the information and suggestions and encouragements he received from the Secretary were really the beginning of what
he, with blushingly modest confession and a caress for himself, calls his "brilliant career."

---

* Mr. Clews relates this whole matter in detail in his *Twenty-
Eight Years in Wall Street* (new edition *Fifty Years*, etc.), in
which noble tome naive conceit and the pleasures of self-contempla-
tion beget an almost equal degree of incautious loquacity and innocent candor.

† By "clear the decks," and "unload," when financial storms
threaten, bankers mean that any soon-to-shrink stocks and bonds
held by them are to be at once sold to (dumped upon) somebody
else, to let somebody else stand the certain loss—just as a sinful
deacon might sell to his neighboring fellow-worshipper a horse he
was sure would die next day, or as an enterprising grocer might
sell a rotten lemon to a blind child. It is "legitimate." It is "opportunity." It is "business." And conscience is a nuisance to some
people when there is "opportunity" to do "business."

Early in life Mr. Clews made a profound impression upon himself—a lasting impression, as his books and speeches always reveal; a not uncommon experience with "prominent people."

Thus Mr. Clews chose the humbler and more healthful rôle in patriotism.

Many of Mr. Clews' old neighbors (hot-headed young men of the War time) are dead. They have been dead a long time. Cannon balls tore some of them to pieces. Bayonets were thrust through some of them. Some were starved to death in prisons. Their once hot blood is mold now. Long ago their flesh was eaten by the battle-grave worms. Time is busy in their nameless graves gnawing at their bones. But, now fifty years after the terrible war began, Mr. Clews is alive and well —he even boasts of his good health and often gives suggestions on how to keep one's health till ripe old age.

And he is still buying bonds.

His special delight is giving advice to—mankind.

Mr. Clews lectures frequently. His favorite themes are "patriotism," "the stars and stripes," "the man behind the gun,"—and "how to succeed." He is a sort of chairman of the committee on wind for patriots in the "greenhorn" stage.

All this space is given to Mr. Clews simply because he is so *perfectly typical* of the shrewd and powerful capitalist *class* who rule—rule by wind and a pompous manner when possible and by lead and steel when "necessary."

His case should be explained carefully to the boys and girls of the working class. In the South such men are Democrats; in the North, Republicans. In both regions the working men are neither, if they understand.

FOURTH ILLUSTRATION: THE SEVEN DAYS' BATTLE— THE "BRAINY" PROMOTERS AND THE BOYS IN BLUE:

A nation in tears is the business man's opportunity.

Any reference by a Thirtieth-of-May orator to the Seven Days' Battle makes "big business men" and statesmen throw out their chests, pat their soft white hands and vociferate with perfectly beautiful patriotism. But let us look a little at the record.

In Chapter Three of the present volume it was briefly stated that one reason for the capitalists' wanting war is that war completely concentrates a nation's attention upon one thing and one thing only; namely, the war; and that while the people are thus "not looking," the business man and the politicians have a perfect opportunity to arrange "good things" for themselves. And here I shall present a sample of American business men filching "good things" while the public's attention is wholly absorbed in war. For shameless, treasonable corruption this sample can not be surpassed with the foulest page in the history of the ancient and rotten pagan Roman Empire.

Washington during the American Civil War was a robber's roost for eminently respectable thieves, industrial "bunco-steerers," and prominent and pious "come-on" financial pirates who were never near the firing line. The very best hotels in the city of Washington were constantly crowded with these patriotic citizens, "brainy men," distinguished business men—from all parts of the North—a continuous thieves' banquet by men who socially despised the humble fellows at the front. Cunningly during the entire war these gilt-edged, gold-dust bandits, far from danger of the firing line, plotted deals and steals and stuffed their pockets with "good things"—while brave men from the farms, mines and factories bled and died on the battlefield,—while working class wives and mothers agonized in their desolated humble homes. President Lincoln hated and dreaded these "hold-up" men, and sometimes he vented his splendid wrath against them in immortal words of warning to the people.*

---

* "It is a well-known fact that the War of the Rebellion was prolonged as a result of the manipulations of the speculators who invested in bonds. While the boys in blue were baring their breasts to the enemy in a heroic struggle to save the Union, for $13 per month, the bond sharks were speculating upon their necessities and the necessities of the Government. At one time President Lincoln was so exasperated by their greedy and unpatriotic actions that he

Washington is such a pleasant place in the kindly, smiling springtime. Business men enjoy that town—while Congress is in session.

For many months preceding July, 1862, a certain group of these broad-clothed money-gluttons camped in Washington—alert as hawks, keen as hungry tigers sniffing warm blood. This precious group of eminently stealthy Christian business men planned and plotted. Cunningly these pirate patriots arranged a specially "good thing"—of which I wish to tell you here.

There was, you remember, one battle in the late Civil War called the Seven Days' Battle. Mark the dates very carefully: June 25 to July 1, 1862—seven days—a bloody, horrible week. For several reasons this battle was regarded as most critical; many thoughtful people, North and South, believed the Union would stand or fall with this battle. President Lincoln ordered General McClellan to capture the Confederate capital, Richmond, or hurry north and protect Washington. As the conflict came closer and closer capitalists and statesmen grew busier—timing a master stroke.

June 24, the nation watched Virginia: one of the most prolonged and savage struggles in the whole history of mankind was imminent.

June 24, therefore, was, for certain men, the last day of special preparation. The cannon would surely begin next day to roar around Richmond.

All was ready (in Washington). . . . The understanding was perfect (in Washington).

"Without a single syllable of debate," a certain bill (precisely as it had been handsomely amended by the Senate) was passed by the House by a vote of 104 to 21. The finishing touch was thus put upon a carefully constructed trap, a trap set by "leading citizens," a trap for big game.

Next day—June 25—the cannon did begin to boom around the Confederate capital.

---

declared they 'ought to have their devilish heads shot off.' "—Congressman Vincent, of Kansas, in the House of Representatives, April 18, 1898.

The first day's struggle—June 25—was awful. The news flashed through the land. Millions turned pale.

But the bandits in Washington were cool. The trap was set. They waited.

The second day was a slaughter.

More smiles and confidence in the best Washington hotels.

The third day of the battle was a butchering contest. The whole people watched, listened. The news flamed north and south. Millions, terrified, read the dead roll.

But the broadcloth gentlemen wept not. They waited—patriotically.

The fourth day was a storm of blood and iron.

But the eminent business men, bankers, statesmen, promoters and other patriotic looters, safe in Washington—far from the firing line—waited, drank fine wine and very confidently waited—waited as lions wait—to spring to the throats of their victims.

Mr. Lincoln held back his signature from that "certain Bill." He was doing his best for the boys in the trenches, and was justly suspicious of the promoter-banker patriotism in Washington.

The fifth day millions looked toward Virginia—and were sickened with grief.

But certain prominent gentlemen in Washington cheerfully jested, ate the best food on earth, lolled in easy chairs, gracefully reclined on elegantly upholstered sofas, craftily plotted—and waited, in calm confidence waited.

The sixth day of the battle was "Death's feast." The nation, North and South, was stupefied with the horror of the war.

But certain "highly respected leading citizens," Christian business men—flag-waving patriots all of them—quaffed their wine, chatted gaily, plotted, and, like reptiles, coiled to strike—waited, confident.

The seventh day, the last day, the baptism of blood and fire broke the nation's heart. As morning dawned the nation's one thought was: The war—the awful battles—the week-long harvest of death in Virginia. Millions sobbed and eagerly sought more news. The storm of death completely absorbed the nation's attention. The Seven Days of slaughter was the nation's one heart-gripping thought.

For this day certain patriots, certain "men of energy and push and enterprise," certain distinguished business men, had patiently and craftily waited. The psychological moment! The nation was blinded with rage, tears and despair. Half insane with an awful joy and a sickening sorrow, the people, millions of them, wildly screamed, sobbed and cursed—on July 1.

Intense day.

The Union army in retreat—defeated.

The President in profound alarm, half crazed with the agony of it all, decided, July 1, to call for 300,000 more soldiers for three years' service.

Supreme moment—for the business man.

Now!

The people are not looking.

Now!

Strike, viper, strike!

Leap, gold-hungry patriot! Leap! Leap now—leap for your country's throat!

Not another hour's delay. . . . Place the final pressure on the President.

"Mr. President! Mr. Lincoln! Sign our bill! Please sign our bill now—right now. Quickly, Mr. President! Don't delay longer. Now!"

Hundreds of cannon were roaring in Virginia. The President was devouring the telegraphic news from the firing line.

Business men—Christian business men—including flag-loving Congressmen, very noble Senators, and many other dollar-mark statesmen, were directly and indirectly urging that the bill be signed—at once, "for the country's welfare," of course.

The President, urged by these money-hungry patriots, urged by these "men of high standing," thus urged, the President, writhing with grief over the Seven Days' slaughter of his brave volunteers, almost sweating blood in his profound fear,—signed the bill, July 1.

What bill?

The bill that legalized a vast and shameless wrong against the wives and children of brave men on the firing line; the bill that legalized a rape of the National Domain and the Federal Treasury by gilded cowards, while from the Atlantic Ocean to the Rocky Mountains, hundreds of thousands of brave men, ill fed, ill clothed, faced hell under the flag on the firing line; the bill that suddenly made plutocrats of Christian statesmen,—made millionaires of flag-waving traitors piously masquerading as patriots; the bill that created the Union Pacific Railway charter, the astounding terms of which are given presently.

The President was numb and dumb with sadness and a thousand worries.

"The news [of the Seven Days' Battle]," says Rhodes,* "was a terrible blow to the President. The finely equipped army which had cost so much exertion and money, had gone forward with high hopes of conquest, and apparently bore the fate of the Union, had been defeated, and was now in danger of destruction or sur-render. This calamity the head of the Nation must face. . . . The elaborate preparations of the North had come to naught. . . . Lincoln grew thin and haggard and his dispatches . . . of these days are an avowal of defeat."

But the business men and the statesmen who were "in on the deal" winked wisely, smiled blandly, and made merry as they quaffed their champagne. They had "turned the trick" —they had made a fine bargain.

"Business is business."

July 2 came. Certain statesmen and business men in Washington were happy, so very, very happy—far from the firing line.

July 2 came. And while a cloud of buzzards circled con-fidently over the Seven Days' battlefield eager for a feast on the rotting flesh of the brave working class soldier boys; while the torn corpses of humble working class men were hurriedly

---

* *History of the United States,* Vol. IV., pp. 44-56.

pitched into the ditches and the dirt and gravel were shoveled upon them; while the grave-worms began their feast and revel in the flesh and blood of the men and boys from the farms, mines and factories; while, July 2, the wounded men and boys screamed under the surgeons' knives and saws in the hospitals; while, July 2, millions mourned;—at such a time, while the Union army was retreating, defeated—the "big, brainy business men" in Washington celebrated *their* victory, the securing of the Union Pacific Railway charter. For months these distinguished patriotic sneaks had been preparing, hatching this "good thing," the Union Pacific charter. After months of patriotic treason and fox-like watchfulness they had "landed" their prize.

They won.

They celebrated.

A nation in tears is the business man's opportunity—for bargains.

This Union Pacific charter was, as shown below, unquestionably one of the most shameless pieces of corruption in the entire history of the civilized, unsocialized world, including even pagan Rome in her most degraded days. The crime was so foul and vast that many of the records were burned later—which, perhaps, saved some eminent gentlemen from being lynched.

Mr. Henry Clews relates :*

"The investigation of the refunding committee of the Pacific railroads at Washington brought the most remarkable evidence from one of the principal witnesses, who stated that the books connected with the construction of the road had been burned or destroyed as useless trash involving the superfluous expense of room rent, though they contained the record of transactions involving hundreds of millions of dollars, a record which became absolutely necessary to the fair settlement between the government and its debtors. Also the fact was put in evidence that a certain party in the interest had testified before another committee, on a former occasion, that he was present when $54,000,000 of profits were divided equally among four partners, himself and three others. None of the books of record containing this valuable information escaped the flames."

* *The Wall Street Point of View,* p. 29.

The charter as originally granted, July 1, 1862, was treasonably generous; but these far-from-the-firing-line patriots were insatiably gluttonous, and they teased and bribed till exactly two years later (July 2, 1864, precisely at a time when the war was terribly intense and especially critical), the liberality of the terms of the charter was almost doubled.

Study the terms—the chief features—of the charter as granted and amended.

Remember the date, June 24 to July 1, 1862,—the week of the Seven Days' Battle. Also look sharply for the patriotism—in the charter.

The terms, in outline, of the Union Pacific charter:

FIRST: At a time when the nation was straining every nerve to carry on the war, at a time when the soldiers in the trenches were paid only 43 cents a day, and even that in depreciated paper money, and were given salt pork and mouldy crackers for rations—at such a time, business men (cunningly assisted by patriotic Congressmen and noble Senators) dipped their greedy hands into the National Treasury and took out a government "loan" to the railway company of $60,000,000 in interest-bearing government bonds worth more than sufficient to build the road. Professor W. Z. Ripley (Harvard University) says:*

"From the books of the Union Pacific and the Credit Mobilier it appears that the expenditures by the Union Pacific directly amounted to $9,746,683.33; and that the actual expenditures under the Hoxie, Ames and Davis contracts were $50,720,957.94, making the total cost of the road $60,467,641.27."

This good-as-cash loan from the government was "assistance" and "incentive" given to the genteel promoters of the Union Pacific Railway: $16,000 per mile from the Missouri River to the Rocky Mountains; $48,000 per mile through the Rocky Mountains; and $32,000 per mile beyond the Rockies. This was a liberal allowance, surely. Collis P. Huntington, long time president of the Southern Pacific, claimed afterward

---

* *Railway Problems,* p. 95.

that the road could be built at an average cost of less than $10,000 per mile. More recently the Union Pacific Railway Company (contending with the State of Utah over tax burdens) proved before the Board of Equalization at Salt Lake City, by the sworn testimony of engineers, that the average cost of the Utah Central line, in a rough country, was only $7,298.20 per mile.

The dear capitalist government was rich enough to stuff the pockets of the glistening, flag-waving traitors with $60,-000,000 in bonds like gold as "assistance" and "incentive" for self-preservation patriotism. But at the same time this dear government could give the "boys in blue" only 43 cents a day in cheap rag money as "incentive." These "enterprising business men" drank champagne and slept in soft beds; but the "boys in blue" drank water from muddy horse-tracks and slept on the ground.

SECOND: The Union Pacific Company, it was cunningly arranged, might make elsewhere a private, cash, mortgage-bonded loan equal to the government loan, $60,000,000.

THIRD: The noble Christian statesmen in Congress and the noble Christian business men (patriots all) cunningly agreed that a *first* mortgage should be given for the *private* loan of $60,000,000.

FOURTH: The government (bunco-steerers inside and outside of Congress) cunningly agreed to take a *second* mortgage on the road for the *government* loan of $60,000,000.

FIFTH: It was cunningly arranged by these business men in politics and these politicians in business that ninety-five per cent. of the government second mortgage loan should not bear interest *till thirty years later;* but that all the private loans should bear interest at once.

SIXTH: The Railway Company was cunningly given permission to sell $100,000,000 in railway stocks.

Stocks were sold to Congressmen and very noble Senators.

Stocks were sold to these very noble statesmen below the market price.

Stocks sold to statesmen—it was cunningly arranged—need not be paid for till after the road was finished and the stocks were paying dividends. For example, Congressman W. B. Allison, afterward Senator Allison, of Iowa (so sly and stealthy that he became known as "Pussy-Foot"), bought some of the stocks "on the quiet," too, from the infamous Ames; he paid out nothing for the stocks, but when he had owned the stocks for only a brief time and while the unfinished road was yet in comparatively poor condition, his dividends more than paid for his stocks.* The Union Pacific scandal snuffed out numerous lesser lights and sadly bedimmed the lustre of twenty-two other "great" names, such as Blaine, Logan, Garfield, Colfax.†

This villainy of the nation's "great" men is worthy of Emerson's interesting flattery of eminent prostitutes:

"When I read the list of men of intellect, of refined pursuits, giants in law, or eminent scholars, or of social distinction, men of wealth and enterprise in the commercial community, and see what they have voted for and what they have suffered to be voted for, I think no community was ever so politely and elegantly betrayed."—("Lecture on Woman.")

One Congressman was given $500,000 for his assistance in getting the charter granted.

"Another [expense]," says Professor Ripley (Harvard University),‡ "of a worse sort concerned a government commissioner, Cornelius Wendell, appointed to examine the road and report whether or not it met the requirements of the law, who flatly demanded $25,000 before he would proceed to perform his duty . . . his demand was paid in the same spirit in which it was made—as so much blood money."

Another authority thus :§

"Oakes Ames, member of Congress, from Massachusetts, and a promoter of the Union Pacific and its bills before the national legislature, distributed Credit Mobilier stock to *influential* Congressmen on the understanding that it should be paid for *out of the dividends*,

---

* See Davis: *The Union Pacific Railway*, p. 187.

† Davis: pp. 89-202.

‡ *Railway Problems*, p. 94.

§ Professor Frank Parsons (Boston University): *The Railways, the Trusts and the People*, p. 64. And see Report of the Wilson Investigating Committee, pp. III, IV, et seq., and Parsons' Chapter on "Railroad Graft." Italics mine. G. R. K.

which dividends depended largely on the passage of the bills giving grants of land and money to the U. P. The bills were passed. The dividends of the very first year paid for the stock and left a balance to the credit of the donees; and the total *construction* profits were $43,925,328 above all expenses, in which profits the stock-holding Congressmen who passed the railroad grants had an important share."

SEVENTH: The statesmen-business men cunningly agreed that when the government used the road (which it had furnished more than sufficient means to construct) one-half the regular rate should be paid in cash and the other half should apply as credit on the government loan.

EIGHTH: The Union Pacific Railway Company, including the Central Pacific (same system),* was cunningly presented —scot free—one-half of all the land within twenty miles of the right-of-way, and "all the timber, iron and coal within six miles" of the right-of-way,—a total of 25,000,000 acres of land. "At $2.50 per acre," says President E. B. Andrews (University of Nebraska),† "the land values alone would more than build the road." The *Northern* Pacific Company received, just two years later, 47,000,000 acres of land as a gift which a land expert‡ estimated to be worth probably $990,000,000 and possibly $1,320,000,000,—which gives us some idea of the value of the 25,000,000 acre gift to the *Union* Pacific.

It is worth the space to add: That "the promoters of the Northern Pacific, through unfair construction contracts and other frauds, made the capitalization of 600 miles of that line constructed down to 1874 amount to 143 millions on an actual expenditure of twenty-two millions."§

NINTH: Again and again the Union Pacific, when it suited its purpose to do so, refused to comply with the treason-

---

* "Similar franchises and subsidies were at the same time given to the Central Pacific Railroad Company."—Parsons: *The Railways, the Trusts and the People*, p. 128.

† *The United States in Our Own Time*, p. 103.

‡ Wilson, for several years Land Commissioner for the Illinois Central Railway Company, cited by Andrews.

§ Parsons: *The Railways, the Trusts and the People*, p. 106.

ably easy terms of its charter; but always the patriots in Washington and the distinguished railway gentlemen cunningly "got together," made some "gentlemen's agreement"—and the charter was not revoked.

As suggested above, this charter, as amended by the Senate and in the form signed by the President, July 1, 1862,—was, when it was finally "considered" in the House of Mis-Representatives, voted 104 to 21 "without a single syllable of debate."*

Professor Parsons sums up the case thus:†

"The promoters got from Congress more than the cost of the road, bonded it again to private investors for all it was worth, issued stock also beyond the cost of construction, sold and gave away a good deal of it, and still had the road and the control of its earnings for themselves."

The magnitude of this statesmen-patriot-thieves' masterpiece ("for love of country and home and God") can not be realized without a further word concerning the land grants.

Seventy-nine land-grant railroads (twenty-one of them "direct beneficiaries of Congress") have been granted 200,000,-000 acres of land (reduced by forfeiture to 158,286,627 acres). "OVER ONE-HALF OF THIS ACREAGE WAS GRANTED BY ACTS PASSED BETWEEN 1862 AND 1864."‡

That is to say, during twenty-four terrible months, just while the nation was sweating blood from every pore, while the people were not looking at anything except the war, precisely at that time, patriotic statesmen gave away to railway promoters who shed no "blood for the flag," gave to these "gentlemen of push and enterprise" a sufficient amount of the people's lands to provide a hundred and twenty-five-acre farm for every one of the 800,000 men mustered out of the Union armies in 1865.

Professor Parsons says "the total *national* land-grants

---

* Davis: *The Union Pacific Railway.*
† *The Railroads, the Trusts and the People*, p. 128.
‡ Professors Cleveland and Powell (University of Pennsylvania): *Railroad Promotion and Capitalization*, p. 250.   **Emphasis mine.** G. R. K.

alone have aggregated 215,000,000 acres"—(15,000,000 acres higher than the estimate by Professors Cleveland and Powell).

"It could be said of more than one railroad company as was said by an English capitalist who inspected . . . the properties of the Illinois Central, 'This is not a railway company; it is a land company.' "*

It is interesting (and instructive) to note that the charter of the *Northern* Pacific Railway with its 47,000,000 acre land gift, with astoundingly liberal amendments to the U. P. charter, was granted July 2, 1864, *precisely at a time* when the nation's attention was again riveted to two specially terrible campaigns which absorbed the nation wholly in the war: Grant and Lee, with immense armies, were fighting bitterly, and Sherman with 98,000 men and Johnston with 45,000 men had been fighting fiercely and almost continuously from June 10 to July 2, 1864. As stated above, the Northern Pacific got 47,000,000 acres of land.†

The three railways, says Professor Parsons in substance,‡ the Union Pacific, the Central Pacific and the Northern Pacific, *cost* somewhat less than $132,000,000, and were *capitalized* at more than $383,000,000—that is to say, about $250,000,000 (*two-thirds* of the capitalization) was fictitious,—a fraud, a lie, *commercial patriotism.*

While at wining and dining tables in closely guarded private parlors in the best hotels in Washington this unmatchable plundering was cunningly arranged ("to develop the country, of course") working class men and boys, half starved and weary, were obediently slaughtering themselves at the word of command—for 43 cents a day, in depreciated paper money forced upon them by pirate patriots.

While the nation is blinded with tears and the common men's blood gushes from their torn veins, the "business" man, with pious patriotism talking grandly of the "glorious flag,"

* See Professors Cleveland and Powell: *Railroad Promotion and Capitalization*, pp. 250, 255.

† See Lalor's *Cyclopedia of Political Science, Political Economy, and United States History*, Vol. III., p. 514.

‡ *The Railways, the Trusts and the People*, p. 107.

cunningly sneaks to the nation's storehouse, a blushless burglar; he climbs aboard the ship of state, a conscienceless pirate.*

FIFTH ILLUSTRATION: "FREEING CUBA"—"REMEMBERING THE MAINE."

So you were—or wished to be—in the Spanish-American War?

Well, I wish to explain why the capitalists excited some young men—carefully excited them—and then sent them to Cuba in 1898.

There were very strong reasons for their doing so.

(1) American capitalists already had investments in Cuban industries, and they knew that if the United States took charge of Cuba, their investments would be more secure, would thus increase in value—and thus yield more profits.

(2) American capitalists wanted Spanish capitalists crowded out in order to give still more opportunity to American capitalists to extend their American capitalism in Cuba —and thus make more profits.

(3) Some American capitalists and craftily noble statesmen also secured some Cuban Revolutionary bonds at extremely low prices or as gifts, and they hoped and struggled to have the interest and principal guaranteed by the United States Government, and thus have these bonds rise in price at least to par—which would mean enormous profits.

(4) There was also at least some possibility (seriously discussed by prominent statesmen in Washington) that Spanish-

---

* The Fourth Illustration was prepared before the appearance of Mr. Gustavus Myers' *History of Great American Fortunes,* in which the reader can find much concerning the land steals. Myers' three volumes are brimful of bombshells for the "noble record" of the glistening barnacles that have clung to the body politic ever since George Washington was under indictment for swearing off his taxes. Mr. Myers has sadly bedimmed the glory of the illustrious "solid men of business." The work serves as a great contribution to the literature on *social parasitism* concerning which the wage-earner should make all haste to get all possible information.

Cuban bonds, said by some to aggregate hundreds of millions, already issued by the Spanish Government against the revenues of the Island of Cuba,—a possibility that these bonds also would be guaranteed by the United States Government.* In case of war these bonds would become doubtful, would fall very low in price, and then they could, of course, be bought up for almost nothing. Then, if guaranteed by our Government, they would rise high in price and become a "good thing" for those who bought them at a sacrifice price and then made all haste to have them thus guaranteed.

Here again the goal was profits.

(5) American capitalists well knew that intervention in Cuba would involve a costly war—so expensive as to make "necessary" the issuing of interest-bearing United States bonds, purchasing which, the buyers could milk the nation in interest for a generation or more. House Bill No. 10,100† actually proposed that our Government should issue, "for Cuban War expenses," $500,000,000 in 3 per cent. untaxable bonds, which, if purchased at par, would annually yield the purchasers the snug little sum of $15,000,000, in profits, besides other immense pecuniary advantages.

"And under the authority to borrow conferred by the Act of June 13, 1898, $200,000,000 of 3 per cent. bonds were actually sold. . . . The total subscriptions [offers for the bonds] amounted to $1,400,000,000. . . . Within a few months the original holdings passed into the possession of a comparatively few persons and corporations."‡

That is, the bond-buying patriots who were not at the front eating canned beef were *willing* to buy *seven times as many bonds as were offered* and thus in tender "love of country," fasten themselves, like leeches, to the social body—profitably.

(6) It was absolutely certain that such a war would vigorously stimulate business—and thus increase profits.

———

* See discussions in Congressional Record of the period.

† See Congressional Records.

‡ D. R. Dewey: *The Financial History of the United States*, p. 467.

(7) A war in Cuba was also certain to make "necessary" a larger standing army. And an army is very useful to the capitalist class in holding down the working class—in the game of profits.

Thus there were seven, or more, patriotic (and profitable) reasons for having Cuba "freed."

They fooled us—didn't they? They shouted: "Remember the Maine!" That made our blood hot—stampeded us—didn't it? But we are cooler now—aren't we? Let us see: Suppose a great ship should sink in a shallow harbor, as the Maine did, and suppose it had on board three dozen young men from the homes of the leading capitalists of America—*millionaires' sons.* What think you—would the vessel be raised or not?

Did you ever think of this? If the Spaniards blew up the Maine with a sunken mine, how can you explain the fact that the Maine's armor-plate was bent *outward* and not *inward* at the points of fracture? *Why does not the United States Government push the investigation to the very limit?* Why stop the investigation very suddenly just as things get extremely interesting?—just as it seems likely that information is about to come out which would astonish the whole world?

Ever think of it? Would it not have been profitable for some American capitalists to have bribed some scoundrel to blow up the Maine from the inside? It *was* profitable for capitalists in the American Civil War to furnish Union soldiers with rifles so defective that thousands of them exploded in the hands of the soldier boys. Thousands of the guns *when sold to the Government and handed on to the soldiers* bore the mark "Condemned." Look this matter up in Gustavus Myers' *History of Great American Fortunes,* Vol. II., pp. 127-38. Then when you hear some "Remember the Maine" music you will not become so violently excited and eager to enlist.

Of course you were told that the purpose of American interference in Cuba was to free the poor, suffering, abused Cubans:—the usual dose of philanthropy, flattery and bombast. Some eloquent speeches were made by Senators and Congressmen, speeches of unusual power and rare beauty. But the beauty and the power and the eloquence did not induce any of the eloquent statesmen to go to the war. Hardly.

If the United States Government had promptly recognized the revolutionary Cubans' right to become a sovereign nation possessing *international rights and privileges,* the Cubans could have freed themselves. France thus recognized the puny, rebellious American Revolutionary government in 1778; and that recognition helped us along wonderfully.

American capitalists in 1897-98 were simply searching the world for an opportunity to line their pockets. Excitable young men and boys came in handy as armed hired hands, hired fists; though, of course, these same hired men were left in the lurch, got disease, broken health—and contemptuous laughter.

Brothers, you veterans of the Cuban War, crafty men excited you, amused you, confused you, then used you and despised you so thoroughly that they gave some of you horse meat while in camp within five miles of Washington on your way to the war—so some of your number have said—and gave you on the battlefield embalmed meat canned years before, meat that even fizzed with a vile odor when the point of a knife-blade was thrust into the can, meat unfit for a mangy cur or a buzzard.

Excited you?

Yes, that is exactly what happened to you.

A man is pretty thoroughly excited and confused—isn't he?—when he is singing "My Country! 'tis of Thee!" at the very time that country is feeding him meat unfit for a dog. Mr. Roosevelt confesses that a special effort was made to excite you, and he also tells us some other things:*

"And from the moment when the regiment began to gather, *the higher officers kept instilling* into those under them the spirit of eagerness for action, of stern determination to *grasp at death* rather than forfeit honor . . . fever sickened and weakened them so that many of them died from it during the few months following their return. . . . We found all our dead and all the badly wounded. . . . One of our own dead and most of the Spanish dead had been

---

* *The Rough Riders,* passim. Italics mine. G. R. K.

found by the vultures before we got to them; and their bodies were mangled, their eyes and wounds being torn. . . . A very touching incident happened in the improvised open-air hospital after the fight, where the wounded were lying. . . . One of them suddenly began to hum, 'My Country, 'Tis of Thee,' and one by one the others joined in the chorus, which swelled out through the tropic, where the victors lay in camp beside their dead."

How lovely—so perfectly sweet of them. So extremely touching—"*grasping* at death."

The buzzards tore out the eyes of some of the brave young fellows and feasted on them; the grave-worms got some of them; vile diseases sickened many thousands of them; and many of them came home to "their *dear* country"—so poor in purse that they had to beg on the streets of Philadelphia, New York and elsewhere.

Their dear country.

They had been "grasping at death" for their dear country.

Remember: The buzzards and the battle-field grave-worms did not get the "prominent people" who actually own this dear country. "Higher officers" can not instill or fill a banker or a manufacturer so full of the "spirit of eagerness" that he becomes eager to "grasp at death" and have his eyeballs ripped out and his shattered body eaten by vultures.

These men were not excited—not in the least.

These men were thinking.

These were not "grasping at death"; they were grasping for Cuba.

Cuba looked good and you looked easy.

These men needed you in their business. And they got you, you Cuban War veterans.

Some items of interest concerning this matter leaked out and got into the papers—into obscure columns of a few of the papers. It improves one's enthusiasm for "patriotism" to read a few of these "leaks." Following are a few of the items, from the New York *Tribune:**

"According to the statement given out by the Cuban Junta yesterday, the Republic of Cuba issued $2,000,000 of bonds, payable

---

* April 1, 6, 9, and 20, 1898.

in gold, at 6 per cent. interest, ten years after the war with Spain had ended. Of this lot $500,000 were sold at an average of 50 per cent. . . . Among the purchasers of these bonds were many prominent financiers of this city; and now the bonds which were originally sold at 50 per cent. of their face value have increased to 60 per cent. . . .

"The disposition of the bonds of the Cuban Republic has been a question discussed in certain quarters during the last few days . . . and the graver charge has been made that the bonds have been given away indiscriminately in the United States to the people of influence who would therefore become interested in seeing the Republic of Cuba on such terms with the United States as would make the bonds valuable pieces of property. Men of business, newspaper and even public officials have been mentioned as having received these bonds as a gift. . . .

"Some interesting facts were developed before the Foreign Affairs Committee of the House today. B. F. Guerra, Deputy-Treasurer of the Cuban Republic, appeared with his books, and they were inspected by the Committee. He explained that of the $10,000,000 in bonds authorized . . . the lowest price at which any were sold was 25 cents on the dollar. . . . One million of the bonds were locked up in the safe of Belmont and Company, of New York, to be sold when the price fixed, 45 cents on the dollar, had been obtained.

" . . . Mr. Guerra was asked about the Spanish-Cuban bonds issued against the revenues of the island. He replied that he did not know their amount, which report placed at $400,000,000. . . . Deputy-Treasurer Guerra was also before the Senate Committee on Foreign Relations today. He said the Cuban bonds which had been sold had been disposed of for an average of about 40 cents on the dollar. . . .

"Some of the Republicans in Congress . . . are investigating the question as to whether the United States under international law, if it intervened in Cuba and cut off the revenues, could be held responsible for the Spanish bonds, said to aggregate $400,000,000, which have been issued against the revenues of the island. Mr. Bromwell says he is looking into the question, and finds some warrant in law for such responsibility. . . .

"Congressman 'Blank'* in the House on Monday, said he had $10,000 worth of Cuban bonds in his pocket . . . while H. H. Kohlsaat, in an editorial in one of the Chicago papers, charges the Junta with offering a bribe of $2,000,000 of Cuban bonds to a Chicago man [to one man!] to use his influence with the administration for the recognition of the provisional government. . . .

---

* See *Tribune* for real name in full.

"Mr. Guerra made the somewhat startling statement that a man representing certain individuals at Washington has sought to coerce the Junta into selling $10,000,000 worth of bonds at 20 cents on the dollar. 'This man practically threatened us that unless we let him have the bonds at the price he quoted, Cuba would never receive recognition. He said he was prepared to pay on the spot $2,000,000 in American money, for $10,000,000 of Cuban bonds, but his offer was refused.' "

As the possibility of "good things" increased, the statesmen's tender hearts were deeply stirred, naturally, and they set up a melodiously patriotic howl for intervention. Many powerful newspapers were turned upon the public to "work" the working class, and soon tens of thousands of humble fellows of the working class were wild with eagerness to rush to the front and "help the poor Cubans."

But a very high authority, Professor McMaster (University of Pennsylvania), assures us* that the outrages committed against the Cubans by the Spanish Government *had been common for more than fifty years.* "The Cubans had rebelled *six times in these fifty years."* But not until American capitalistic interests were well developed did it seem "noble" and "grand" and "the will of God" to intervene. But by the year 1895 "upwards of $50,000,000 of American money were invested in mines, railroads and plantations there. Our yearly trade with the Cubans was valued at $96,000,000."

It was time to weep—profitably.

Hence the tearful orations and powerful editorials for intervention. How the orators and business men far from the firing line loved "the men behind the guns." Here is some more evidence :†

"The canned roast meat . . . a great majority of the men found it uneatable. It was coarse, stringy and tasteless and very disagreeable in appearance, and so unpalatable that the effort [!] to eat it made some of the men sick. Most of them preferred to be hungry rather than eat it. . . . As nine-tenths of the men were more or less sick, the unattractiveness of the travel-rations was doubly unfortunate. . . . In some respects the Spanish rations were preferable to ours. . . . We had nothing whatever in the way of

---

* *School History of the United States*, p. 476.

† Roosevelt: *The Rough Riders*, passim.

proper nourishing food for our sick and wounded men during most
of the time. . . . On the day of the big fight, July 1, as far as we
could find out there were but two ambulances with the army in
condition to work—neither of which did we see. . . . On several
occasions I visited the big hospitals in the rear. Their condition
was frightful beyond description from lack of supplies, lack of medicine, lack of doctors, nurses, and attendants. . . . The wounded and
the sick who were sent back [to the hospitals] suffered so much
that, whenever possible, they returned to the front. . . . The fever
began to make heavy ravages among our men . . . not more than
half our men could carry their rolls. . . . But instead of this the
soldiers were issued horrible stuff called 'canned fresh beef.' . . . At
best it was stringy and tasteless, at the worst it was nauseating. Not
one-fourth of it was ever eaten at all even when the men became
very hungry. . . . The canned beef proved to be practically uneatable. . . . When we were mustered out, many of the men had lost
their jobs, and were too weak to go to work at once. Of course
there were a few weaklings among them; and there were others,
entirely brave and self-sufficient, who from wounds or fevers were
so reduced that they had to apply for aid. . . ."

While our government was feeding its soldiers on meat
unfit for a dog, our export trade included millions of pounds
of the best meat on earth—sent to Europe to be eaten by the
aristocratic snobs of the *"better* class."

Shakespeare has asked the thoughtful man's question:

"What would you have me do? Go to the wars, would you?
Where a man may serve seven years for the loss of a leg, and have
not money in the end to buy a wooden one."

"Freeing Cuba" was—was what? A change of masters for
the Cuban working class, and a "fool's errand" for the American working class soldiers, as many of them have confessed
—confessed with curses for the crafty prominent people who
seduced them to the battlefields.

SIXTH ILLUSTRATION: STANDING AT ATTENTION FOR CIVIL-
IZED CANNIBALS:

Consider a moment the recent war between Christian
Russia and pagan Japan, a war for the capitalist control of
Manchuria, the working class of course doing the fighting—
as usual.

It is well-known that the economic interests of the pagan

Japanese capitalists in Manchuria inspired the Japanese statesmen to the recent war with Russia. The Christian Russian capitalists had precisely the same sort of inspiration for the war. Here are presented some facts to be considered by the spiritual followers of Christ who presume to scorn the "sordid materialism of the 'unsaved' pagan Japanese":

(1) For years preceding 1903 the Christian Tsar and the Christian Empress and many of their Christian friends had opposed the threatening war in Manchuria.

(2) In 1903 the Royal Timber Company was organized to scoop up many millions of dollars in profits to be made out of the vast lumber forests in the Yalu River valley "secured" from the pagan Corean government.

(3) In 1903 the Tsar and the Empress and many of their friends joined the Royal Timber Company, taking stock to the amount of many millions of dollars.

(4) Having become involved in Corea *as capitalists* with *economic* interests to be protected, the Tsar, the Empress and their friends immediately and completely reversed their position on the question of war—vigorously favored the war which now seemed to be necessary to protect their Yalu River lumber interests. It now, of course, became perfectly clear that "the kingdom of Christ could be advanced among the heathen"—on the point of the bayonet.

Hence the two years of butchering of brothers by brothers —who were duly informed that they were "enemies."*

It seems barely possible that the 47,387 Japanese soldiers who were killed in that war could have no proper appreciation of the Tsar's spiritual motives in promoting the war; but, on the other hand, during the war 320,000 sick and wounded were sent from Manchurian battlefields to Japan. These, while nursing their festering wounds and their wasting health, had some leisure to have explained to them the somewhat elusively spiritual element of a Christian war inaugurated for "Jesus' sake" and the protection of a saw-mill enterprise.

This terrible war lasted two years. But it would certainly

---

* See *McClure's Magazine*, Sept., 1908.

have closed in six months because of lack of funds—if Christian business men and gentle, "cultivated" Christian women of the world had refused to lend money to the two sleek groups of official brutes in Japan and Russia who were forcing hundreds of thousands of humble working men into Manchuria to slaughter one another. Just charge up twenty-four months of that ferocious blood-spilling—charge it, not only to the Christian barbarians the Tsar and his friends, and the un-Christian Mikado and his pagan capitalist friends, but also to the civilized, fur-lined, orthodox savages of Western Europe and of the United States who were so wolfishly eager for un-earned incomes in interest on war bonds that they were willing, by lending money to fan the flames of war,—willing to foster wholesale murder, willing to wet the earth with working class blood and tears—willing thus to sink their industrial tusks deep into the quivering flesh of the toilers of Japan and Russia. Always there is a reason.

At one time in the war Japanese statesmen offered interest-bearing, Japanese national bonds for sale in San Francisco. There was instantly a swinish scramble by lily-fingered Christian ladies and gentlemen of that city to buy those pagan blood-wet bonds; the bonds were thus purchased immediately —with the unblushing promptness of greed. The offers of cash vastly exceeded the amount of the bonds offered. And now these "leading Christian citizens," having thus stuck out their tongues in scorn at the Christ of Peace, having thus given the loud laugh of contempt for the noble sentiment of the brotherhood of man,—these eminently respectable cannibals by means of their bond purchases having adjusted their scornful lips to the veins of the far-away working class of Japan—*are satisfied;* and for a generation they will suck and tug—like beautiful tigers at the throats of common work horses—will suck the industrial blood of the working class they despise.

This blood-sucking process will be called "business."

The blood they suck will be called "interest."

These gilt-edged cannibals will continue to be called "the very best people of San Francisco."

Their occasional contribution to Christian missionary work in Japan will be called "splendid generosity."

Their "views" on the "harmony of capital and labor" will be quoted in many capitalist newspapers as "sound advice."

And, strangely enough, these smooth murderers—particeps criminis—will actually go unhung, such is the irony of the present order.

And these distinguished abettors of international assassination will—with crafty thoughtfulness—occasionally visit the armories and barracks in San Francisco and carefully flatter the working class militia and the working class "regulars," flatter them into the folly of standing guard for those who despise and betray and bleed the working class of the whole world.

Brothers, will *you* be tricked to the trenches, march in the mud, murder your class and bleed yourselves for such as these? Will you stand at "attention" for these international leeches? What about loyalty to your own class?

Concerning these international bond-buying leeches the Reverend Dr. Walter Walsh writes:*

"By the very condition of its existence international capitalism has no country—save Eldorado; no king—save Mammon; no politics—save Business. . . . Mammon worshippers of all nations forswear every allegiance whensoever and in whatsoever part of the world it clashes with their allegiance to capital and interest; that heterogeneous and polyglot crowd of millionaires, exploiters, money-lenders, gamblers . . . or the adoring circle of political women who worship them—being moved by no other consideration than profit and loss. . . . By the transference of its investments from native to foreign countries capitalism ceases to be national . . . this bloated order of capitalism."

The English philosopher, Frederic Harrison, hands these international profit-gluttons the following compliment:†

"Turn which way we will, it all comes back to this—that we are to go to war really for the money interests of certain rich men. . . . All this is very desirable to the persons themselves. But it is not the concern of this country to guarantee them these profits,

---

* *The Moral Damage of War,* pp. 332-33.
† *National and Social Problems,* pp. 211-12.

privileges and places. It would be blood guilt in this country to enforce these guarantees at the cost of war. The interests of these rich and adventurous persons are not British interests; but the interests of certain British subjects. And between their interests and war and conquest, domination and annexation—how vast is the gulf."

"War seldom enters but where wealth allures."—Dryden: "Hind and Panther."

"Gold and power the chief causes of war."—Tacitus: *History*, Book 4.

"A great and lasting war can never be supported on this principle [patriotism] alone."—George Washington: In a letter to John Bannister, April 21, 1778.

> "Let the gulled fool the toils of war pursue
> Where bleed the many to enrich the few."
> —Shenstone: "Judgment of Hercules."

"When wars do come, they fall upon the many, the producing class, who are the sufferers."*

SEVENTH ILLUSTRATION: THE AMERICAN COSSACK.†

"The man on horseback" has always typified despotism. He means "Silence!" to all opposition. He is the assassin of discussion and the destroyer of democracy. Historically he has usually been the ambitious general usurping political powers and becoming an autocrat. He has always been dreaded by all who have worked for the progress of freedom. "The man on horseback" has ceased to be a myth in America. He has been recreated by the Neros of American capitalism whom he proudly serves for rations and flattery, the pet of the "captains of industry."

The Tsars of Russia have used the Cossack and recommend, him to all the rulers of the world.

The American Cossack has been on duty for several years in some parts of the United States. He is shameless, dangerous, effective. He will probably be multiplied by thousands, in numbers, and by infinity, in insolence,—within the next ten years—in the United States. *He must be understood— by the working class.* Here is a sample:

---

* Gen. U. S. Grant. Compare also Grant's comment on the cause of the Mexican War: *Memoirs*, Vol. I.

† See Chapters Seven, Section 7-12.

In the anthracite coal strike of 1902, 145,000 humble miners whose average income was $1.29 per day, struggled for a few pennies more for their toil with which to feed and clothe themselves and their families. In that strike the following brave deed was done by a mounted militiaman, an American Cossack, in the service of the tyrants who own the vast stores of anthracite coal.

A mounted militiaman, armed with a modern rifle and a powerful revolver, a double row of cartridges and a club in his belt, rode pompously through the street of a mining village, bravely daring the unarmed toilers and heroically glaring at the humble women and the helpless little children at the cabin doors. *Ready*—with him fed, petted, armed, mounted and brutal—the *capitalists* were *ready,* ready though the capitalists themselves were a hundred miles or ten thousand miles away. That AUTOMATIC TUSK of the capitalist class was on duty. Suddenly he cried out to an old man, a "mine helper," on strike, an old veteran of the Civil War: "Halt!"

Then, pointing down the dusty road, "the man on horseback," the American Cossack, said to the hungry old man: "March! Git! Damn you, git! Right down that road right now—and keep marching—straight ahead of me! Mind you —I'll be right behind you, you damned lazy scoundrel! Walk pretty—damn you! If you make a mis-step or even look sidewise, I'll put a bullet through you! Now march!"

The march began at once. Thus this well-dressed, well-mounted, well-armed young working man, an American Cossack, rode hour after hour—for half a day—a few steps behind the weary old wage-slave, a veteran of the Civil War,— on and on in the hot sun for many weary miles, down the Susquehanna River (in the direction of Gettysburg). Finally, after the long march, the noble hero on horseback called out to the old hero on foot, "Halt! Do you see that trail over yon mountain? Yes? Well, now, you damned old cheap skate, you scratch gravel over that mountain—quick, too! And let me tell you one thing—if you ever show your damned skinny old face in the anthracite coal region again, we'll shoot you like a dog. Now, you old gray-headed —— —— —, git

up that mountain—git up that mountain and out of sight or
I'll shoot you. Go!"

Wearily the old Union veteran climbed the mountain.
When he finally got away from his noble tormentor he sat
down to rest—and think—to think of "our free country."

Long ago that old gray man—when in his excitable
youth—had marched proudly under the "Stars and Stripes"
on gory battlefields, risking all, all, to defend "his country,"
and his dear "Old Glory." Once, he told me, the flag was
reddened with his own blood. . . . But now "Old Glory"
mocked him. Captains of industry, capitalists, industrial
Caesars, had captured the flag and with devilish craftiness
used that same flag to defend their industrial despotism.
Sons and grandsons of veterans of the Civil War were now
shrewdly flattered and bribed into the ignoble rôle of Russian-
izing America. Sons and grandsons were becoming Cossacks,
and they cursed his gray hairs for demanding of American
capitalists a few more pennies a day for ill-fed, ill-clad, ill-
housed women and children in the dismal homes of the miners.
. . . A cursing Cossack wearing khaki and flying the flag virtually spat in the old veteran's face.

"A cold-blooded organization that [Pennsylvania] State Constabulary."*

When Decoration Day comes, when the Fourth of July
is to be celebrated, when "patriotic" displays are to be made
—at such times—bankers, big business men, politicians and
statesmen—many of these—should put on black masks, wrap
themselves in black flags, and sneak (blushingly, if possible)
down into dark cellars and stay there during the celebration—
with their memories crowded with soldiers, widows and orphans brutally wronged,—with their memories crowded with
congresses corrupted, treasuries looted, lands stolen, charters,
privileges and "good things" shamelessly raped from the un-
seeing public while brave but deluded working men agonized
on bloody battlefields.

And on such days the working class should shout less

* New York *Evening Sun*, Editorial, Feb. 24, 1910.

and think more. "The man on horseback" should have some special thought.

And the working class are thinking to-day more than ever before. And, thinking, they begin to see that hand-clapping, fife-playing, drum-beating and buncombe from a prostituted orator are neither freedom nor justice, nor even the *sign* of such; but are, rather, just what Mark Twain called them*— a "bastard patriotism."

The motive of the young men who voluntarily join the army or the militia is possibly, in many cases, a good motive. Perhaps they do not see the tricks of the string-pullers behind the scenes, the powerful motives of the industrial masters behind the curtains. *It is not always easy for the young man to realize that he is to be used to punish the half-nourished, pale-faced working class baby that vainly tugs weak-lipped at the withered and milkless breasts of the ill-fed, ill-clothed, discouraged working class mother.* However, the cheap rôle of the armed protector of industrial parasites is becoming more and more clearly understood, and consequently more and more disgusting to the entire working class—including both the militia and the regulars themselves. LIGHT IS BREAKING IN THE TOILERS' MIND. THE HIDEOUS BUSINESS OF STANDING READY TO BAYONET THE MILLIONS OF MEN AND BOYS AND WOMEN AND GIRLS WHOSE LIVES ARE MADE UP OF MEANLY PAID DRUDGERY—THIS VILE BUSINESS IS RAPIDLY SINKING BELOW THE LEVEL OF CONTEMPT. STRONG YOUNG FELLOWS IN THE ARMY AND THE MILITIA AND THE NAVY INCLINE MORE AND MORE TO LINE UP WITH THEIR OWN CLASS, THE WORKING CLASS, AND REFUSE TO ASSASSINATE THEIR BROTHERS WHO ARE STRUGGLING FOR A FEW PENNIES ADVANCE IN WAGES.

They see the trick.

Some of the militiamen resigned in the anthracite coal strike of 1902, resigned when they realized that they were being used simply as watchdogs for industrial masters who were cheating even the little ten-year-old boys in the coal-breakers, cheating even these little fellows whose fingers, worn

---

* In an address, New York, May 25, 1908.

through the skin, were bleeding on the coal they sorted with their hands.

That was in Republican Pennsylvania.

Not long ago when the street railway union men were on strike in New Orleans some of the militiamen, with splendid contempt and defiance, threw their rifles down on the cobblestones rather than obey orders to shoot their old neighbors who were struggling for a larger share of life.

That was in Democratic Louisiana.

Workingmen, both Democrats and Republicans, begin to see the trick.

Thousands of young men desert—and thousands more would like to desert—the United States army every year. They cannot stand the snubs and sneers of their "superior officers," and the contempt now increasingly felt by the working class for the armed handy man serving as a fist for the ruling class.

So many young men in America understand the working class soldier's disloyalty to his own class that the Department of Murder now has much difficulty in keeping the ranks full. The Government now has to tease and coax young men to join the army and the navy. In the autumn of 1907, the capitalist press began to discuss boldly the necessity of *conscription* for filling the ranks of our standing army, the European plan of forcing young men to assume the rôle of armed flunkies. But just as the capitalist papers began to discuss and commend compulsory military service, the panic, the hard times, broke upon the country; hundreds of thousands were suddenly thrown out of employment. Instantly the Government and the capitalist papers ceased discussion of conscription, knowing well that thousands of jobless men could easily be recruited to save themselves from rags and hunger. At the same time Congress *advanced the pay of regular soldiers*—while millions of toilers were out of work, millions were reduced to "part time," millions had their wages cut: the destroyers' wages were advanced, but the producers' wages were cut down.

These facts made millions think. Thinking whets the edge of the working class mind. This sharpened mind cuts through the noisy mockery and the glittering sham of capitalist patriotism.

The workers wake. They see the trick.

Volunteers?

"The British volunteer army is in reality recruited to the extent of 80 per cent. by the peril of starvation. The yearly average of desertions from the British Regular Army is 7,000."* The writer of the present volume has heard of young men volunteering for the American Regular Army who enlisted in the fall and deserted in the spring, some of them doing this even three times.† The capitalists would not hire them and they were too proud to beg. They "wintered" in the army. But they despised the whole thing.

They see the trap.

A WORKINGMAN'S MEDITATIONS: "WE APPRECIATE IT."

In time of peace the "leading citizens" give us horny-handed working people the cold gaze—socially. We are not invited to dine with them—socially, or dance with them—socially, or otherwise visit with them—socially. They say we are ignorant and coarse-grained—socially; and they turn us down "cold and hard"—socially, *in time of peace.* But in time of *war* these "very best people" don't neglect us so much —and we appreciate it. *Then* the "best people" give us glad, stimulating glances and speak up kindly—and we appreciate it. They tell us we are brave and intelligent and patriotic— and we appreciate it. They tell us that soldier clothes look good (on us)—and we appreciate it. When our newly en-listed working class company are ready to go away to war the bankers and the other big business men chip in a quarter apiece to get the brass band out to give us a "send off"—and we appreciate it. The bankers and the big business men and the band go down to the railway station with us: we grin, then they smile—and we appreciate it. As our train of dirty

---

* British authority for this statement; but exact citation un-fortunately lost.

† But see Index: "Desertion."

old second-class coaches pulls away we look out through the car windows and see the bankers and the other leading citizens waving their soft white hands and sweetly smiling at us, saying, "You are the very *thing*"—and we appreciate it. The "best people" know we are going to feast on embalmed beef and show our patriotism: they wipe their eyes sympathetically —and we appreciate it. The "best people" modestly and courteously remain at home in order that we working people may have all the honor and glory of butchering and being butchered—and we appreciate it. The "best people," with beautiful forethought, give us working people the blessed privilege of leaving our homes lonely, leaving our wives desolate and widowed, our children orphaned—and we appreciate it. The "leading citizens" fraternally let us working people do the fighting and the bleeding and the dying for the country—and we appreciate it *so* much. With gracious manner these "prominent people" show us a "hot time" and tell us to "*go* to it"—and we appreciate it. With melting tenderness the "*very best people*" give us working people the "hot air" and the "frosty lemons"—and we begin to appreciate the trick.

When the southern slave-driver gave the slave fifteen lashes instead of sixteen the slave appreciated it.

Reader, in nearly every country in Europe, in America—in all parts of the civilized world—the workers are having their eyes opened. They begin to understand the crafty flattery of the dollar-marked patriots who never get on the firing line.

A SPECIAL WARNING TO THE WORKING CLASS OF THE UNITED STATES:

Open wide your eyes, brothers—and sisters.

The next trick-to-the-trenches is being prepared.

There is *talk* of peace—but *preparation* for war.

For more than twenty-five hundred years the great sea wars have been fought on the Atlantic Ocean and the Mediterranean Sea. The bottoms of these oceans are strewn with shattered ships and human bones.

But the vast butcherings at sea in the near future will probably be, most of them, on the Pacific Ocean.

Like hungry wolves hotly eager in sight of prey, like clouds of vultures swooping confidently over a field strewn with a vile feast—thus the capitalist nations are gathering together their drums, their rifles, cannon, dynamite, lyddite, embalmed beef, hospitals, soldiers, marines, battleships, and boat-destroyers, preparing to assemble on the Pacific Ocean for bloody struggles.

There is *talk* of peace—but *preparation* for war.

What for?

Simply to secure more opportunity to make more profits for more money-hungry cowards, who will loll at home—safe —while the "brave boys" do the fighting.

There is talk of peace—and preparation for war.

What for?

Eastern Asia is the prize.

Working-class boys everywhere who are socially snubbed at home—and even turned down at the factory—these boys will join the armies and the navies of the world for these future struggles. Huge guns will roar, big shells will boom across the waves, splendid ships will shudder, then plunge to the bottom of the deep, filled with boys enticed from the homes of the humble. The sharks will send the innocents to the sea.

It will be "great" and "glorious." Very.

And especially profitable: which is the main thing.

Perhaps your own bones or your son's bones will bleach at the bottom of the Pacific Ocean.

The *fundamental* cause of these future wars on the Pacific Ocean and in Eastern Asia, the cause, will be ignored or concealed by all International Peace Conferences and Conventions. And, afraid to admit the cause, they can not treat the cause of these wars; they will thus be unable to prevent these wars—these wolfish struggles for Eastern Asia as a capitalist prize. The leading capitalist citizens of the world have no confidence in these International Peace Conferences. Therefore they continue building more cannon, more battleships and more than ever they are teasing the boys—our own younger brothers of the working class—teasing them on board these great butchering machines.

Warn your neighbor—right away.

More and more defiantly the purpose is announced. In the year 1908 the President of the great American "Republic" uttered an imperial fiat—and lo! 18 battleships, 8 armored cruisers and a flock of torpedo-boat destroyers, with thousands of cheap and humble young fellows on board,—a fleet of butchering machines with the butchers aboard—pompously steamed 'round the earth on a forty-five thousand-mile cruise and carouse, meaning—meaning what? Precisely this:

The capitalists of the United States are prepared with "civilized" weapons, a shark's appetite and a tiger's methods, to conquer a lion's share of the vast profits to be wrung from Eastern Asia if they can find enough gullible jackies to do the fighting.

Be warned—you toilers in the mills and mines and on the farms.

"During the last half century," writes Dr. Josiah Strong,* "European manufactures have risen from $5,000,000,000 to $15,000,-000,000. This increase of production has led the European Powers to acquire tropical regions nearly one-half greater than Europe. But while European manufactures were increasing threefold, ours increased sixfold, and we, too, must find an outlet.

"All this means that the great manufacturing peoples are about entering on an industrial conflict which is likely to be much more than a 'thirty years' war,' and like all war will cause measureless misery and loss."

The interocean Panama Canal, costing our country hundreds of millions of dollars, is simply *one part* of the American plutocrats' plan to dominate the Pacific, bleed Asia, convert the "Republic" into a still less veiled despotism for conquest, commerce and profits to stuff the pockets of the modern Caesars who talk of patriotism and always lust for gold.

Mr. William H. Taft, in an interview, spoke thus threateningly in 1908:

"The foremost issue of the coming campaign will be the question of expansion and the affairs of our insular possessions.

"The American Chinese trade is sufficiently great to require the government of the United States to take every legitimate means to

---

* *Expansion*, pp. 101-2.

protect it against diminution or injury by any political preference of any of its competitors.

"*The merchants of the United States are being aroused to the importance of their Chinese export trade and will view political obstacles to its expansion with deep concern. This feeling of theirs would be likely to find its expression in the attitude of the United States Government.*

"The Japanese have no more to do with our policy as a people than any other nation. If they have or develop a policy that conflicts with ours, that is another matter. . . .

"I am an advocate of a larger navy."*

There is *talk* of peace—but *preparation* for war.

But mark it well, brothers of the working class: Mr. Taft's sons will not be butchered as cheap American marines fighting on the Pacific Ocean for a larger market for American capitalists. No capitalist shark shall make a sucker of his sons and tease them to the sea. Mr. Roosevelt's sons, Mr. Bryan's sons, and the sons of Senators and of Congressmen, the sons of bankers, great merchants and manufacturers—the flesh of these will never rot at the bottom of the Pacific Ocean. No, oh, no. Scarcely. They are too proud and shrewd to do anything of the sort—for fifty cents a day. The mothers and sisters and sweethearts of these thoroughbred boys will never weep in homes made desolate by the thoughts of skulls of loved ones shining and grinning at the bottom of the Pacific Ocean.

Brothers, I warn you.

"Tell them who are so fond of touring around the globe to import—(I would rather say to inflict)—their civilization on the backward nations and tribes," says Mr. Frederic Harrison,† "tell them that you want civilization here at home, if you can get it genuine. . . . Tell them that there are fifty burning social questions at home to solve. . . . Tell these noisy philanthropists . . . whilst 'civilization' is making the tour of the world on board iron-clads, with eighty-ton guns, civilization is terribly wanted . . . at home. . . . Therefore it is, I say, that peace, international justice, and quiet relations with all our neighbors, are first of all the interest of the workingmen . . . they lose most heavily by war, both in what they immediately suffer and in what they have to surrender. They may leave their bones to wither in distant lands, but they bring

---

* Italics mine. G. R. K.

† *National and Social Problems,* pp. 186-88.

back no fortunes, no honors . . . no new honors for their class. They only can speak out boldly and with the irresistible voice of conscience, because they only have no interest in injustice, nothing to gain by conquest, and everything to lose by interference."

Refuse, brothers, refuse. Be proud. Refuse. Stand by your own class. Refuse. Bankers refuse. Manufacturers refuse. All the shrewd "prominent people" refuse. You also should refuse to let your flesh rot and your bones bleach at the bottom of the ocean in the interest of these international leeches.

Lift up your meek faces, you tricked toilers of the world. The war trenches are yawning for your lives—a gulf in which the hopes, the happiness, the blood and the tears of your class will be swallowed.

Refuse.

When you understand, brothers, you will defend yourselves.

The day is dawning when the working class will not only shrewdly refuse to be tricked to the trenches, but will also proudly seize all the powers of government in defense of the working class. The working class must defend the working class. The state, the school, the press, the lecture platform, and even part of the church, all these powerful institutions, are at present used to fasten and hold the burdens of toil and the curse of war on the backs of the brutalized and despised working-class producers and the working-class destroyers.

It is our move, brothers. Have we sense enough for self-defense? See Chapter Ten: "Now What Shall We Do About It?"

CHAPTER SEVEN.

For Father and the Boys.

Following are "Topics for Discussion," commended especially to working men as themes for conversations by fathers (and mothers) and sons, daughters also. It is hoped, too, that many of these themes may be brought up for discussion by labor union bodies.

The reader will kindly refer to the footnote on page 13.

The divisions—or "sections"—of the present chapter and of the succeeding chapter are not always materially related, and for the author's purpose it is not necessary that they should be. The section numbering is for convenience in cross reference and for indexing.

(**1**) The Tsar of Russia and Germany's famous general Von Moltke positively refused to permit the young soldiers to see Verestchagin's pictures of war. Why? Because the pictures are true: they look like hell. Hell is not alluring.

"If my soldiers should think carefully, not one of them would remain in the ranks."—Frederick II.

Did you ever notice the attractive pictures of well-dressed, well-fed soldiers and marines displayed as our government's advertisements for army and navy recruits? The pictures are lovely. They are intended to make war look good to the young and hungry wage-earners, especially to those out of a job. But let me tell you: Recently when a crowded transport reached San Francisco back from the Philippines, some of the soldiers, on seeing again the advertising pictures displayed as decoys in San Francisco, shook their fists at the pictures and loudly and bitterly cursed them as part of the bait used to lure them to the hell of war. They had been thinking it all over. A good time to think it over is *before* you enlist—before you agree to go to hell.

(2) Comment on war:

German proverb: "When war comes the devil makes hell larger."

The Rev. Doctor Albert Barnes: "War resembles hell."

Bishop Warburton: "The blackest mischief ever breathed from hell."

Lord Clarendon: "War . . . an emblem of hell."

William Shakespeare: "O, War, thou son of hell."

General W. T. Sherman: "War is hell."

Well, really, it does seem as if the workingmen should at least be sharp enough to stay out of hell.

Now, since "war is hell" and the business men want hell and the politicians declare hell—why not let these gentlemen go to hell?

(3) Suppose we should have two laws passed and suppose we were in political position to rigidly enforce these two laws:—

FIRST LAW,—Requiring that when Congressmen and Senators are elected there shall be elected at the same time an alternate for each and every one of the Congressmen and Senators elected—to fill easily and promptly any vacancies that may occur from any cause.

SECOND LAW,—Requiring that all Senators and Congressmen who vote for war and thus "declare war" shall be forced, according to this law, to instantly resign their offices, and, by special draft provided for in this law, be forced to join the army immediately, infantry department, and, with the common instruments of war (rifles, swords, etc.), fight on the firing line, as privates, without promotion, till the war is finished or till they themselves are slaughtered.

It is significant that:

"Universal military service, adopted by all the great states on the Continent, in imitation of Germany [following the Franco-Prussian War], has, by making the young men of wealthy families join the army, personally interested the members of the governments and parliaments in avoiding war."*

---

* Charles Seignobos: *Political History of Europe Since* 1815, p. 819.

When, in 1909, the Spanish War in Africa became intense and dangerous, the Spanish government renewed an old "exemption" law permitting wealthy and "noble" and elegant Spanish gentlemen to send substitutes to the war and thus avoid the hell of the firing line themselves.*

Our "Dick" Military Law, passed by Congress in 1903, exempts Congressmen, Senators, judges, etc.,—also (by agreement with the State laws) preachers and priests—exempts all these from the clutches of the War Department, though that same law *sweeps millions of other men*—all able-bodied, male citizens over eighteen and under forty-five years of age—*sweeps millions more than before* into the absolute control of the Department of Slaughter. (See Section 11, below.)

Does it not seem that if war is good enough to vote for or pray for it is good enough to go to rifle in hand? If not, why not?

Those who vote for or pray for blood-stained victories should be forced to go after them. (See Chapter Eight, Section 14.)

(4) Mr. Workingman, would you for any reason permit any statesman or other leading citizen to compel you personally and individually to go out into a neighboring pasture-field and open fire with a Winchester upon your neighbor who had done you no injury, against whom you felt no enmity? Scorn the thought!

Well, suppose you are multiplied by 500,000 and your neighbor is also multiplied by 500,000, and instead of a neighboring pasture-field you have a neighboring territory on the other side of some national boundary line, and no quarrel, no enmity, no injury to be righted between the two groups of 500,000 workingmen—what then? Can't you see the point—till you have a bayonet thrust into you?

Suppose the Congress of the United States and the Diet of Japan should declare war against each other. Why not have all the fighting and the bleeding and the dying done by the Mikado and the national legislature of Japan and our President and our national legislature? Simply have these

---

* Similar practice was common in our Civil War.

two small groups of glistening strutters forced to face each other with rifles, swords and Gatling guns out on some nice level county fair-ground or big cornfield—forced to furnish the blood, cripples, corpses and funerals. This plan would be far more fun and less worry and less work—for the working class; it would require so much less time and money and blood and tears.

Take the last great war between Germany and France, in 1870-71. The King of Prussia and the Emperor of France had a personal quarrel about who should be or who should not be the new King of Spain—which was none of their business. They got "real mad." War was declared. The "honor" of this precious pair of handsome parasites was at stake. Nothing but blood would wash out the stain upon their "honor." Of course, royal blood was too precious for this laundering process. "Noble blood" was, of course, not available—for such purposes. The blood of common working class men would do very well for these two brutes to do their washing in. They were too cowardly to take each a sword and a Winchester and go out behind the barn or into the woodshed and "settle it," risking their own putrid blood. . . . No—oh, no! The red ooze of kings and nobles is not to be wasted as long as a lot of cheap wage-slaves are standing around willing to be butchered—with pride,—for the experience and honor of it.

"To the front! To the front! A million men to the front!"

Instantly a multitude of the strong men of the working class blindly rushed to the front—as ordered, and *asking no more questions* about the *justice* of the war than the cavalry horses asked.*

Did the working people of France and Germany have any grudge against one another? Not the slightest. But they butchered one another by the tens of thousands.

It is true that the King of Prussia and the Emperor of France were actually in this war, "at the front" (somewhat—or "as it were"). But the working class reader should not be

* But see Index: "Four Historic Events."

deceived by that fact. The King and the Emperor were rarely in any danger whatever—up *very* close. They *"enjoyed"* the battles from the high ground overlooking the slaughter—watching bravely through telescopes.

"How, then, did the Germans capture the Emperor at the Battle of Sedan?"

His troops were overwhelmed by the Germans. His soldiers swept back—crowded into Sedan. Five hundred German cannon pounding the town made the Emperor long for home. He did his grandest deeds of heroism—in trying to escape. He hadn't time to get out of the way. Bravely he dressed *in women's clothes* in order not to be recognized, hoping by a perfectly ladylike manner to get back to his throne on which his heroism would be more apparent and his martial spirit more assertive.

(**5**) Well-paid federal injunction judges, well-paid generals and naval officers (and their widows) are provided with liberal old-age government pensions—to make sure that *their* last years may be *absolutely secured* against toil and worry and the humiliation and social damnation of poverty. Now if these well-paid men, receiving salaries of from $2,000 to $12,500 a year for many years,—if these and those they love should be carefully protected against want and worry in their gray old age, then why should not useful industrial workers who serve long and well in the mills and mines and on the farms and railroads for a meagre living where their lives are full of risk—why should not these also be made absolutely secure when the sunset of their lives draws near? Why not?

The present annual cost of our two Departments of Murder—the Army and the Navy—(including interest on war bonds and the loss of the "regular" soldiers' labor-power, but *not* including the military pensions) would furnish an annual old-age industrial pension of more than $290 each for one million four hundred and fifty thousand people. You old men and old women of the working class, wouldn't it give you a feeling of peace and confidence if you were absolutely certain that, after a life of useful labor in the grand army of industry, you, every pair of you, would receive yearly, not as charity, but as a right provided for all, over $580? The lives of many working class men and women are to-day filled with fear of hunger and rags and shelterless, helpless days when they pass the capitalists' deadline, the employers' "age-limit."

Says the New York *World*:*

"The unemployed of New York ask that on Decoration Day there be a service in the honor of the workingmen who have lost their lives at the post of duty. Not much attention has been paid to the suggestion. . . . These are the legacies which a people devoted to industry have received from an ancestry devoted to war. The heroes most honored in all ages have been warriors, and yet every generation has produced countless examples of devotion and sacrifice remote from the field of carnage.

"More than any other great nation this republic might be expected to glorify the martyrs of industry, whose lives have been as truly for progress as any of those sacrificed in the ranks of armies. There are many dangerous callings in which the risks are as great as those of war. *There are hundreds of thousands of working men and women fighting fiercer battles daily than many a soldier ever knew.* On the *industrial* firing line, *where no quarter is given to the invalid or the incompetent,* courage is not sustained by excitement and passion, and there are no illusions of fame to strengthen the faltering toiler when he comes face to face with defeat and death.

"It is well that we should remember the fine patriotism of our citizen soldiers, but even they were workers before they were warriors. *If we would celebrate heroism it is to be found all about us in the humble stations among the men and women—even the children—who toil.*"

Think about this matter, carefully, you men and women of the working class. Discuss it with your children and your neighbors.

(**6**) The owner of a factory, protected by law, by the constitution, by the flag, by the politicians and the soldiers and militia, can "turn down" a skilful, effective wage-earner because his hair is gray, because he is "too old," is "past the age limit"—even though his old wife starve for support. The "glorious flag" protects even such vile industrial tyranny. The flag that the old man has worshipped, the constitution he defended, and the politicians he voted for—all these are no

* May 21, 1909. Italics mine. G. R. K.

protection for him. Thus our old industrial soldiers are helpless even though the industrial tyrant spit on their gray beard.

(**7**) The patriotic militiamen and the "regulars" often
say: "We believe in protecting property in time of strikes."

How much property have you? And what kind of property
is it? Is your property in danger? Indeed, was your property
even remotely threatened? Do those who own the property
you protect actually help you in protecting their property—
help you in actual struggles where the lead flies?

American capitalists often refer to the "splendid service"
of the militia and the regular troops in Chicago in 1894 in
"protecting railway property from being burned by the strikers." But let us see:

Certain railway companies in 1894 knew that the government of Chicago could be forced or "persuaded" to pay for
all the cars destroyed within the city limits during the strike
by claiming insufficient protection of property had been furnished. If, then, hundreds of old worn-out cars worth "old-
iron" prices could be destroyed by fire within the city limits
during the strike, and if the railway companies could by trick-
ery collect from the city, say, $500 for each such car burnt, it
would be "good business" to have such cars set on fire by paid
incendiaries. The burning of this precious property would
also create powerful sentiment against the strikers when
"played up" luridly by the capitalist newspapers. Thus there
was powerful motive for having the precious property burnt.
It would be both awful and profitable. Employees of some of
the railways entering Chicago have told the writer that old
worn-out cars from railway shop towns far out in Iowa were
actually hauled to Chicago and burnt within the city limits
in 1894.

Did you know that in 1895 in court the railway union men
were charged with burning the cars during the strike; and
did you know that when the union men brought into court
the proof that detectives were caught in the act of setting fire
to cars, *court adjourned,* and the case has never been called
since, though there has been a standing challenge to the courts
to do so? Thousands of such facts as these are suppressed.

"It is in evidence and uncontradicted," says Carroll D. Wright,* "that no violence or destruction of property by strikers or sympathizers took place in Pullman [Illinois], and that until July 3d [when the federal troops came upon the scene] no extraordinary protection was had from the police or military against even anticipated disorder."

(8) In 1907 there was a bitter strike at the iron mines in northern Minnesota. In all the "strike" mining towns, *except one,* armed men, "special guards," were officially placed on duty at once—ready to "keep order," ready to "quell the riots," etc. In Sparta, an iron-mining town, there were over three hundred men on strike, hotly eager to win the strike. But the strikers and the town officials united in an urgent request that no special armed guards be sent to Sparta. The strikers and the town officials agreed that "the guards only stir up trouble," and without the guards they could and would keep order themselves.

Guards were sent to all the "strike" towns but Sparta.

Turmoil and bitterness promptly broke out and continued for weeks in every "strike" town except Sparta.

There was no trouble whatever in Sparta during the entire strike. The only man arrested in Sparta for disorder during the entire strike was a special guard that sneaked into the town and got viciously drunk. He was promptly thrust into jail by the police, with the glad sanction of the strikers, and on the following morning he was escorted to the town limits and forced to get away and stay away. Another day during the strike several special guards came to the borders of the town, plainly seeking trouble. They were promptly forced to leave.

Well-fed, well-paid, well-armed men in a strike town ready to bayonet poor fellows struggling for crusts against a brutal corporation—simply stir up trouble. And the capitalist employers know this well.

Surely you have noticed that during troublous times of strike the chief use made of police, militia, cossacks and "regulars" is to protect the haughty employer who blurts out:

---

* Report of the United States Pullman Strike Commission: Carroll D. Wright, Chairman.

"Nothing to arbitrate!" He would promptly come to terms—
there would instantly be "something to arbitrate"—if he did
not feel sure that the toilers would be promptly jailed or shot
if they became maddened in their fear and hunger and humiliation.

(**9**) You must have noticed that in turbulent strike times
in your community hungry, humiliated, angry men never for
a moment think of doing the least damage to the publicly-
owned school houses, the publicly-owned libraries and the
publicly-owned art galleries and the State University and the
publicly-owned park. You see, the workers are in a more
social relation to this *social property*. And if the mills, mines,
factories, and railways and the like were socially owned and
socially controlled, the workers would also be in a far more
social relation toward this *socialized industrial property*.
Then there would be no *class* war raging around the mines
and shops. Then this property would need no protection from
cheated, hungry, humiliated, maddened working people nor
from detective crooks in the service of capitalists as incendiaries. Then the workers could not be haughtily turned down
with the brutal "Nothing to arbitrate!" Then indeed there
would be no industrial kings and emperors to demand: "Bring
out the Gatling guns and the cossacks! This is *our* business!"

Notice:

Political justice is impossible under a political despotism.

Political democracy is the *only* known cure for political
despotism.

Industrial justice is impossible under an industrial despotism.

Industrial democracy is the only cure for industrial despotism.

Industrial democracy would end the civil war in industry.

"The right to rule the political state is *mine!*"—says the
king.

"You are wrong!" answer the most enlightened people.

The king steps down. He must.

The people step—up—to power. They must.

This is progress.

"The right to rule in industry is *ours!*" say the capitalist industrial masters, the industrial kings.

"You are wrong!" is the increasing answer of the increasing multitude of the increasingly intelligent members of the working class.

The kings of capitalism will come down. They must.

The working class will go up—to industrial democracy. They must.

This will be progress.

IF DESPOTISM IS ALL WRONG IN POLITICS, IT CAN NOT BE ALL RIGHT IN INDUSTRY.

INCREASING DEMOCRACY IS ON THE INCREASING PROGRAM OF MANKIND.

The master of ceremonies is the *political party* of the working *class* to secure, to inaugurate, to "render the next number on the program,"—industrial democracy.

This is the "road to power."

Forward! Forward! On!—to the last great battle in the civil war in industry.

"Evolution makes hope scientific."

Evolution leads to revolution.

That is a law of nature.

Laws of nature cannot be ignored, suspended, amended or repealed.

Learn the road to power, great splendid multitude of toilers.

The world is ours just as soon as we learn the road to power.

Prepare for the revolution—and Life.*

(**10**) That there is civil war in industry under capitalism has concrete illustration in the facts of strikes and lockouts. Here are some of them for a short term of years—in our own country:—

From 1881 to 1901 there were in the United States 22,793 strikes, which involved 117,509 establishments, threw 6,105,-694 persons out of employment for an average of 21 and 8/10

* See Chapter Ten on "What Shall We Do About It?"

THE WAR
IS THE
CLASS WAR

days, lost these workers in wages $257,863,478, consumed $16,174,793 in assistance from labor organizations, and lost to the employers over $122,731,121. Of these strikes less than 51 per cent. succeeded, slightly more than 13 per cent. partly succeeded, and over 36 per cent. failed altogether. During these same years there were 1,005 lockouts which involved 9,933 establishments, threw 504,307 persons out of employment for an average of 97 days, lost $48,819,745 in wages, cost $3,451,745 in assistance from labor organizations, lost for the employers $19,927,983. About 51 per cent. of these lockouts succeeded, less than 7 per cent. partly succeeded, and about 43 per cent. failed.*

"In legalizing labor wars," says Waldo F. Cook,† "the state virtually recognizes industrial classes as belligerents; and enough time has now elapsed to enable one to say that the long series of these wars and their highly probable continuance for an indefinite period under present conditions, establishes the presumption that the wage-system is a failure and must sometime be replaced by another, which will not produce industrial classes with hostile interests and exacerbate society by their class antagonisms and hates. For the labor war, no less than the war between nations, cultivates prejudice, bitterness and hatred—only these feelings affect classes within a nation rather than the nations themselves in their relations with each other. . . . Law makes violence by nations right; law makes violence by strikes wrong."

"War is a collision of interests."—General Von der Goltz. (Quoted by Mr. Cook, above.)

(**11**) THE DICK MILITIA LAW: A QUIET REVOLUTION. Everywhere our capitalist government prepares to serve the capitalist interests in the "collision of interests,"—in the civil war in industry.

The highest literary honor that can come to an officer of the United States Army is the Gold Medal of the Military Service Institution. This honor was won in the year 1908 by Captain Bjornstad of the Twenty-Eighth Infantry—with

---

* See article by Labor Commissioner C. D. Wright: *North American Review*, June, 1902; also R. T. Ely: *Outlines of Economics*, Edition of 1908, pp. 397-98.

† *International Journal of Ethics*, April, 1908.

an essay urging a standing army of 250,000 men and a reserve army of 750,000 men.

Would not the following be a fruitful subject for discussion in the labor union halls: What is the connection between
the threatening increase in the insulted, starving army of the
unemployed and the threatening increase of the bribed standing army?

Study and discuss this matter till our class realize that
strong men of the working class are bribed with bread to slay
those who earn bread.

All working men should read the Annual Report made by
Mr. Elihu Root, Secretary of War, in 1902-3. Mr. Root,
shrewd, shameless and powerful lackey of the capitalist class,
forcibly set forth in his Report the great advantages that
would result (to the capitalist class) from certain almost
revolutionary changes that could be easily made by vastly
increasing the "State" militia forces and at the same time
constituting these "State" forces as an organic, instantly
commandable part of the national army—to be used precisely
like "regular" troops for any purpose desired by the capitalists
in control of the national government. Mr. Root's Report
attracted instant wide and favorable attention. The capitalists were delighted. The workers were deluded. Immediately
the Report became the basis of the "Dick Militia Law" which
was passed in 1903.

The author of *War—What For?* has urged capitalist
editors all over the United States to publish this law. He
has offered to pay for space at liberal advertising rates in
which to print from ten to one hundred lines of this law. He
has not succeeded in finding a capitalist editor who would thus
reveal the treachery of his class lurking in this law. This
law is a rough-ground sword against the rousing, rising
working class in the United States, a law more important to
the working class than any other law passed since the middle
of the nineteenth century. This law is loaded with death for
the workers when in future years the army of the unemployed or the ill-paid toilers gather around the mines and
factories and roar for work or bread. Instead of work they

will get sneers. Instead of bread they will get lead and steel
—provided for by this Dick Militia Law.

The capitalists do not dare permit the working class to read
and study this "Dick" law in the newspapers. Note some of
the features of this law:

The purpose: "An Act to promote the efficiency of the
militia and *for other purposes.*"

What is meant by "other purposes" will become clearer
as the army of the unemployed grows larger. "Other purposes"—exactly: food for reflection when out of work and
hungry.

SECTION 1,—"The militia shall consist of every able-
bodied male citizen of the respective States, Territories, and
the District of Columbia . . . who is more than eighteen and
less than forty-five years of age."

The males of military age, all from eighteen to forty-five inclusive, in 1890 numbered 13,230,168.*

SECTION 4,—". . . It shall be lawful for the President
to call forth for a period not exceeding nine months such
number of the militia as *he* may deem necessary . . . and
to issue his orders . . . as he may think proper."

The law was amended with an iron hand during the winter and spring of the hard times of 1907-8, when millions
were thrown out of employment and into the muttering,
angry army of the unemployed. For example, the nine-
months limit was struck out of Section 4, which is more food
for reflection—for any one who has brains enough to reflect
with.

SECTION 7,—"Any officer or enlisted man of the militia
who shall refuse or neglect to present himself to such muster-
ing officer upon being called forth . . . shall be subject to
trial by court martial, and shall be punished as such court
martial may direct."

The law creates a vast reserve army now rapidly being
perfected. The law, especially as amended recently, gives the
President power greater than is possessed by some of the

* C. D. Wright: *Practical Sociology*, p. 38.

most dangerous and hated tyrants on earth to-day. Issuing a general order by telegraph and post, the President could suddenly place under orders from five to ten millions of the strongest men in the land—including the strikers themselves; and to neglect or refuse to obey such orders would mean a "court-martial" trial with rigorous punishment. A court-martial jury is not noted for gentleness; famously different from a jury of one's "old neighbors."

SECTION 9,—"The militia, when called into actual service of the United States, shall be subject to the same rules and articles of war as the regular troops." That is to say, for the time they are "on call," they are virtually federal soldiers.

The law as amended by Congress in May, 1908, provides "that every officer and enlisted man of the militia who shall be called forth in the manner hereinbefore prescribed shall be mustered for service *without further enlistment.*" [Italics in Report.]

"The call of the President will, therefore, of itself accomplish the transfer of the organized militia which is called forth by him from its state relations to its federal relations. It becomes part of the Army of the United States and the President becomes its commander-in-chief.

"The *President* is the *exclusive judge* of the existence of an emergency which would justify the calling forth of the Organized Militia."*

This law contains twenty-six sections, every one of which should be studied carefully by the working class of the United States. The Union labor bodies should urge local newspapers to publish parts of the law selected by the unions. The more the law is examined the more food for reflection will be found in it.†

The English capitalist government has also recently enacted a new military law, a species of "Dick" law, called the

---

* See Report of Secretary of War, 1908, p. 155. Italics mine. G. R. K.

† An excellent edition of the law with notes, analysis, history, and suggestions by Mr. Ernest Untermann, can be had for 5 cents, of any Socialist literature agent.

Territorial Force Act. This law transforms a "voluntary citizen soldier" into a "regular" soldier. Says *Justice:**

"Under the new act the Volunteer must 'enlist' and serve under 'military law.' He will be as much a regular soldier as a Life Guard or a Lancer, and can be called out to shoot down strikers in labor disputes as was actually done at Featherstone . . . and at Belfast only a few months ago."

"The Volunteer," says the *Morning Post*, "will no longer be a citizen soldier, he will be a soldier without the blur of citizenship. . . . He may be mechanic; many of the best Volunteers are mechanics. If there is a strike in his works, ordered by the trade union to which he subscribes, and if the Mayor is afraid of the Strikers, and wants soldiers to shoot them, in case of need, the Volunteer, renamed 'man of the Territorial Force,' is just the man he wants; and the bill empowers the Mayor to call him out for the purpose."

The "Dick" law was passed by capitalist "friends of labor," of course, both Republicans and Democrats; and the "Territorial Force Act" was similarly passed by capitalist "friends of labor," both Liberals and Conservatives. As the unarmed army of the unemployed grows threateningly larger and the armed army of bribed butchers grows larger—ready to murder those who starve—it is in order, in "Old England," in "New America," everywhere in order, for the working class to give more careful attention to the "good men" who are so tearfully and fearfully "friendly to labor."

(**12**) Why should the working class give the capitalist governments a free hand in the murder of the workers? Why not rigorously restrict the power to call millions of men to arms?

What would happen if the working class should refuse to fight?

"That 'the government can not put the whole population in prison, and if it could, it would still be without material for an army, and without money for its support,' is an almost irrefutable argument. We see here ['in passive resistance, not simply in theory, but in practice'] at least the beginnings of a sentiment that shall, if sufficiently developed, make war impossible to an entire people. . . ."†

* London, March 21, 1908.

† Miss Jane Addams: *Newer Ideals of Peace*, p. 232.

Four points to be emphasized here:

(1) Require all the school teachers to teach all the children to despise and hate war.

(2) Arm everybody or nobody.

(3) Train everybody or nobody.

(4) "The right of the people to bear arms shall not be infringed."—*Constitution of the United States: Third Amendment.*

(5) The working class should diligently study the folly of requiring one regiment of the working class to fight the united and class-loyal capitalist class in strikes.

These four propositions suggest a plan that would, even under capitalism, render the working class far less helpless and hopeless than they are at present in their class struggle against the capitalist class of masters who may legally order the working class soldiers to fire on the working class.

However, the triumphantly effective work can be accomplished in this matter when—and not until—the working class have seized the powers of government. (See Chapter Ten, which is wholly devoted to the fundamentals of "What to do.")

It is significant that the first Secretary of War, Henry Knox, appointed by President Washington, made a Report January 18, 1790, on the proper basis for the military defense of the United States. His plan was "to reject a standing army, as possessing too fierce an aspect and being hostile to the principles of liberty."

A scholar of world-renown, Francis Lieber, German-American soldier, historian, economist and publicist, has this to say of standing armies:*

"Standing armies are not only dangerous to civil liberty because depending upon the executive. They have the additional evil effect that they infuse into the whole nation . . . a spirit directly opposed to that which ought to be the general spirit of a free people devoted to self-government. Habits of disobedience and contempt for the citizens are produced, and a view of government is induced which is contrary to liberty, self-reliance, self-government. . . .

---

* *Civil Liberty,* pp. 116-117.

Where the people worship the army, an opinion is engendered as if courage in battle were really the highest phase of humanity; and the army, in turn, more than aught else, leads to the worship of one man—so detrimental."

(**13**) "For the French and Italians and especially the German and Russian adolescent of the lower classes . . . the army is called . . . the poor man's university."*

"The poor man's university!"—in which he is drilled and kicked into spineless subserviency and is taught the noble art of killing himself, his class, scientifically. The degraded, docile, and despised millions of the working class men of the standing armies of the world are indeed educated when they are willing to wade in their own blood in defense of the parasitic capitalist class who rule, ride and ruin the toilers of all the world.

A standing army is a joke and a yoke on the working class. A standing army is a compound human machine educated to spank the working class when it cries for milk—and bread and meat. A soldier, a militiaman, is an educated boot with which the employers kick the working class.

(**14**) Do not rich men's sons sometimes voluntarily join the militia?

Yes, sometimes—but very, very rarely. One of the bluest-blooded Vanderbilts of New York was recently a captain in a specially handsome Regiment. But, mark you—in ninety-nine cases in a hundred, well-armed, well-trained militiamen fight unarmed, untrained workingmen (and women), which is not so very, very dangerous—for the militiamen. To an intelligent rich man an unarmed wage-earner on strike for an extra nickel to buy bread, as "the enemy," and an armed trained soldier whose business is murder, as "the enemy,"—these look different, you know.

For years New York millionaires and all the other "best people" "pointed with pride" to the famous Seventh Regiment of the National Guard, the "rich men's regiment," the "gilt-edged regiment" of lovely young millionaires, many of whom rode to the armory for drill in their automobiles. This regi-

---

* G. Stanley Hall: *Adolescence*, Vol. I., pp. 222-23.

ment of the American nobility of lard-and-tallow-steel-coal-and-railway millionaires, ready at any moment to defend and save the dear country from "the enemy,"—this regiment was, indeed, the pride of the village called New York. These glistening patricians taught the common people patriotism. "So they did."

Until the Spanish War broke out.

Then these fakir patriots—what did they do—then?

Resigned.

Or they did what amounted to the same thing—*voted* not to go to the war.

Certainly they did. Promptly, too—and intelligently.

Why not?

Surely you do not expect a lot of *intelligent* men to leave their happy homes, go to hell and make themselves ridiculous, do you? Why, the cost of a rubber tire for one wheel of an automobile would pay the war wages of a cheap man of the "lower classes" for six months.

(15) "Didn't one millionaire go to the war in Cuba?"

Yes. Out of our six thousand patriotic, flag-waving millionaires, one, just one, a young green one, went to the war in Cuba—"for a little excitement and a lark," he said. He found large quantities of excitement "all right," and some cold lead. He was killed. As a millionaire "patriotically" going to war his case is an exception, clearly an exception, a conspicuously lonely, vain and stupid exception; and that exception will never be imitated. Too much intelligence—among the millionaires. Even his millionaire friends laughed at him for going to war. But he wanted a "hot time." He got the "hot time"—and the cold lead.

There were several thousand other millionaire flag-wavers instructively conspicuous in that war—by their intelligent patriotic absence.

It is instructively significant that the capitalist newspapers gave more than a hundred times as much space to the death of the one millionaire soldier in the Spanish-American war as they gave to the death

OF ANY HUNDRED HUMBLE WORKING CLASS SOLDIERS WHO
WERE SLAUGHTERED IN THE SAME WAR.

(**16**) Were not some of the rich men of to-day soldiers
at one time—"years ago"?

Yes. Some of the rich men of to-day were soldiers at
one time—years ago; but they are not soldiers now when they
are rich, and they were not rich when, years ago, they were
soldiers.

(**17**) If politicians do not go to war, what about Mr.
Bryan's case? Didn't Mr. Bryan patriotically go to the war
in Cuba?

No. Mr. Bryan did not go *to* the war in Cuba. He simply went *toward* the war.

Mr. Bryan was, of course, patriotic, fervently, noisily so;
but, like the intelligent people of his class, he always had his
enthusiasm under perfect control. Mr. Bryan at no time
showed an unmanageable desire to get *up close in front, on
the firing line.* And his class was true to him, respected
his strong preference for war five hundred miles from the
flaming, snarling Gatling gun; and, accordingly, his class—
in power at Washington—kept him well out of danger. At
one time he got the impression he was in danger of being sent
to the front. At once he cried out, "It's politics!" and
promptly resigned his noble command, double quick, patriotically. Mr. Bryan, mounted on a splendid horse, with uplifted sword in hand, grandly vowing to "defend the flag
against the enemy" as he headed his noble braves, assembled
for review, and admiration, before the *Omaha Bee* building,
ready to start *toward* the front—at that sublime moment
Colonel William Jennings Bryan was, well, simply beautiful,
not to say pretty. As the golden tones of this Nebraskan
Achilles, this Alexander from the Platte Valley, rolled forth
in his heroic vow to bleed (if necessary) for his flag, the
nation was comforted—felt saved already.

Patriotism *is,* after all, *worth all it costs*—that is, worth
all it costs Mr. Bryan. Mr. Bryan, like Mr. Hearst and
many others, is patriotic, even intemperately so—with his
mouth.

But the reader may ask, "Was not Mr. Roosevelt in the Cuban War a case of a politician actually on the firing line?"

Clearly an exception. Name a few other "great statesmen" or international noises who went to the Cuban War—to the actual firing line.

Mr. Roosevelt loves excitement and danger. And what indescribable dangers there were for the Americans in the Cuban War! The mightiest "republic" on earth was pitted against the most toothless, decadent old political grandma in Europe. The dangers?—equal to those that threaten an armed, athletic hunter alone and face to face with a sucking fawn. Mr. Roosevelt himself has heroically—and carefully—recounted and printed his own brave deeds in that war. With Christian love and humility, with charming modesty and delicacy, with the diffident ingenuousness of a blushing schoolgirl, characteristic of him, Mr. Roosevelt tenderly recites one of his noble deeds as follows :*

"Lieutenant Davis's First Sergeant, Clarence Gould, killed a Spaniard with his revolver. . . . At about the same time I also shot one. . . . Two Spaniards leaped from the trenches . . . not ten yards away. As they turned to run I closed in and fired twice, missing the first and killing the second [Oh, joy!]. . . . At the same time I did not know of Gould's exploit, and I supposed my feat to be unique."

Surely it requires courage, rare and noble courage, for a wealthy graduate of Harvard University to boast in print that he shot a poor, ignorant fleeing Spanish soldier—very probably a humble working man drafted to war, torn from his weeping wife and children—that he shot such a man, *in the back*. Oh, bliss—elation—ecstasy divine! "I *got* him! with my *revolver* too! in the *back!*" Manly pastime of an American gentleman, a mongrel mixture of patrician and brute. Yes, reader, Mr. Roosevelt, politician, was in the Cuban War—with a purpose; and secured a military title and a "war record" worth at least 75,000 votes in his campaign for the governorship of New York which immediately followed the war. For details consult *The Rough Rider.*

* *The Rough Riders*, p. 139.

With shrewd patriotism, political foresight, rare courage—
and girlish bashfulness—Mr. Roosevelt's picture is repeatedly
presented in the book, the poses expressing his usual audible
modesty and ferocious gentleness.

Emerson finely says: "Every hero becomes a bore at last."

(**18**) The noble Professor Paulsen (Berlin University)
wrote:*

"Hate impels men to seek quarrels, and pride turns their heads.
. . . Nay, arrogance and hatred are really always the signs of an
irritable, diseased self-consciousness. . . . [That] selfish, arrogant,
vain and narrow-minded self-conceit, which the flatterers of the
popular passion call patriotism."

The distinguished Italian historian, G. Ferrero, has
written:†

"Thus in destroying or creating, man can procure for himself
strong emotions, and persuade himself of his own superiority. . . .
Two passions have divided the human heart throughout the annals
of human history: the divine passion for creation, and the diabolical
passion for destruction. . . . Nineteenth-century man may seek after
violent and inebriating emotions that permit him to assert his superiority over his fellows. . . ."

Robert G. Ingersoll understood the hero-brute mongrel:

"Courage without conscience is a wild beast. Patriotism without principle is the prejudice of birth, the animal attachment to
place."

Thus Victor Hugo:‡

"To be, materially, a great man, to be pompously violent, to
reign by virtue of the sword-knot and cockade . . . to possess a
genius for brutality—this is to be great, if you will, but it is a
coarse way of being great."

The cannon's roar, the bayonet's thrust, the crush of flesh,
the splash of blood,—such things in battle make men gentle,
tender, gallant, even heroic, fit subjects for the adoration of
women.§ For example: When the Christian heroes captured
Magdeburg:

---

* *System of Ethics*, p. 660.

† *Militarism*, pp. 60-61.

‡ *William Shakespeare*, Pt. 3, Bk. 3, Ch. I.

§ See Chapter Eight, Section 11,—of special interest to women
who incline to be "perfectly delighted" with soldiers.

"Now began a scene of massacre and outrage which history has no language, and poetry no pencil, to portray. Neither the innocence of childhood nor the helplessness of old age, neither youth nor sex, neither rank nor beauty, could disarm the fury of the conquerors. Wives were dishonored in the very arms of their husbands, daughters at the feet of their parents, and the defenseless sex exposed to the double loss of virtue and life. . . . Fifty-three women were found in one church with their heads cut off. The Croats amused themselves by throwing children into the flames, and Pappenheim's Walloons with stabbing infants at their mothers' breasts."*

But it may be said that those things were done far back in the seventeenth century. Consider, then, the fact that in the French civil war of 1871 the government's noble heroes, having conquered the revolutionists, took thousands of un-armed prisoners—men, women, and children—to an open space at the city limits of Paris and shot them, children and all; in many cases the brave, armed ruffians stood up rows of helpless prisoners one behind the other and amused themselves by testing their rifles on living human flesh, noting how many men, women and children could be butchered with one bullet. Many of the "better class," "refined ladies and gentlemen," "leading citizens," conspicuous by their elegance of manners and dress, were present *watching the fun,* smiling encouragement and making helpful suggestions to the "civilized" butchers.

And still more recently:

A British hero thus describes a "funny" incident in the South African war: "Really, sir, I never saw anything quite so funny in all my life. Just fancy, I saw a Kaffir woman pick up the headless body of her baby and strap it on her back. Funny, oh, Lord! It makes me laugh when I think of it now." The same authority (the *Westminster Review,* quoted by Walter Walsh) also gives the following case of Christian military heroism: "A contingent of German scouts [in South Africa] took five native women prisoners . . . an officer ordered ten men to fix bayonets. Five stood in front and five behind the women, and stabbed the women to death."

---

* Quoted by Thomas E. Will, *Arena,* Dec., 1894.

Ten armed, Christian heroes with bayonets ripping the breasts of *five unarmed women.* Great! Isn't it? At least it is war. One scarcely knows which to despise the more—the soldiers or the lazy parasites for whom they committed a thousand crimes of basest cruelty and cowardice. Dr. Walter Walsh[*] lets the soldiers tell in their own heroic language of their manly deeds—thus:

" 'Our progress was like the old-time forays in Scotland two centuries ago. . . . We moved on from valley to valley . . . burning, looting and turning out the women and children to sit and cry beside the ruins of their once beautiful farmsteads . . . my men fetched bundles of straw. The women cried, and the children stood holding to them and looking with large frightened eyes at the burning house. . . . The people had thought we had come for refreshments, and one of them went to get milk. . . . We then set the whole place on fire. They dropped on their knees and prayed and sang, weeping bitterly the while. One of the poor women went raving mad. When the flames burst from the doomed place the poor woman threw herself on her knees, tore open her bodice, and bared her breasts, screaming, "Shoot me, shoot me, I've nothing to live for, now that my husband is gone, and our farm is burnt, and our cattle taken!" ' "

These foul deeds are samples of thousands.

"War, is it?" says Dr. Walsh. "Be it war: then an army is a manufactory for cowards and a school for cowards."

"A war hero," says the distinguished Roman Catholic Bishop John Spaulding,[†] "supposes a barbarous condition of the race; and when all shall be civilized, they who know and love the most shall be held to be the greatest and the best."

And Robert Ingersoll thus:

"Every good man, every good woman, should try to do away with war, to stop the appeal to savage force. Man in a savage state relies upon his strength, and decides for himself what is right and what is wrong."[‡]

"Nothing is plainer," says Emerson, "than that sympathy with war is a juvenile and temporary state."[§]

---

[*] *Moral Damage of War*, pp. 146-47.
[†] *Education and the Higher Life*, p. 171.
[‡] *Works*, Vol. IV., Dresden Edition, p. 124.
[§] "Lecture on War."

Dr. John Fiske, historian and philosopher, makes the following observations on the slow grand march from brutality to brotherhood.*

"For thousands of generations, and until very recent times, one of the chief occupations of men has been to plunder, bruise and kill one another. The . . . ugly passions . . . have had but little opportunity to grow weak from disuse. The tender and unselfish feelings, which are a later product of evolution, have too seldom been allowed to grow strong from exercise . . . the whims and prejudices of militant barbarism are slow in dying out. . . . The coarser forms of cruelty are disappearing and the butchery of men has greatly diminished . . . in the more barbarous times the hero was he who had slain his thousands. . . . And thus we see what human progress means. It means throwing off the brute inheritance, gradually throwing it off through ages of struggle that are by and by to make struggles needless. Man is slowly passing from a primitive social state . . . toward an ultimate social state in which his character shall have become so transformed that nothing of the brute can be detected in it. The ape and the tiger in human nature will be extinct."

How encouraging! We can confidently look forward to a time when not even a pervert candidate for the presidency of a great Christian "republic" will be either tiger enough to butcher a human being or peacock and monkey enough to brag of doing so.

> "Who loves war for war's own sake
> Is fool, or crazed, or worse."—Tennyson.

"One of the commonest popular mistakes is to confound aggressiveness and belligerency with genius. These qualities are almost in inverse proportion. . . . But usually great energy and determination, and especially combative qualities are associated with rather meagre abilities."†

There is really too much bull-dog greatness.

> "No blood-stained victory, in story bright,
> Can give the philosophical mind delight;
> No triumph please, while rage and death destroy:
> Reflection sickens at the monstrous joy."‡

---

* *The Destiny of Man,* pp. 100-103.
† Lester F. Ward: *Applied Sociology,* p. 264.
‡ Bloomfield: "Farmer's Boy."

> "Cursed is the man, and void of law and right;
> Unworthy property, unworthy light,
> Unfit for public rule, or private care,—
> That wretch, that monster, who delights in war."*

Imagine a Sioux Indian chief, pagan Alexander, pagan Cæsar, Christian Napoleon, also the Christian bullies Emperor William and Theodore Roosevelt, also the quiet Christ—imagine these seven "not only willing, but anxious to fight," mounted on foam-stained horses galloping across a bloody battlefield strewn with wounded and slaughtered men and boys, imagine these seven galloping, bravely and boisterously galloping, waving red-stained swords, yelling, squawking, yawping, hurrahing for war, "glorious" war—the iron-shod hoofs of their rushing horses crushing into the breasts and faces of dead and dying young men and boys.

The savage Sioux, the immortal pagan brutes Alexander and Cæsar, the renowned Christian bullies Napoleon, William and Theodore—these six "geniuses," these coarse-grained, blood-stained egotists fit that picture perfectly, as a shark fits the ocean, as a wolf fits the forest, as a tiger fits the jungle, as a savage fits a cannibal feast,—as the Devil fits Hell.

But Christ, Christ in whose breast lurked no tiger and no savage,—Christ with a long sword, a hero's butcher-knife in hand, plunging it into the breast of his brothers, screaming like the "dee-lighted" brute, calling it "great," "splendid," "bully!"—

Impossible!

But why impossible for Christ and "dee-lightful" for the other six?

Because, simply because, these six blood-lusting heroes are savage or at best only civilized; but Christ was socialized.

Socialization opposes assassination—both wholesale and retail.

Christ is immortal—by his wide love and brotherhood.

The "great general" is promoted and immortalized for his narrow hates and brilliant brutalities.

(19) Has not war been natural and necessary in the

---

* Pope's Homer's "Iliad."

life of the human race, and has not war been a potent factor
in the intellectual development of mankind?

Professor Ferrero has this to say:*

"Thus the duty of every well-meaning man to-day is to diffuse
knowledge of the fact that war no longer serves the purpose it once
served in the struggle for civilization.

"War necessary to civilization?"

Well, for a long time in the life of the human race nature
was so ill understood, man had such insufficient knowledge
and control of nature, that it was extremely difficult to get a
living for all. Our ancestors naturally quarreled; perhaps
it was necessary for some of them to kill others in order that
some of them might live—ignorant as the people were in
those times of how to make nature yield bountifully and
easily for all. And no doubt the struggle developed the
race—the part that did not get killed. In those struggles
were developed, at first, strong muscles, skin-ripping claws
or knife-like finger-nails, tusks in the mouth, and thick skins;
and, later, clubs, spears, cross-bows, bows-and-arrows; and
still later, rifles, cannon, battleships and lignite shells, and
also the methods and tactics of struggle;—all these were
developed. Always, too, cunning, deception, malignance,
egoism, egotism, coarse-grained dispositions, cheap ambitions,
swaggering manners, fierce eyes, and the soft, bull-like military voices and hero worship—all these were developed.

The muscles and the mentality thus developed are still
extremely useful. Indeed, the mentality, developed in war
(but neither wholly nor chiefly in war), is worth all it cost,
whatever it did cost, because with this godlike mentality, and
only with this mentality, we can now have the higher and finer
forms and phases of life, the pleasures that distinguish man
from the brutes; that is, with this mentality we can have
these more glorious forms of life: *Provided,* that the low
cunning, deception, malignance, egoism, egotism and the
coarse-grained strain of the ancient brute are not even yet
too strong in our veins and characters. In spite of one's in-

---

* *Militarism,* p. 316.

telligence he may be "not only willing, but anxious to fight."
Such a person may no longer have the skin-ripping finger-
claws, but he has the skin-ripping disposition that was developed when the skin-ripping finger-claws were developed,
and developed in the same way.

Now, of course, we still need the muscle and the intelligence, every one of us. But we do not any longer need the
skin-rippers, or the tusks, or the club, the "big stick," the
spear, the bow and arrow, the rifle and the battleship; nor do
we any longer need the arrogant egotism, the cheap cunning,
the prize-fighter ambitions or the tiger's readiness to take
blood. Nor should we any longer need the ancient method
of struggle, every-fellow-for-himself, in the industrial process
of life—in a *rationally* organized society, with our *present*
control of nature. And we should no longer enjoy any of
these brute means and methods if we were civilized in the
noblest sense, that is, if we were decently socialized.

"Are you ready for the question?" This is the question:

Can you use, do you prefer to use—your developed mentality like a brute, like a savage, or like a truth-seeking, socialized man? Are you "not only willing, but anxious to
fight," or are the business and the methods of the brute disgusting to you? What o'clock is it in your personal evolution? Do you prefer a library to an armory, books rather
than bayonets? Is a fight natural, or necessary, or helpful
in your personal development? If a fight, actual part in a
fight rifle-in-hand, is not necessary to the preacher, the senator, the professor, the banker or the manufacturer, why should
it seem necessary in your case—and why should you permit
these "better class" citizens to have you ordered and led
around like a prize-winning bull-dog to fight in the international prize-ring called the struggle for the world market?
War as a developer and a civilizer is a flat failure *in your
case* if the capitalist class can seduce you for fifty cents a
day to fight for a foreign market for American porterhouse
steak while you and your father and mother are fed on
third-rate meat, beans, cheap syrup and mock-coffee without
cream. Brother, you may indeed be a "brave boy," and a

"good shot," and you may have heroically stained your hands in other men's blood; but, really, the "upper class" have marked you as an easy victim, a useable cheap "guy" of the "lower class."

(**20**) John Ruskin keenly appreciated the capitalist's craftiness and the workingman's buffoonery in "a war for civilization." He wrote:*

"Capitalists, when they do not know what to do with their money, persuade the peasants that the said peasants want guns to shoot each other with. The peasants accordingly borrow guns, out of the manufacture of which the capitalists get a percentage, and men of science much amusement and credit. Then the peasants shoot a certain number of each other until they get tired, and burn each other's houses down in various places. Then they put the guns back into towns, arsenals, etc., in ornamental patterns, and the victorious party put also some ragged flags in churches. And then the capitalists tax both annually, ever afterwards, to pay interest on the loan of the guns and powder."

The Italian historian Ferrero sees the swinish snout of the ruling class greed in the wars of three thousand years of "civilization." He writes:†

"During those thirty centuries from which dates our historical knowledge, war has been more a social system than a cruel pastime for kings—the first most violent and brutal means adopted by ruling minorities to acquire wealth."

(**21**) Is it said that wars always have been and always will be?

That wars always have been is an unproved proposition.‡

That "wars always will be" depends upon the working class. The clouds of confusion are clearing from the mind of the working class. A revolution is ripening in the toilers' thought on war.§

(**22**) Is it said by the leading citizens that wars are necessary in order to kill off the surplus population?

---

* Quoted by John A. Hobson: *John Ruskin: Social Reformer,* p. 346.

† *Militarism,* p. 317.

‡ See Chapter Eleven.

§ See Chapter Ten, also Index: "Revolution of Opinion."

If wars are necessary for such purpose, why not have Mr. Leading Citizen and his friends classified as a part of the surplus population on the ground that they are criminally unsocial, and have them taken out to the battlefield and forced to shoot one another? The theory of having the surplus population killed off would thus quickly lose its popularity with the "upper classes."

(**23**) It may be said that the Napoleonic wars removed more than 7,500,000 men from competition in the labor market;* and it might be argued by the working man that since war reduces the competition among the workers, the working class should on this account welcome war.

Let us see: If four men are competing for two jobs, should two of them be satisfied, and even glad, to have the competition for the jobs reduced by having the other two climb upon their backs and cease to bid for the jobs? It should be kept distinctly in mind that the workers who do not go to war support those who do go to war—always, everywhere, absolutely no exceptions.

(**24**) There is a somewhat popular, and simian, assumption that in war—even in beautiful Christian war—the results are "the survival of the fittest," meaning, in the case of modern wars, the survival of "the more highly civilized," also the biologically "best."

Of course a "bullet carefully selects its victim."

And do not statesmen tell us on the Fourth of July all about the "splendid intelligence" and the "noble spirit" and the "superiority" of the "brave boys who *died* in battle"?

Does not the recruiting officer try to get the *soundest* men for slaughter?

Let the orthodox worshippers answer: Is pagan Japan more fit for survival than Christian Russia?

What show for survival would Belgium have in a contest with Turkey, Spain or Russia?†

---

* See McCabe and Darien: *Can We Disarm?* p. 56.

† See Index: "What War Decides"; also "Blood Cost of War."

(**25**) A kindred and stupid assumption in all wars is this: *Might makes right.*

But if might makes right between two warring nations, then why does not might make right when a strong man by force compels a weaker man to hand over his pocket-book?

(**26**) A Scotch philosopher on the "brave boys":*

"Omitting much, let us impart what follows: Horrible enough! A whole marchfield strewed with shell-splinters, cannon-shots, ruined tumbrils and dead men and horses; stragglers remaining not so much as buried. And those red mound-heaps: aye, there lie the Shells of Men, out of which the life and virtue have been blown; and now they are swept together and crammed down out of sight, like blown Eggshells! . . . How has thy breast, fair plain, been defaced and defiled! The green sward is torn up, hedge-rows and pleasant dwellings blown away with gunpowder, and the kind seed-field lies a desolate Place of Skulls. Nevertheless, Nature is at work . . . all that gore and carnage will be shrouded in, absorbed into manure. . . .

"What, speaking in quite unofficial language, is the net purport and upshot of the war? To my own knowledge, for example, there dwell and toil, in the British village of Dumrudge, usually some five hundred souls. From these, by certain 'natural enemies' of the French, there are successively selected, during the French war, say thirty able-bodied men: Dumrudge, at her own expense, has suckled and nursed them; she has, not without difficulty and sorrow, fed them up to manhood, and even trained them up to crafts, so that one can weave, another build, another hammer, and the weakest can stand under thirty stone avoirdupois. Nevertheless, amid much weeping and swearing, they are selected; all dressed in red and shipped away, at the public charges, some two thousand miles, or say only to the south of Spain, and fed there till wanted. And now to that same spot in the south of Spain, are thirty similar French artisans—in like manner wending their ways; till at length, after infinite effort, the two parties come into actual juxtaposition, and thirty stand facing thirty, each with his gun in hand. Straightway the word 'Fire!' is given, and they blow the souls out of one another; and in the place of sixty brisk, useful craftsmen, the world has sixty dead carcasses, which it must bury, and anew shed tears for.

"Had these men any quarrel? Busy as the Devil is, not the smallest! They lived far enough apart; were the entirest strangers;

---

* Thomas Carlyle: *Sartor Resartus*, Book II., Chapter 8.

nay, in so wide a universe, there was even, unconsciously, by commerce, some mutual helpfulness between them.

"How then?

"Simpleton! Their governors had fallen out; and instead of
shooting one another, had these poor blockheads shoot."

(27) In that part of biology treating of parasitic life
the technical terms "host" and "guest" are used. The host
is the living thing that furnishes a living not only for itself,
but also for the life-filching intruder which fastens itself
upon the body of the "host." The intruder, the robber resid-
ing upon the body of the "host," is the "guest," that is, the
parasite.

Now one of the strangest things in the entire live world
is this: When in some life-forms a certain stage of parasitism is reached, when the guest has permanently fastened
itself upon the body of the host and the host has become
thoroughly accustomed to and adjusted to the parasitic
arrangement, the host stupidly inclines to *defend the parasitic guest.* It is remarkable (and discouraging) that this
law of nature, this tendency, is found in operation in the
social life of man. For thousands of years multitudes of
men, women and children have been held in the grip of this
law, mentally strangled in their effort to think Justice and
Freedom; the vast majority of the working class are always
quickly and easily rendered "peaceful," "law-abiding," and
"satisfied," and "patriotic." Millions of chattel slaves have
"loyally" defended their parasitic masters. Millions of serfs
have "loyally" defended their landlords-and-masters. And
to-day tens of millions of wage-earners strongly incline to
"loyally" defend their parasitic employer masters. Moreover,
the employer, by craftily praising the wage-earner, can induce
the wage-earner to ignorantly, blindly, stupidly praise and
defend not only the employer, but also the whole wage-system
of robbery and social parasitism. Not only that, the employers, by controlling certain institutions such as the school,
the library, the press, and the lecture platform, can have the
wage-earning hosts taught to teach their own children to defend and praise the parasitic employer guests and the para-

sitic social system under which their lives are belittled by being sucked up as rent, interest and profits and fed to the parasitic capitalist class.

What the employer calls a contented and loyal working man is simply a stupidly acquiescent "host," biologically considered. And a working class man with a rifle in his hand defending the class that, as social parasites, rob the working class—such a workingman is the best possible illustration of the fact that the great laws of nature are careless of the so-called "dignity of man," totally careless of the ridiculous spectacle of a human being reverting to the behavior of creatures far, far down below even the simian cousins of the human race. Nature does not care whether a man behaves like a crab or a sucker, a tiger or a monkey, a sycophantic slave or a defiantly self-respecting man.*

(**28**) Toward the prideless working class as a social "host" defending the ruling class, the defended ruling class take nature's contemptuous attitude. And the working-class soldier as professional defender of the parasitic capitalist class, tho' much flattered, is cordially despised.

What the United States government thinks of the soldier may be seen, for example, in the fact that a Civil Service employee, in the Weather Department, travelling about on duty on long trips, is allowed one dollar, and even more than a dollar per meal in his expense account; while the "brave boys" in khaki who agree to stand ready to butcher their brothers for a living are lucky if they get a thirty-cent meal at any time. In this connection the following from Mr. Taft's Report as Secretary of War for 1907 (p. 92-93) is of interest. Under the head of "Rations" we find:

"The present ration, while *liberal and suitable*, falls considerably short of the Navy ration in variety. Butter, milk and molasses, or *syrup, at least*, should be *added* to the garrison ration. These are articles *almost* necessary in the preparation of desserts. . . . They are part of the ration in Alaska and they should be everywhere."†

---

* See Index: "Parasites."

† Italics mine. G. R. K.

The present ration "liberal and suitable," yet lacking butter, milk and molasses and even syrup. Such things are *"almost* necessary!"

The reckless epicureanism thus proposed by "the great secretary" in offering some *cheap syrup* as an *addition* to the *dessert* gives us an illuminating suggestion as to the War Department's estimate of the cheapness of the hungry greenhorn who can be lured into the rulers' "service" with cheap syrup. An *ordinary* house fly can be coaxed into a trap with syrup—good syrup.

The United States soldier's meals are estimated by the War Department to be worth six and two-thirds cents apiece, as will appear from the following passage taken from the Report of the War Department for 1907, page 85: "The pay of the private, at present, is 43 and one-third cents a day. Adding the [daily] cost of his ration as 20 cents, clothing allowance and right to quarters each at 15 cents, and his remaining privileges at, say, six and two-thirds cents, his present pay still falls 25 cents short of the average laborer throughout the United States." This is the War Department's estimate of the soldier's average total daily income in cash and allowances, made by the Department in order to compare the soldier's incentive with that of the *farm hand and general day laborer.* On page 84 of the same Report is the Government's estimate of the average daily income of the "farm and the general laborer": For 1902 the average for these two classes was (according to the Report) $1.20 a day; and "allowing for the increase in wages since 1902" *the government's estimate for the "farm and general laborer" in 1907 was $1.25 per day.* This, the Report says, is $7.50 per month better than the soldier's incentive in 1907.

It is matter of common knowledge that the United States soldiers and marines are forced to spend a considerable portion of their cash incomes for food that the Government is too stingy to furnish. That is, the ruling class have such contempt for their human "watch dogs" that they furnish them a meaner living than is received by the most meanly paid group of the working class over whom they stand guard

and stand ready to murder if they strike and struggle for
more.

In the same Report, under the heading "Quarters," is
this:

"The fact that he is living in a $40,000 building impresses the
soldier less if he finds in it only iron bunks, cheap chairs, and un-
painted tables—the absolute necessities for his use and nothing for
his comfort. The barrack is the home of the soldier while he remains in the service. It is possible that he might think oftener
of continuing there if it presented more the appearance of a home.
So far as the squad rooms are concerned, mere room adornment is
neither necessary nor advisable [!]. . . . The squad rooms are sleeping rooms only. There is space only for bunks, lockers and a few
chairs; but these last might in part be something more than the
present cheap and uncomfortable article. But it is the reading and
amusement rooms that are meant particularly. There is no reason
why they should not be made habitable. [Indeed! Really, Mr.
Taft! How daring of you!] A few barrack chairs and rough
tables, with possibly a billiard table, ordinarily constitute their
furniture now. There is little to tempt a man to stay there.
["Tempt" is good.] . . . These rooms might be made comfortable
and pleasant. A rug on the floor, a few prints on the walls, substantial chairs, a few writing tables and writing materials could
all be supplied at no serious expense to the United States. . . .
There is nothing degenerating in such furnishings; there is much
that is homelike." [Like *whose* home?]

"A few prints"—not many of course, and cheap ones, let
us say about ten cents each; and "a rug"—a dull, unexciting
mat of rags—simply these and nothing more, lest the degenerating influences of fine art should soften the syrup-baited
lads' blood-lusting temper too much for the more glorious
art of butchering. As Mr. Taft profoundly remarks, "There
is little to tempt a man to *stay* there" at present; but, as he
sagaciously suggests, about 98 cents expended in baiting the
bunk-room trap with a few original Italian, or, say, Dutch,
masterpieces, and a few imported Persian fascinations of emotional red—this 98 cents for the seductions of fine art added to
a nickel's worth of skimmed milk and molasses *would* be an
effective allurement for the khaki heroes to re-enlist and "stay
there."

Recently Congressmen and Senators advanced their own

salaries from $5,000 up to $7,500 per year. This is one sign of self-respect. This advance of $2,500 per year will of course be sufficient to provide a fair quality of syrup and skimmed milk for the statesmen's dessert.

Does it seem probable that cheap molasses added to the dessert of the soldier's ration and a few ten-cent prints hung on the walls of the soldiers' living rooms will attract Taft's sons or Roosevelt's sons or the sons of Senators and Congressmen and the sons of the "better class leading citizens" to the dreary, barren barracks provided for men who stand ready to slaughter for less than 50 cents a day and cheap "keep"?

Says Major-General J. F. Bell, Chief of Staff :*

"That men enlist believing they will love the life is likely, but their mental picture is oftentimes so different from the reality that disappointment is the almost inevitable consequence."

Fifty-eight per cent. of all the desertions from the military service in the year 1906 were desertions of men in their first year of service, and considerably more than half of these desertions were during the first six months of service.†

Twenty-six times as many enlisted men in our army committed suicide in 1908 as in 1907, and *thirty-nine times* as many of the "tempted" and trapped young men in our army committed suicide in 1909 as in 1907. No suicides are reported for the years 1901 to 1906 inclusive. The record for the three years 1907, '08, '09 is 1, 26, 39, respectively.‡

It would seem likely that a young fellow whose loathing for the army life had become unendurable would desert rather than commit suicide to escape the hideous business. But no doubt the following line from the Report of the Secretary of War, Mr. Wright, in 1908, will help explain somewhat the increase of suicide in the army. Mr. Wright says (page 19) : "An elaborate system . . . now almost perfected is well calculated to secure *swift and certain apprehension and pun-*

---

* *Report*, 1907, p. 73.

† See Report of Department of War, 1906.

‡ See Annual Reports of the Secretaries of War for the years named; also Preface of the present volume.

ishment of deserters and will . . . have a marked effect in reducing the crime to a minimum."* An illustrative feature of this "highly perfected system" is to furnish the run-away soldiers' pictures to the police of a city to which the lads can be traced, and offer the police $50 a head cash for the arrest of the soldiers. The $50 results in a human "blood-hound" search. This "highly perfected system" makes a young man's enlistment a good deal like swallowing a barbed fish-hook. A great number of the boys go insane. In 1908 *insanity ranked third* in the long list of causes of discharge from the army for disability.†

Army service, even in time of peace, is not exactly a picnic dream. On this point General Frederick Funston offers some helpful information, thus:‡

"There is too much of the everlasting grind of drill and practice marches, and at some of the posts too much 'fatigue' in the way of keeping the reservations in apple-pie order. It is pretty much of a shock to many of the men who have entered the army service to taste the delights of military life to find that, from the stand-point of the post-commanders, the most important part of their training consists in cutting brush and weeds."

In his Report of 1907, page 14, Mr. Taft said:

"A noteworthy feature in the recruitment of the Army under present conditions is the increasing number of men who fail to re-enlist and of those who leave the Army before the expiration of their term of service by purchasing their discharge. . . . The fact cannot be disregarded nor explained away that for some reason or other the life of the soldier as at present constituted is not one to attract the best and most desirable class of men."

In the excerpt just quoted Mr. Taft makes it pretty clear that in his judgment the present enlisted men in the "regular" army are "undesirable citizens." Hence the "great secretary's" recommendation of milk-and-syrup additions to the soldier's dessert, a few cheap prints on the walls, and a coat of paint on the tables used by the soldiers—in order to catch a

---

* Italics mine. G. R. K.

† See *Report of the War Department*, 1908, p. 21; see also Index: "Insanity."

§ *The World's Work*, May, 1907.

better and more desirable class of men; that is, a better and more desirable class of workingmen; for be it remembered the Government does not expect to get any well-fed capitalist class men into the army by means of cheap syrup and cheap milk and cheap 'print' pictures and the like." "The soldier in peace," says the Report just quoted, "is better fed and better clothed than the average man of *his class* in civil life."*
How interesting and instructive!

In 1905 almost 73 per cent., and in 1906 almost 74 per cent. of the applicants for examination for enlistment in our army "were rejected as lacking either mental, moral or physical qualifications."†

President Roosevelt, in his Message of December, 1907, virtually ridiculed the patriotism of the men in the army and those who may contemplate entering the army. He wrote:

"The prime need of our present Army and Navy is to secure and retain competent non-commissioned officers. The difficulty rests fundamentally on the question of pay."

"Fundamentally on the question of pay." How suggestively patriotic! Did Colonel Roosevelt join the army for the cash there was in it? "Oh, certainly not." But why should he insultingly say that, for other men, joining the army is fundamentally a question of cold cash?

The War Department, with Mr. Taft at the head, in 1907, joined Mr. Roosevelt in his sneering contempt for the soldier's motive in joining the army. The Report runs:‡

"Under a voluntary system men enlist either to aid their country or to promote their own ends; that is, through self-sacrifice or self-interest. . . . Self-sacrifice of this sort is patriotism, an emotion necessary to arouse. . . . To keep it through long periods of peace at a pitch high enough to maintain an army would be impossible. . . . *Self-interest* is, therefore, the *only* cause of enlistment necessary to consider; . . ."*

It thus appears that, in the judgment of the "great secre-

---

* Italics mine. G. R. K.

† See Reports of the Department of War for the respective years.

‡ *Report of the Secretary of War,* 1907, p. 72.

tary," now President, patriotism is not at all a matter of brains, of reason steadily sustained by logic, but is, on the contrary, a matter of emotion, passion, "brainstorm," induced with fife and drum and sustained with godlike sky-climbing aspiration to have one's stomach filled with "butter, milk and molasses, or syrup, at least"—as "dessert." The two Presidents, the anti-labor injunction judge and the lion-hunting monkey murderer,* agree that what *looks* like patriotism in the long-service "regular" is after all simply a matter of getting less than fifty cents a day and "keep." Of course, such things as this are not mentioned on the Fourth of July nor in campaign speeches when the "great secretary" or his chattering predecessor is courting the 'brave boys' for their votes.

(**29**) When a young man joins the army or the navy he virtually agrees to pocket his pride and submit to a series of insults from his "superior" officers for a term of years. The recruiting officer is to some degree, at least temporarily, a man of pleasant manners, and the callow patriot taking the bait in the recruiting office is treated alluringly. But when the youth signs his name in the books and becomes a soldier patriot, matters take a change. It is a case of being "stuck" or "stung." For following the hour of his enlistment, humble, prideless submission to strutting, swaggering bosses is the soldier's portion. From "superior" officers he must meekly accept insults for which, in private life, he would promptly knock a man down. In the service he must bend his neck and take the yoke for years. Here is a sample of the spirit of the haughty airs assumed by the "superiors."

Mr. Taft, speaking as Secretary of War, February 14, 1908, to the young men at West Point Military School, said:

"The plainest of your duties is to keep your mouths shut and obey orders. As a soldier you must forego the privilege of free

---

* Mr. Roosevelt's kill-for-pleasure hunting trip in Africa in 1909-10 included, according to the press reports, "a splendid time," "a corking time," shooting monkeys—murdering his ancestral cousins, so to speak—"a careful count being kept of the exact number" of the jolly, playful little creatures butchered for the brave and noble gentleman's amusement on his "old home" trip.

speech. . . . You will meet with injustices, others will get all to
which they seem entitled. Your wives will have heart-burnings.
Your children will have heart-burnings. In spite of all that you
must do your duty, honestly and devotedly."

Here is a soldier's letter:*

". . . We are supposed to work eight hours a day, but we get
dismissed when the officers see fit to let us go—all for fifty-two
cents a day. The negroes working at Panama get more money and
are better treated than the enlisted men out here. Our 'little brown
brothers' are treated better over here. And to cap the climax,
over comes a high statesman [Mr. Taft?] and makes a speech to a
mob of our 'little brown brothers' and tells them not to judge
the Americans by the enlisted men, as the enlisted men are composed of the roughest elements in the States. . . ."

President David Starr Jordan (Leland Stanford University) writes of the contemptuous treatment of the men in
the ranks by the "superior" officers:†

"One soldier [in the Philippines] says, 'If the United States
were on fire from end to end, I would never raise my hand to put
it out.' Another would 'toss in a blanket the officials at Washington, as we toss a cheating corporal.' Another says in print, referring to the abuse of the soldiers by their superiors in pay: 'Yes,
I knew that war would be hell before I got into it. But I did
not know that war would be hell deliberately and fanatically in-
flicted. I expected to sleep in mud puddles with my head on a
stone for a pillow, and go hungry for days on forced marches and
away from a base of supplies. But I never dreamed that I would
have to sleep in a leaky and exposed shed when there was plenty
of good shelter elsewhere, and when thirty officers had fine apart-
ments in which there was room for five hundred men; neither did
I expect to be fed on coffee-grounds and foul canned meat for
weeks when we were right next to a base of supplies, and when our
officers lived on the choice of the commissary's department.' "

But the question naturally occurs to one: Why shouldn't
the working class soldiers be treated thus? Surely it is to be
expected that the great majority class will *get what they
permit* from their "superiors."

_____

* A private, writing from the Philippines, in *Everybody's
Magazine*, April, 1908.
† *Imperial Democracy*, p. 272.

Note how the soldier boys are snubbed and bull-dozed in the German army. Says Dr. Walsh:*

"In a trial reported Dec. 17, 1903, a lieutenant of the infantry has been convicted of 618 cases of maltreatment and 57 cases of improper treatment of soldiers under him, and a sergeant in another regiment has been convicted of 1,520 cases of maltreatment and 100 cases of improper treatment. . . . The men deposed were so afraid, that nobody ventured to complain."

There is a yearly average of 7,000 desertions from the English regular army. Quite naturally. Frozen, starved and despised, the thirty-cent patriots make a break for bread and freedom from the "noble" snobbery of the aristocratic pets in control.

The record of desertions from the American Army is, for the years 1907, 1908, and 1909, respectively, 4,534, 4,525, 5,023.

(**30**) How is it possible to interest young men in the brutal business of war?

There are some paragraphs on this matter in the chapter following, "For Mother and the Boys." Here the matter of military parades is suggested for consideration by "father and the boys."

Sometimes the boys' interest in war begins in so simple a thing as a parade. A military parade is a trap—for the working class. A writer in the New York *Tribune,* April 22, 1908, makes several artful suggestions as to the value of military parades in snaring young toilers into the army. He suggests:

That "parades, so far as circumstances permit, be through or near . . . sections [of the city] . . . where they may encourage enlistment among a . . . class of prospective recruits . . . instead of on Riverside Drive [where the 'better classes' live], to which the public has access with difficulty and which is not frequented by the class of young men to whom the National Guard appeals. . . . These suggestions reflect the views of many citizens . . . with whom the writer has conferred."

The writer also points out that bright-colored uniforms

---

* *The Moral Damage of War,* pp. 150-51

for the paraders have excellent effect on the imagination of the prospective recruits.

There can be no doubt that the masters are well aware of the hypnotizing influence of marching loud, gay-colored bands, festively uniformed infantry, and fascinating cavalry-men through the streets where they may be seen and admired by the working class, admired by many thousands of ill-fed, ill-clothed, meanly sheltered young men and women whose lives are dull and sad, consumed with the killing monotony and hurry of the factory. A cavalry captain in the United States Army, a part of whose business is to wheedle the gullibles into the dreary army life, has this to say of parades:

"The good influence in popularizing the army by having it stationed in large cities is exemplified in London. The various guards and other bodies of troops marching through the streets, preceded by their gorgeously dressed bands, all the uniforms recalling traditions of brave, gallant deeds, gain friends every time."

The best known butcher of modern times (Napoleon) also understood this matter.

"You call these toys? Well, you manage men with toys!" said that red-stained egoist, speaking of the ribbons and crosses and other gewgaws of his Legion of Honor.*

When at the street-side a boy of seven, watching a military parade, shouts in gleeful admiration and claps his small hands in happy hurrahs, Mars, the bloody god of war, begins to fasten his clutches on the little fellow, the child's imagination takes fire with visions and hopes, his soul begins to thrill with the kill-lust, then and there he is being prepared to enlist —when he "gets big." How different it would be for the small boys if, when soldiers were marched through a city, these armed slayers of their kind should march at night with all lights out and with the rumble of drums and the frequent boom of cannon in the darkness making the air tremble. The working class mother might well consider this matter. She has all to lose.†

---

* Quoted by Professor E. A. Ross, in his *Social Control*, p. 89.
† See Chapter Eight: "For Mother and the Boys," Section 1.

In the average parade-and-review the workingman is made ridiculous. Did you ever see prominent bankers or other "better class" business men in large numbers trudging along a-foot in the middle of the dusty or muddy street, marching and sweating miles and miles past a gay-colored reviewing-stand to be "reviewed" and grinned at by a bunch of sugar-coated crooks in the "reviewers' stand"? No! And you never will. The trudging and the sweating, as usual, are handed over to the "common people," chiefly the wage-slaves. When the "very *best* people" do take part in the parading before the "grand-stand," they ride, up front, in carriages or on horse-back. They laugh and chat and gaily enjoy the stupid gullibility of the working men as the humble fellows are thus "bell-weathered" through the dirt and heat. On the occasion of a recent great parade in New York City a well-known capitalist gliding along in a handsome automobile swaggeringly called out, "We've got the ships, we've got the men, and we've got the money too!" A seedy, hungry-looking young man proudly answered back, "You bet we have!" On the same occasion thousands of ten-dollar-a-week clerks and factory workers were charmed into hand-clapping as the gaudily dressed soldiers marched by carrying the very rifles they were ready to use to crush the admiring toilers if they should strike and struggle for justice.

The usual "review" is a pompous occasion on which hundreds or thousands of meek, ill-fed, cotton-lined, callous-palmed working men "hoof it" for an hour or so past a "reviewing-stand" occupied by some grinning, well-fed, silk-lined, lily-fingered, decorated "great" men who scorn even the thought of the working class having a political party of their own for their own self-defense.

(**31**) A great many fathers and sons are thinking a good deal about an "era of peace" to be ushered in mainly through the good offices of peace societies. The Hague Peace Conference is, in the judgment of many people, "the hope of the world."*

---

* See Index: "Bankruptcy, Danger of."

The first meeting of the Hague Conference was called—in Jesus' name, of course—by the most infamous blood-stained butcher of feeble old men and women and thoughtful, aspiring young men and women, in all the world,—that is, by the Tsar of Russia. The sincerity of this crowned murderer may in some measure be realized by a brief study of his gross inconsistency in the year 1903 and in the years immediately preceding. (See Chapter Six, and Sixth Illustration.)

The second meeting of the Society was held in 1907, and another is scheduled for the year 1915.

The serene confidence the world's rulers have in the Society is easily seen in their frantic efforts to increase their armies and navies. They are bleeding their people white with taxes to make the enormously expensive preparations for what is likely to be the most vast and terrible butchering of the working class by the working class that has ever horrified mankind. Secretly the crowned and uncrowned ruling butchers of the world have nothing but contempt for the Conference at The Hague. Very naturally, however, they are all shrewd enough to make a large and beautiful profession of faith and desire for peace through the Conference, while at the same time they all "want for soldiers young men who are not only willing, but anxious to fight." The man who inaugurated the Conference promptly scorned the Conference when he believed his interests would be served by a war with Japan. The famous French anti-militarist G. Hervé shrewdly pointed out the hopelessly weak place in the "authority" of the capitalist Hague Peace Court:*

"Governments so far are unanimous in *withdrawing from The Hague Tribunal all questions affecting 'the honor and vital interests of the country,'* a convenient formula permitting them to *refuse* arbitration when they please."

And here is a frank admission:

"The Hague Tribunal has nothing compulsory about it; all its members are left in perfect freedom as to whether they submit questions to it or not. . . . In all treaties hitherto the Great

---

* *The International*, July, 1908. Italics mine. G. R. K.

Powers have retained power to withhold submission of questions affecting 'their honor or vital interest.' "*

"Honor and vital interests,"—convenient phrase—a matter of business—cash and commerce, "plain dollars and cents," —under capitalism.

It is of interest to note that another peace society, The Peace Society, founded in London in 1816, has been busy for almost a hundred years trying to mop up the blood, so to speak, never daring, or not knowing how, to uncover the fundamental cause of war.

In at least some respects a "Conference" of The Hague Peace Society is, itself, hopelessly ridiculous and, in appearance, wickedly insincere. For example, at the "Conference" of 1907 the delegates learnedly and laughably discussed the "Humanizing of War,"† and, after much brain-fagging effort, the delegates to the fakirs' feast duly and heavily concluded as follows:

"It is especially prohibited to employ poison or poisoned arms."

WELL BE IT KNOWN:—

THAT KLEPTOMANIACS' PERIODICAL LUNCHEON, OR "THIEVES' SUPPER," CALLED THE HAGUE CONFERENCE, WOULD HAVE NO MORE WORK TO DO FOR THE NEXT THOUSAND YEARS, WOULD NEVER AGAIN HAVE ANYTHING WHATEVER TO MEET FOR, IF ALL BULLETS AND ALL SWORDS AND ALL BAYONETS USED IN ALL THE ARMIES WERE DIPPED IN A DEADLY POISON; FOR, IN THAT CASE, THE WORKING CLASS OF THE WHOLE WORLD WOULD FLATLY REFUSE TO VOLUNTEER OR BE DRAFTED TO SERVE IN ANY WAR ANYWHERE UNDER ANY CIRCUMSTANCES. AND, OF COURSE, THE SOFT-VOICED, WELL-FED "HUMANIZERS OF WAR" WOULD NOT GO TO WAR—POISON OR NO POISON. THE UNIVERSAL USE OF POISONED BULLETS, SWORDS AND BAYONETS WOULD MAKE WAR ABSOLUTELY IMPOSSIBLE, BECAUSE THE INAUGURATION OF SUCH A POLICY WOULD MAKE THE WORKING CLASS THINK.

---

* *Documents of the American Association for International Conciliation*, 1907-08, p. 22.

† See *The Peace Conference at The Hague*, pp. 93-120, and 151.

A thinking slave is the terror of the plunder-bloated rulers of the world—always.

When the workers once think about war they will promptly do two things:

First, They will refuse to go to war;

Second, They will find the cause of war, and will remove it.

Of course, it requires the deep and prayerful investigation of "great" and "prominent Christian" gentlemen in peace conference assembled to discover that it *is* wrong for men to butcher men with swords and bullets dipped in poison, but that it is *not* wrong for men to destroy men with clean lead and clean steel, their souls charged with hate as an adder's fang jetting venom into its victim's flesh; to discover that it *is* wrong to have soldiers thrust poison-dipped bayonets into one another's stomachs, but that it is *not* wrong for a "Christian business men's" government to feed its soldiers on poisoned canned beef. The poor dupes who butcher one another at the word of command are, of course, too "common" and ignorant to understand the logical legerdemain of these prayerfully discovered distinctions; but the learned and prominent gentlemen in peace conference assembled, far, far from the battle line, smoking 50-cent cigars, quaffing the world's costliest champagne—these noble braves, these bottle-scarred heroes, can tell us all about it.

Certainly.

With thoughtful tenderness many Christian governments, influenced by peace societies, have made an international agreement that, in case of war, no bullet used weighing 14 ounces or less shall be an explosive bullet,—that is, a bullet that easily expands, flattens and shatters *when it strikes flesh.* However, these same "more refined and civilized" nations are all at perfect liberty to use a cannon bullet, or shell, weighing hundreds of pounds, charged with explosives, flesh-tearing materials and deadly gases, arranged with time-fuses in order to explode over the heads of, or among, a great body of men on the field, or in the midst of men when it has pierced the armor of a war vessel.

It is not definitely known how these wise Christian statesmen and scholars discovered that a three-hundred pound explosive bullet might properly and lovingly be used by gently
sensitive Christian butchers, but that a thirteen-ounce explosive bullet might not with propriety be used by these loving
followers of the gentle Jesus. Possibly the discovery was
made by some deep-seeing pot-house statesmen and scholars
after a prayerful study of the Sermon on the Mount,—with
champagne on the side.

War is "human" or "inhuman" according to the orations,
discussions, confusions, delusions, conclusions, decisions and
provisions of these perfumed, patent-leathered fighters after a
long fast—on terrapin, porter-house and "Mumm's Extra
Dry."

The eloquence of the Hague Peace Conference literature
concerning its long list of extremely "glorious achievements"
would lead the uninstructed to suppose that till this organization came on the field there had never been a dispute settled without war. It modestly claims everything in view.

Note here the fact that:

*"There is no period known to history in which instances
are not found of arbitration as a substitute for force, and we
can only wonder when we consider the historical antiquity of
the former that the latter should have maintained its hold so
long, so constantly and so fiercely."* *

> "Where are thy portents, Peace?
>   What sign on land or sea
>   Of thy great coming, of thy rule to be?
> The fighting and the drumming do not cease;
> Gun-thunder smites the air,
>   And shakes the earth beneath.
> Bait we not the war-dogs in their lair,
>   And toil at harvesting of dragon's teeth? . . .
>
> Must it forever be a poet's dream—
> The land secure, the mind at rest,

---

* *Harper's Magazine*, Vol. 87.   See International Conciliation
—Documents of the American Association for International Conciliation, 1907-08: Third Paper—"A League of Peace."

The cut-throat tamed and laboring at an oar,
The braggart silent and ashamed,
The toiler as a monarch seem,
The woman with her baby at her breast,
Aglow with joy that war shall be no more? . . ."
—J. I. C. Clarke, in New York *Times.*

Prominent people—prominent chiefly because they are elevated upon the shoulders of the working class—have been *talking* about peace for a long time. But peace born of *justice,* peace founded upon *fairness,*—that is neither thought of nor talked of, by the ruling class, in the pompous and pretentious peace conferences; it is not on the program.

Father and the boys of the working class will themselves have to place peace on the program of mankind. And one of the first things to do is to bring up the subject of war and peace in every working class organization in the world—*for discussion.* (See pages 272, 283-289. Index: "Carnegie.")

A Special Notice to the Hague Peace Society:

As to "limited armaments"—whether the swords are long or short, the working class more and more clearly see that you intend that the working class shall continue to do all the fighting in case of war.

A Special Challenge to the Hague Peace Society:

That all delegates to the Conferences shall discuss, not the problems of "disarmament," but (1) the problem of striking the bands from the wrists of the wage-slaves; (2) the artificial arbitrary restriction placed upon the consuming power of the wage-earners, out of which fact grows the imminent world-struggle for the "world-market."

A Second Special Challenge to the Hague Peace Society:

That the Society shall frankly announce in all its Conferences, in all its Reports, in all its leaflets, in all its lectures and sermons, that the Socialist Party's method of preventing war is to frankly and loudly WARN THE VICTIMS OF WAR, the working class, just what war always means to the working class; and that this method has succeeded in preventing two wars in recent years in cases where the Hague Peace Society was powerless.

A Third Special Challenge to the Hague Peace Society:

That the Society shall explain why the Capitalist masters of the Hague Peace Society will not *permit* their vassals in the Conferences to accept the Second Challenge.

THE BENEFICIARIES OF HELL, FLIRTING WITH "HEAVEN"

CHAPTER EIGHT.

For Mother and the Boys and Girls.

Topics for consideration, especially by the mothers in the working class.*

(**1**) "Will there be, indeed, more wars?"

Yes, undoubtedly.†

"What shall be done about it?"

There are two things to be done, by the mother, right away: Think about war and talk about war with other mothers and the boys—also with the girls.

Let us see:

In the next war whose sons shall be shot?

The aristocrat's wife is not worrying about whose children are to be destroyed in the next war. She knows already that her sons will not be destroyed in battle; her sons will not stand before Gatling guns; her sons will not be torn and lie bleeding, groaning, screaming and cursing on the steel-swept battlefield by day or through the long night; her sons will not fester and sicken and die in dismal battlefield hospitals; she knows that her sons will not be pitched into nameless trenches—buried like dogs; her flesh and blood, her slain sons, will not be brought home to mock her aching heart.

That is settled—positively.

She belongs to the *ruling* class.

The ruling class protect her and the men and boys she loves—loyally.

But the working class mother—the humble mother of wage-slaves—she feels no such security. Herod and Mars invade her home to steal the men and boys she loves. The rude fist of war is ever ready to crush her. This humble woman

---

* See foot-note on page 13; and also introductory paragraph, Chapter Seven, preceding Section 1.

† See Index: "Another War."

is wholly unprotected against war by the ruling class. She is also unprotected against war by the voting men of her own class.

This woman must protect herself—for the present.

Let it be remembered that in the gentle heart of a humble mother whose loving sons have been butchered in battle, it is always winter. The cheap rhetoric and hypocritical compliments of the coarse-grained political orator, the honeyed words of any man in any profession—sacred or secular—craftily exempted from the war which slew her loved ones, these can not charm the wintry desolation of her life into rare June weather. Nor can the wound in her mother heart be healed with a stingy quarterly allowance of filthy money called a pension. When her loved ones were slaughtered her joys were slain.

This woman must indeed protect herself; and she can protect herself, somewhat,—if she will.

She can do this: She can teach her child to hate—to hate war.*

(**2**) Mother, is your five-year-old son strong, healthy and handsome? Yes? Well, that is fine. But think of him at the age of twenty in slaughtering clothes, being transformed into a swaggering armed bully. Mother, if he should be tricked into the army and butchered and his torn corpse should be brought home to you, you would then know what *other* mothers feel when their boys, whom your son butchers, are brought home to them. Then, perhaps, war would seem quite different—far less "great" and "glorious" to you. You see, mother, in a war *some* mothers' boys must be butchered. Perhaps a false patriotism has been taught to you—just as a false patriotism is taught your sons. Both the mother and her sons are confused. To get the working class boy ready for war the capitalist must first confuse and trick the mother.

Kings, emperors, presidents, tsars, and capitalists of all lands are lovingly interested in the problem of "race suicide," the problem of small families,—interested in the "food-for-

---

* See Chapter Seven, Section 30.

powder" crop, the "bullet-stopper" crop,—EAGER THAT EVERY
WORKING CLASS MOTHER SHOULD BECOME A BREEDER. After
Napoleon Bonaparte had had multitudes of the men and
boys of France butchered, making it difficult to find soldiers,
he impatiently exclaimed, "What France needs is mothers!"
What he meant was that France needed more human breeders
flattered into bearing and rearing more butchers for Napoleon. Of course Napoleon was shrewd enough to confuse the
humble mothers with plenty of cheap flattery concerning their
"patriotism." * Capitalists to-day want larger working class
families for more soldiers, also for a larger army of unemployed—in order that the capitalists may, in the industrial
civil war, more tyrannically dictate the wage terms to the
workers and also more easily secure substitutes in case of a
war.

And to this end the capitalists are willing to pay the
price; that is, willing to pay for the social chloroform, for
the false teachings, necessary to beget a slave's blind enthusiasm for the master that betrays him—called patriotism.

(3) Thomas Carlyle called working class soldiers simple-
tons. A person of good mind, however, *if caught young,* can
be confused till he will actually volunteer to butcher his fel-
lowman. This can be done in many ways; for example, take
Fitchburg, Massachusetts, May 29-30, 1908. The very small
children, also ten-year-olds, and those still older, were assembled, according to age, in halls, churches, the Young Men's
Christian auditorium, and elsewhere, May 29; and for long
weary hours gory stories of "bravery" in war were recited to
them, horrible pictures were displayed before them, blood-
curdling suggestions were urged upon them, cheap lusts for
cheap glory were inspired in the helpless youngsters,—just
as a savage might teach his little sons to rip the scalp from
a screaming victim's skull And humble mothers of the
working class were tricked into co-operating in this anti-social
"patriotism."

Such abominable performances stunt the children. Their

* See Index: "Napoleon."

social development is arrested. They become jingoists, ignorant little bigots—utterly incapable of sincere international love. Their political philosophy is a shallow and silly "Hurrah!" Their "patriotism" becomes a belittling conceit and a readiness for cruel deeds.

Everybody, of course, loves a frank, finely social child. International and national murder is a coarse and unsocial thought; and when parents, teachers, preachers, or lecturers, speak enthusiastically of wholesale murder or of famous national and international murderers in the presence of a child, the child's social development is checked, stunted; when a few suggestions of international jealousy and malice have been ignorantly (or cunningly) thrust into a child's mind it becomes simply impossible for the child to develop into an "international man," a finely social person sincerely loving his fellowmen. This would be a charming world if all men and women were social—socialized, unblasted, unstung by shriveling national jealousy and malice; but everywhere the vile business of blasting the social nature of the rising generation is being extended. The school, even, is invaded. The Rev. Dr. Walter Walsh warns parents thus:*

"The school has become not only the training ground, but actually a recruiting ground for the army. The British War Office issues a circular pressing secondary schools to teach boys over twelve the use of the rifle; issues Morris tube carbines to schools having suitable ranges; and supplies ammunition at cost price. The inevitable next step is the formation of cadet corps in the schools, with inspection by military chiefs. . . . The capture of the schools by the militarists is one of the most ominous signs of the times. The militarist has long looked with wistful eye at this happy hunting grounds. . . . Parliaments have already been strongly urged to make military drill compulsory in all public schools. . . . The scholar is rapidly transformed into the conscript."

The shameless audacity of using a socializing institution, the school, to cultivate national malice in the helpless children!

(4) If only the children could get one good look at the hell behind the curtain it would be more difficult to beguile and betray them.

---

* *The Moral Damage of War*, pp. 97-99.

Let the wonderful Zola tell what the boys in the public schools are *not* taught and are *not permitted to realize* till later when they are grown up and are seduced to the battlefield with the crafty cry, "Follow the flag!"

Here following are some paragraphs on the battlefield hospital. A military hospital, it may be said, is an institution in which sick and shell-torn men are hastily repaired in order that they may go again to the battle line—perchance to faint or be ripped to pieces again. Thus Zola: *

". . . Outside in the shed the preparations were of another nature: the chests were opened and the contents arranged in order. . . . On another table were the surgical cases with their blood-curdling array of glittering instruments, probes, forceps, bistouries, scalpels, scissors, saws, an arsenal of implements of every imaginable shape adapted to pierce, cut, clice, rend, crush. . . . The wagons kept driving up to the entrance in an unbroken stream. . . . The regular ambulance wagons of the medical department, two-wheeled and four-wheeled, were too few in number to meet the demand . . . provision vans, everything on wheels that could be picked up on the battlefield, came rolling up with their ghastly loads; and later in the day carrioles and market-gardeners' carts were pressed into the service and harnessed to horses that were found straying along the roads. . . . It was a sight to move the most callous to behold the unloading of those poor wretches, some with the greenish pallor on their faces, others suffused with the purple hue that denotes congestion; many were in a state of coma, others uttered piercing cries of anguish . . . the keen knife flashed in the air, there was the faint rasping of the saw barely audible, the blood spurted in short sharp jets. . . . As soon as the subject had been operated on another was brought in, and they followed one another in such quick succession that there was barely time to pass the sponge over the protecting oil-cloth. At the extremity of the grass plot, screened from sight by a clump of lilac bushes, they had set up a kind of morgue whither they carried the bodies of the dead, which were removed from the beds without a moment's delay in order to make room for the living, and this receptacle also served to receive the amputated legs and arms, whatever débris of flesh and bone remained upon the table. . . . Rents in tattered, shell-torn uniforms disclosed gaping wounds, some of which had received a hasty dressing on the battle-

<hr>

* See *The Downfall*, passim, Part II., also p. 446. This powerful story (published by the Macmillan Company, New York) is here again heartily commended to all readers of *War—What For?* Again the author thanks the publishers for reprint privileges.

field, while others were still raw and bleeding. There were feet, still encased in their coarse shoes, crushed into a mass like jelly; from knees and elbows, that were as if they had been smashed by a hammer, depended inert limbs. There were broken hands, and fingers almost severed, ready to drop, retained only by a strip of skin. Most numerous among the casualties were the fractures; the poor arms and legs, red and swollen, throbbed intolerably and were as heavy as lead. But the most dangerous hurts were those in the abdomen, chest, and head. There were yawning fissures that laid open the entire flank, the knotted viscera were drawn into great hard lumps beneath the tight-drawn skin, while as the effect of certain wounds the patient frothed at the mouth and writhed like an epileptic. . . . And finally the head, more than any other portion of the frame, gave evidence of hard treatment; a broken jaw, the mouth a pulp of teeth and bleeding tongue, an eye torn from its socket and exposed upon the cheek, a cloven skull that showed the palpitating brain beneath. . . . Although the sponge was kept constantly at work the tables were always red. . . . The buckets . . . were emptied over a bed of daisies a few steps away. . . . Some seemed to have left the world with a sneer on their faces, their eyes retroverted till naught was visible but the whites, the grinning lips parted over the glistening teeth, while in others with faces unspeakably sorrowful, big tears still stood on the cheeks. One, a mere boy, short and slight, half whose face had been shot away by a cannon ball, had his two hands clasped convulsively above his heart, and in them a woman's photograph, one of those pale, blurred pictures that are made in the quarters of the poor, bedabbled with his blood. And at the feet of the dead had been thrown in a promiscuous pile the amputated arms and legs, the refuse of the knife and the saw of the operating table, just as the butcher sweeps into a corner of his shop the offal, the worthless odds and ends of flesh and bone. . . . Bourouche, brandishing the long, keen knife, cried: 'Raise him!' seized the deltoid with his left hand and with a swift movement of the right cut through the flesh of the arm and severed the muscle; then, with a deft rear-ward cut, he disarticulated the joint at a single stroke, and, presto! the arm fell on the table, taken off in three motions. . . . 'Let him down!' . . . he had done it in thirty seconds. . . . Their strength all gone, reduced to skeletons, with ashen, clayey faces, the miserable wretches suffered the torments of the damned. . . . The patients writhed and shrieked in unceasing delirium, or sat erect in bed with the look of spectres. . . . There were others again who maintained a continuous howling. . . . Often gangrene kept mounting higher and higher, and the amputation had to be repeated until the entire limb was gone."

And that is hell—for which your children are prepared.

This phase of war is shrewdly kept from the children. No child's mind could be poisoned, no child's imagination could be set on fire for war, no child's heart could be made to lust for the "glory" of the battlefield of carnage—if he were shown *this* side of war.

But the child is an easy victim. Even some cheap jingo jingle called patriotic poetry renders the working class the easy, fooled tool of despots. The victimizing of the helpless child is rendered especially easy when the mother, blindfold with flattery, gullibly lends assistance in strangling the child's sociability. (See Chapter Seven, Section 30.)

(**5**) Here is a specimen of the poison craftily used in the public schools under the control of the capitalist class:

> "A soldier is the grandest man
>   That ever yet was made.
> He's valiant on the battlefield
>   And handsome on parade.
> By strict attention to my drill
>   It should not take me long
> For me to be an officer
>   When I am big and strong.
> Then, when my country needs me,
>   In case of war's alarms,
> I'd run and get my uniform*
>   And call the boys to arms!
> With sword in hand I'd lead the charg
>   My orders I would yell
> Above the noise of cannon's roar
>   And storms of shot and shell.
> We'd dash upon the foreign foe,
>   As Teddy did of yore,
> Who took the hill while covered with
>   Dust, victory and gore!
> With banners gay, while bugles play,
>   We'd seek our native land.
> Upon a horse I'd ride that day,
>   The General in Command!"†

---

* Precisely! Never stopping to inquire: Who declared this war? or what for?

† Quoted by George Allan England, in *New York Daily Call*, Dec. 2, 1909.

Will the mothers protect their children's nature against the unsocial small souls who are always ignorantly or maliciously ready to thrust fangs and venom into the generous natures of frank and social children by having them recite stupid praise of distinguished human butchers and "famous victories"?

An American literary man of great eminence, Dr. Edward Everett Hale, thus rebuked the poisoners of school children:

> "But even now, think how much more care you give to the study of the histories of war than to the histories of peace. There are ten times as many people who know who commanded at the Battle of New Orleans as there are who could tell me the name of the great apostle who made freedom the law for Ohio, Indiana, Illinois, Iowa, Wisconsin, Minnesota, North Dakota, South Dakota and Michigan. This man died leaving no memorial."*

(**6**) The working class should speedily get control of public libraries and throw out and keep out books written especially to exalt war and puff the brilliant butchers who have guided millions of working men to death on blood-soaked battlefields,—throw out and burn all books designed to praise the Christian or pagan cannibalism, or the civilized savagery called war. LABOR UNIONS AND ALL OTHER WORKING CLASS BODIES SHOULD MAKE FORMAL AND VIGOROUS PROTEST AGAINST HAVING ANYTHING SAID IN THE PUBLIC SCHOOLS IN PRAISE OF WAR AND IN PRAISE OF DISTINGUISHED BUTCHERS. Let them reflect too that military drills, given *as such,* with martial songs and war tales, cultivate blood lust in the children, blind them to the true meaning of war, make them an easy prey, later, to the crafty cowards who will seek to use them in future savage contests, and are thus an outrage on the children. For a dozen reasons the working class should get control of local school boards.†

(**7**) The following lines from a poem written by an ele-

---

* See Lucia A. Mead's *Patriotism and the New Internationalism,* p. 22.

† Read Walter Walsh's *Moral Damage of War,* Chapter Three on the "Moral Damage of War to the Children." The chapter is of startling importance.

gant coward, are often used in the primary grades of the public schools:

> "Form! Form! Riflemen, fòrm!
> Ready! be ready to meet the storm!
> Riflemen! Riflemen! Riflemen, form!"

A SCHOOL TEACHER CAN MAKE A FOOL AND A MURDERER OF A BOY OF EIGHT OR TEN YEARS WITH SUCH LINES. REMEMBER THAT POETS AND TEACHERS WHO FURNISH THE WAR-SONG CHLOROFORM FOR SCHOOL CHILDREN USUALLY "SIDE-STEP" WHEN THE STORM BREAKS—NO RIFLE BUSINESS FOR THEM—THEY LET OTHERS "MEET THE STORM" WHICH THEIR POETRY AND TEACHING HELPED STIR UP. THE WAR-SONG POET AND THE WAR-SONG SCHOOL TEACHER, IF YOU PLEASE, ARE TOO "CULTIVATED AND RESPECTABLE" TO BE PATRIOTICALLY BUTCHERED.

Under no circumstances should a working class father and mother keep silent while a public school teacher or a Sunday-school teacher thrills the children's blood and blasts the glorious sentiments of human brotherhood with recitals of war-tales and fulsome praise of men whose "glory" is red with the blood of tens of thousands of working class men. Such stories and such praise scar and brutalize the social natures of the children as distinctly as a hot branding iron would disfigure their tender faces.

(8) The little lovers, the children, who are conceived in love, born in love, and live on love, who hunger for love, long to love, glorify the home with love and make the sad world hope for—almost mad for—love, one generation of these sweet little lovers, these prattling sweethearts of mankind, would, when grown up, fill the world with an international love, *if they were not bitten by the viper of petty, local patriotism.*

The mother who will think about this matter somewhat will promptly realize that there is something disastrously wrong with the education which stings her little lovers with a murderer's aspiration. There is something wrong when the gracious neighborliness and charming sociability of children give way to swaggering insolence and savage blood-lust.

Let the mother think of it: Even their playthings, their toys, are craftily used to sting, to debauch the imagination of the children, to write the hopes of brutes in the hearts of gentle children. Lately there has been enormous increase in the business of manufacturing toy soldiers, toy cavalry horses, toy cannon and toy Gatling guns, also khaki soldier clothing for children. "120,000 bales of scrap tin from the Puget Sound canneries were sent recently to Hamburg, Germany, to be made into toy soldiers."* There can be no doubt about the results of using such garb and playthings. That the child is thus scarred is revealed when the tiny boy assumes the attitudes and the strut and swagger of the professional man-slaughterer. His very conversation with his military toys shows he is marked—*ready.*†

William Lloyd Garrison wrote:

"My country is the world, my countrymen are all mankind."

But the stung child can not learn the meaning of Garrison's noble words.

(9) Boy, kill one human being, and you will be called a murderer—despised and hanged. But kill a thousand human beings in war—and you become "great"! Deluded women smile upon you, little children gape at you, preachers praise you, politicians pet you, orators glorify you, capitalists grin at you, universities honor you, and the Government medals and pensions you;—but lonely, war-orphaned children and war-robbed widows, *these despise you exactly in proportion as they understand you.*

Remember, boy, the soldier's sword reaches through the slaughtered father to others—reaches the hearts of helpless women and helpless children.

Which would you rather be, boy, a dead and useless slaughterer of men, or a live and useful man of peace?—a dead butcher or a live brother?

---

* New York *World*, editorial, May 6, 1910.

† See New York *Times*, October 31, 1908, long article on the increasing manufacture of such toys.

(**10**) Here, of course, the thought of patriotism occurs. A great American, Ralph Waldo Emerson, wrote:

"We hesitate to employ a word so much abused as patriotism, whose true sense is almost the reverse of the popular sense. We have no sympathy with that boyish egotism, hoarse with cheering for one side, for one state, for one town; the right patriotism consists in the delight which springs from contributing our peculiar legitimate advantages to the benefit of humanity."

And thus James Russell Lowell:*

"There is a patriotism of the soul whose claim absolves us from our other and terrene fealty. . . . When, therefore, one would have us throw up our caps and shout with the multitude, 'Our country, however bounded!' he demands of us that we sacrifice the larger to the less, the higher to the lower, and that we yield to the imaginary claims of a few acres of soil our duty and privilege as liegemen of Truth. Our true country is bounded on the north and the south, on the east and the west, by justice. . . . Veiling our faces, we must take silently the hand of Duty to follow her."

The fallacy of false patriotism is exploded in the following quotation by James Mackaye:†

"There is a school of patriotism more or less popular which teaches that a man owes to his country a duty which he owes to no other aggregate of the human race, and that he should render service to the constituted authorities thereof, whatever policies they may choose to pursue. The motto of this school is 'My country, right or wrong.' Had this been the motto of Washington and his compatriots the United States would still be a part of the British Empire. The particular aggregate of men which constitutes a nation is a matter of the merest accident. . . . Indeed the patriotism whose dictum is 'My country, right or wrong' is but one degree of egotism, for if my country right or wrong, why not my state right or wrong; if my state right or wrong, why not my town . . . my neighborhood . . . my family . . . my great uncle . . . or why not myself right or wrong?"

George Washington was disloyal to his own government, the greatest national government in the world in his day, simply because that government did not do things to suit *him.*

---

* Quoted by Walter Walsh: *Moral Damage of War*, p. 380.
† *The Economy of Happiness*, pp. 519-20.

Washington *took up arms against his own government* because it did not suit him. Washington was *unpatriotic* toward his great national government because it did not please him. Washington *even trampled upon the flag* of his own national government because that government's policy did not suit him.

But Washington was loyal to his own interests. He was patriotic toward the new *revolutionary* government that did suit him. He *transferred his allegiance* to a *new* flag and a *new* constitution and a *new* government and thus *protected his economic interests.*

And all these things are true, strictly true, of almost every *great* American in the times of Washington. Nearly every "leading citizen" in England at that time thought the behavior of the great Americans was "simply awful," "outlandishly anarchistic."

The "patriotic" great men in England were protecting their *economic* interests and *used their government* to protect those interests.

The "unpatriotic" Americans were protecting their economic interests, and they despised the government that would not protect their interests, and they straightway constructed a government which they *could* use in protecting their interests. Then they became patriotic toward the new government which they were using to protect their interests.

Always those in possession of the powers of government use the Government to protect themselves—that is, to protect their interests; and they never fail to shrewdly shout, "Patriotism!" and teach "patriotism"; nor do they ever fail to shout, "Unpatriotic!" at any group or class who seek to reorganize government in self-defense.

"Patriotism!" "Love of our country!" Yes, indeed! But, doesn't the average American working class man look ridiculous shouting, "Hurrah for our country—our land of the free"? He has no voice in the control of the factory where he works; has no voice as to the use of the militia and the soldiers; has *no right to demand a job and thus defend his life;* he could not have the service of one petty village marshal, to open up a "shut-down" factory, even though the opening of the factory would save him and five thousand other men and their twenty-five thousand women and children from starvation; in the mill and mine and factory he has no voice as to who shall be his foreman or superintendent any more than black chattel slaves in Georgia cotton fields in 1850.

Our country! Land of the free! Where the president of the American Federation of Labor could be clapped into jail if he should use the "freedom of the press" to publish even a short list of boycotted industrial tyrants; where the officers of the Western Federation of Miners were kidnapped and the kidnapping was declared to be constitutional by the highest court in the land, and the untried prisoners (constitutionally entitled to all the presumptions of innocence) were declared guilty by the cheap President of the political mockery called a "free republic."

(**11**) Mothers and fathers are not permitted to learn of many of the foul things happening at barracks or far away whither their sons have been "flimflammed" for bullet-stoppers.

For President William H. Taft's official testimony on the sexual degradation of the soldier sons of loving mothers, see Chapter Four, Section One, of the present volume.

"On the 17th of July, 1899, the staff correspondents of American newspapers stationed in Manila stated unitedly in public protest:

" 'The [Press] censorship has compelled us to participate in this misrepresentation by excising or altering uncontroverted statements of fact, on the plea, as General Otis said, that "they would alarm the people at home," or "have the people of the United States by the ears." ' "*

Some things, you know, must be concealed. President D. S. Jordan (Leland Stanford University) writes:†

"Does the *Outlook* [editor] know what Manila is becoming under military rule? We hear of four hundred saloons on the Escolta, where two were before; that twenty-one per cent. of our soldiers are attacked with venereal disease, that according to the belief of the soldiers, 'even the pigs and dogs have the syphilis.' "

Following the Spanish war, venereal diseases as cause of

---

* Walter Walsh: *Moral Damage of War,* p. 376.
† *Imperial Democracy,* p. 270.

ineffectiveness and cause for discharge from the army increased two and a half fold; that is, *two hundred and fifty per cent.** The statement by the Secretary of War, Mr. Dickinson (Report for 1909, p. 17) is sufficient to disgust and anger every woman in the land with the entire filthy business of militarism. For the startling statement see Chapter Four, Section One, of present volume.

In this connection read the words of an officer in the Department of War, Col. John Van Rensselaer:†

"I have but one word to say. I am an officer of the Medical Corps of the Army, and will speak on this important subject from that standpoint.

"Every soldier excused from duty on account of sickness of any kind has a record made of his case. By reason of this fact, I believe I may safely say that military vital statistics, including venereal diseases, are the most complete extant.

"The authorities observing that there has been in recent years a progressive increase of these diseases in the Army, until the non-efficiency from them with us now exceeds that of any other army, and despairing of help from the civil control of prostitution, have instituted a plan within the service by which they hope to reduce the excessive non-efficiency from venereal. Medical officers are required to instruct the men in the nature and dangers of these diseases, the non-necessity of exposure to them. . . .

"Such instruction is valuable to a certain extent, but only to a certain extent. . . . We cannot, therefore, expect all of our men, so many of whom are at the age of highest virility, to avoid exposure by reason of any moral suasion we may bring to bear. Some certainly will not, so we say to them, 'Be continent, but if you cannot, then protect yourself!' *And we tell them how to do it.*"

How splendid, how grandly noble, it must have been to see a regular army physician, wearing the official professional uniform marked "U. S.," going, officially, at stated intervals, to the officially "segregated" houses of prostitution in Manila

---

* See Annual Report of the Secretary of War, 1908, p. 22.

† See *Social Diseases*, p. 24, March, 1910; Contents—A Symposium concerning a phase of venereal diseases, being addresses and discussions at a meeting of the American Society of Sanitary and Moral Prophylaxis, held at the New York Academy of Medicine, December 9th, 1909. Address: Social Diseases, 9 East 42d Street, New York. Italics mine. G. R. K.

to officially examine the condition of professional prostitutes, and, having examined them, officially report them "unfit" (for whom?)—or "fit" (for whom?). How sublime! How patriotic! How lovingly Christian! Great flag-waving, constitutional government, performing a noble function nobly and, of course, constitutionally! All in the name of Christ, of course—for "This is a Christian nation"—officially.

Life on board a war vessel is unnatural. So far as social and sex relations are concerned the men are virtually kept in solitary confinement for weeks, even months, at a time. *Under such profoundly unnatural conditions human beings behave unnaturally.* Many strong characters and all the weak ones collapse, utterly collapse; and the wild, ugly, worse than brute monster, *Perverted* Sex Appetite, has a vile festival weeks at a time, enticing, embracing, befouling, devouring many of the finest youths in the land.

It is said to be common knowledge with many who know and with many it is a source of horrible jest—that under such unnatural conditions on board a battleship men *sexually* associate *with men* in ways worse (if possible) than the most degrading ways mentioned (and cursed) in the Old Testament. And when, after weeks or months at sea, the warship touches at a port for a few days or weeks, there is a wild rush of unfortunate boys for unfortunate women whose diseased condition is an unspeakable abomination. And this should be known too: Certain Christian and un-Christian governments' officials *provide the boys with certain preventive chemicals (as they leave the ship for a "lark" on shore),* knowing that the boys, many of them, are *sure to be the victims of victims reeking with disease.*

And then if the reader could witness the "round-up" the night before the ship sets out to sea again,—could see scores of fine young marines, pride of loving mothers,—if the reader could see them taken on board dead drunk and horribly befouled, taken on board in wheel barrows and dumped like big lumps of diseased, drunken, snoring and slobbering flesh, to be sobered up and "treated" when the ship gets out to sea, —if the reader could see all this and very much more, for example in New York harbor, he would then better under-stand why very few of "our very *best* people" of the "upper class" are not easily wheedled into giving up their own sons to defend our great and glorious country on board a big steel fighting machine called a battleship—to cruise and carouse around the world.   Just in proportion as the working class mother thinks about this matter her sons will be safer from the wheedling seductions of the recruiting officer.

Mothers, what is the blind sentiment that makes you clap your hands in admiration of the "great statesmen" or the "great government" that has prostitutes examined for the sons you bore and carefully reared and tenderly love?

"LEAD US NOT INTO TEMPTATION," SAID JESUS CHRIST. YET A "CIVILIZED" CHRISTIAN GOVERNMENT RECENTLY NOT ONLY EXAMINED, BUT PROVIDED PROSTITUTES FOR THE SOL-DIER BOYS.   THE GREAT BRITISH GOVERNMENT WITHIN RECENT YEARS PROVIDED PROSTITUTES FOR HER SOLDIERS IN INDIA.   Circular memoranda were sent to all the cantonments of India by Quarter-Master General Chapman, in the name of the commander-in-chief of the army of India (Lord Rob-erts).   Here are three excerpts from those documents and from official reports :*

"In regimental bazaars it is *necessary* to have a *sufficient num-ber* of women; to take care that they are SUFFICIENTLY ATTRACTIVE; to *provide* them with proper houses, and above all to insist upon means of ablution being always available [to prevent venereal dis-eases]. . . . If *young* soldiers are *carefully advised* in regard to the *advantages* of ablution, and recognize that *convenient arrangements exist in the regimental bazaar* (that is, in the chacla, or brothel), they may be expected to avoid the risks involved in association with women who are not recognized [that is, not examined and licensed] by the regimental authorities."

Another commanding officer writes in his report:

"PLEASE SEND YOUNG AND ATTRACTIVE WOMEN AS LAID DOWN IN THE QUARTER-MASTER GENERAL'S CIRCULAR, NO. 21A. . . . THERE ARE NOT WOMEN ENOUGH; THEY ARE NOT ATTRACTIVE ENOUGH.   MORE AND YOUNGER WOMEN ARE REQUIRED. . . . I HAVE ORDERED THE NUM-

---

* See Walter Walsh: *Moral Damage of War*, pp. 151-52.   Em-phasis mine.   G. R. K.

BER OF PROSTITUTES TO BE INCREASED . . . AND HAVE GIVEN SPECIAL
INSTRUCTIONS AS TO ADDITIONAL WOMEN BEING YOUNG AND OF AT-
TRACTIVE APPEARANCE."

And this: "The total number of admissions to hospital of
cases of venereal diseases amongst troops in India rose in
1895 to 522 per 1,000."

And this from another authority:*

"In 1902, in India, the enormous number of 12,686 men were
admitted into hospitals suffering from sexual diseases alone; more
than 1,000 military victims were always in the hospital—and the
report from which these figures are taken deals with the healthiest
year for 20 years past. In the Home Army . . . in a single period
of twelve months, of 154,000 troops, there were 24,176 sexual complaint cases—or one in every six. In the author's judgment, 80
per cent. of the entire British Army in India, and a proportion
slightly smaller for the Home Army, have been at some time
affected."

"The worst of war and war service is that the soldier is a
ruined man."†

General Sherman has spoken on the refining influences of
war:

"Long after the Civil War, General Sherman, defending the
conduct of his troops in South Carolina, said to Carl Schurz: 'Before
we got out of that state the men had so accustomed themselves
to destroying everything along the line of march that sometimes,
when I had my headquarters in a house, that house began to burn
before I was fairly out of it. The truth is—human nature is human
nature. You take the best lot of young men—all church members
if you please—and put them into an army and let them invade an
enemy's country and let them live upon it for any length, and
they will gradually lose all principle‡ and self-restraint to a degree
beyond the control of discipline. It has always been so and always
will be so.' "§

(12) An anonymous author writes thus:‖

"Real war is a very different thing from the painted image that
you see at a parade or review. But it is the painted image that

---

* Edmondson: *John Bull's Army from Within.*

† Elbert Hubbard: *Health and Wealth*, quoted in the *New Age*,
August 5, 1909. See Index: "Venereal Diseases."

‡ See Chapter Seven, Section 18.

§ *International Journal of Ethics*, April, 1908.

‖ *Arbeiter in Council*, pp. 38-39.

makes it popular. The waving plumes, the gay uniforms, the flashing swords, the disciplined march of innumerable feet, the clear-voiced trumpet, the intoxicating strains of martial music, the pomp, the sound, and the spectacle—these are the incitements to war and to the profession of the soldier. They are not what they are. But they still form a popular prelude to a woeful pandemonium. And when war bursts out it is at first, as a rule, but a small minority even of the peoples engaged that really sees and feels its horrors. The populace is fed by excitements; the defeats are covered up; in most countries the lists of killed and wounded are suppressed or postponed; victories are magnified; successful generals are acclaimed, and the military hero becomes the idol of the people. The over-fed, seedy malingerers of a small society join with the starving loiterers about the gin palace in applauding the execution of ruin. If their heroes are successful, what are their trophies?—prisons crowded with captives, hospitals filled with sick and wounded, towns sacked, farms burnt, fields laid waste, taxes raised, plenty converted to scarcity or famine, and vast debts accumulated for posterity. Then when these [military] heroes have done their work, the heroes of peace . . . appear, and by long and patient labor amid scenes of universal lamentation seek to mitigate the suffering of their repentant fellow-countrymen."

The poet Byron was in a war and described war thus:
"All the mind would shrink from of excesses;
All the body perpetrates of bad;
All that we read, hear, dream, of man's distresses;
All that the devil would do if run stark mad;
All that defies the worst which pen expresses;
All that by which hell is peopled, or is sad
As hell—mere mortals who their power abuse—
Was here (as heretofore and since) let loose. . . .
War's a brain-spattering art."*

(**13**) In connection with the foregoing section 12 examine Chapter Seven, Section 18.

"War! War! War! . . . God send the women sleep in the long, long night, when the breasts on whose strength they leaned heave no more."†

Wives and mothers of the working class, as soon as the government has had your choicest sons slaughtered, the gov-

---

* *Don Juan*, VIII., IX.

† E. C. Stedman: "Alice of Monmouth."

ernment is *through with you*—except to send you a miserable, blood-stained, silver sop, a sort of cash bribe, once a quarter. Then as you receive the vile cash, you can, in imagination, hear the shrieks of your dead loved ones. The government seeks to win your approval and to silence your hearts' protests against human butchery with the cheap jingle of some filthy dollars—as if you had sold your sons and husbands for a price. Such a pension is a form of hush money.

"If the stroke of war fell certain on the guilty heads, none else . . . but alas!

> That undistinguishing and deathful storm
> Beats heaviest on the exposed and innocent;
> And they that stir its fury, while it raves
> Safe at a distance send their mandates forth."—Crowe.

Robert G. Ingersoll wrote:*

"Nations sustain the relations of savages to each other. . . .

"No man has imagination enough to paint the agonies, the horrors, the cruelties, of war. Think of sending shot and shell crashing through the bodies of men! Think of the widows and orphans! Think of the maimed, the mutilated, the mangled! . . ."

Let the working class mothers beware of crafty and cowardly politicians and business men seeking to excite them with the shallow cry: "The flag! Our country! Our homes!" For the mothers' sake it is worth the space to restate the fact here: *That more than half of all the mothers in the United States have no homes of their own and must live in rented homes, and more than one-eighth of them live in mortgaged homes.*† And vast numbers of the mothers in the United States live in mean, small houses with scarcely a single modern convenience.

Mothers, keep your eyes on the bankers and the manufacturers and the other "leading citizens": they and their sons and sons-in-law are not shedding a large quantity of

---

* *Works,* passim.

† See Census Report, 1900, Vol. 2, p. CXCII.

their "blue" blood for "our" country and "our" homes and "our" flag; *and they can not be wheedled into doing so.* Watch them closely, mothers, both before a war and during a war. Don't get excited. Remember Christ's "Put up thy sword."

St. Paul said, "Follow peace with all men."

You have heard of this doctrine: "Thou shalt not kill."

"War has no pity," said Schiller.

"God is forgotten in war, and every principle of Christianity is trampled under foot," said Sidney Smith.

> "To be tender-minded
> Does not become a sword."—Shakespeare.

"War is one of the greatest plagues that can afflict humanity; it destroys religion . . . it destroys families. Any scourge, in fact, is preferable to it. . . . Cannon and firearms are cruel and damnable machines."—Martin Luther.

The gentle and charming lover of little children, Eugene Field, wrote:: "I hate wars, armies, soldiers, guns, and fireworks."*

"And he shall judge among the nations, and he shall rebuke many people. And they shall beat their swords into ploughshares and their spears into pruning hooks: nation shall not lift sword against nation, neither shall they learn war any more."†

James Russell Lowell :‡

> "The laborin' man and laborin' woman
> Have one glory and one shame;
> Ev'y thin' thet's done inhuman
> Ingers all on 'em the same."

And Tolstoi thus :§

"Every war—even the briefest—with its accompaniment of ruinous expenses, destruction of harvests, thefts, plunder, murders, and unchecked debauchery, with the false justifications of its necessity and justice, the glorification and praise of military exploits, of patriotism and devotion to the flag, with the pretense of care

---

* *Autobiographical Note.*
† Isaiah: Chapter II., par. 4.
‡ "Biglow Papers."
§ *The Kingdom of God.*

for the wounded, etc.,—will, in one year, demoralize men incomparably more than thousands of thefts, arsons and murders committed in the course of centuries by individual men under the influence of passion."

Let the women's literary clubs and circles, many of them devotees of John Ruskin, consider the following lines from his pen:*

"But Occult Theft—Theft which hides itself even from itself, and is legal, respectable, and cowardly,—corrupts the body and soul of man, and to the last fibre of them. *And the guilty thieves of Europe, the real sources of all deadly war in it, are the Capitalists,* —that is to say, those who live by percentages on the labor of others.—The *Real* war in Europe—is between these thieves and the workman, *such as these thieves have made him.* They have kept him poor, ignorant, and sinful, that they might without his knowledge gather for themselves the produce of his toil. At last a dim insight into the fact of this begins to dawn upon him."

As to thieves: Think of stealing several years of a man's life when he is in the prime of young manhood, by tearing him from his own friends and loved ones, forcing a rifle into his hands, and compelling him for years to learn the vile science and art of human butchery. Thus are the best years of millions of the choicest young men in Europe stolen— stolen by a class,—a class of prominent kidnappers, industrial and political thieves, "leading citizens" hypocritically wearing a mask called "Patriotism." Think of many millions thus stolen—stolen from their parents, stolen from their brothers and sisters, stolen from their wives and children.

When the working class think about war and see the vast theft of their lives they will astound the world with their protest.

And the mothers will take part in this protest.

(**14**) Didn't Christ say in substance: "I came not to send peace, but a sword?"

Yes. At least that is what some of the gentle Christ's followers are said to have reported that they heard he had been reported to have been heard to say. And it is true, too,

---

* Quoted by John A. Hobson: *John Ruskin—Social Reformer,* p. 346. Italics mine except for "The *Real* War." G. R. K.

that tyrants, hypocritically mumbling *interpolated* malignance *ascribed* to Christ, draw the sword to combat the brotherhood of man—as, doubtless, Christ expected they would do. But it is worse than blasphemous nonsense to teach children—young or old—that Christ, the Great Lover of Mankind, was a cheap jingoist, recommended the sword and counseled wholesale butchery of brothers by brothers. The distinguished intellectual prostitutes who argue Christ into the same butchers' list with Alexander, Caesar, Napoleon and the Tough Rider, are pridelessly down on their faces in the dust cringing before their industrial masters; they are simply betraying Christ again for "thirty pieces" of blood-stained silver called salaries.*

Christ, according to the reports, also said: "Blessed are the peacemakers: for they shall be called the children of God." Also: "Ye have heard it hath been said: 'An eye for an eye, and a tooth for a tooth'; but I say unto you: 'That ye resist not evil.'" And this: "They that take up the sword, shall by the sword perish."

And this on authority: "Thou shalt not steal."

One of the most eminent bishops in the United States went, in the winter of 1907-8, before a Congressional Committee and argued eloquently for a large cash donation from Congress for a certain "boys' academy" managed by his church. His chief argument was that the little fellows "are carefully trained *in the use of arms* and would be *ready for use in case of trouble.*"

Many schools thus prepare boys to murder hungry working men who are out on strike for a few pennies a day to feed their families—which is a "case of trouble." Now imagine Christ training tender boys for human butchery and teasing the brutal government of his time for cash with which to buy spears and swords for the children!

"There is a powerful section of the Christian church which teaches its entire membership that the Church has a

---

* See Index: "Christ."

right to exempt them—the clergy—from the usual duties of citizenship, and especially from military duty."*

Now, it does not matter what church we may or may not be members of, all the men and all the women of the *working* class—*in all the churches and out of the churches*—should band together in a *world-wide fellowship and effort* of the *working* class to drive war from the world and thus protect the helpless women and children. Remember, mothers, it is not fair that your husbands and sons should be torn from your homes, have cruel rifles thrust into their hands, and be forced into a war where they may be destroyed,—and you be thus widowed and your younger children be left fatherless; and, at the same time, the minister who by prayer and public speech exerted powerful influence to bring about the war,—that *he* should be exempted from the horrors of the battlefield, the horrors *up close,* where human blood and brains are pounded into the mud by cannon balls and the hoofs of horses. Remember, too, that tens of thousands of ministers have no wives and no children to be desolated. Does it not seem rather that these wifeless, childless men who want war should themselves go to the war instead of having your lovers go?

It should be repeated:

No MATTER WHAT DENOMINATION THEY BELONG TO, THOSE MEN WHO PRAY FOR WAR OR PRAY FOR VICTORIES IN WAR, OR HELP TRAIN BOYS FOR WAR—THOSE MEN SHOULD GO AND FIGHT THE WAR.

IF A WAR IS GOOD ENOUGH TO PRAY FOR IT IS GOOD ENOUGH TO GO TO. THOSE WHO WANT "GREAT VICTORIES" SHOULD BE FORCED TO GO AFTER THEM, RIGHT UP TO THE FRONT TOO, WHERE CANNON SHELLS BURST STRIKING HUNDREDS WITH DEATH—UP TO THE FRONT, INTO "HELL'S HURRICANES."

How does this matter seem to you, mother? Won't you think it over and bring up the subject for friendly and earnest *discussion in your community?* Why not urge all women everywhere to take up this subject—and thus *chain the atten-*

* See *The World To-Day*, p. 956, Sept., 1905.

*tion of society to this subject of the degradation and slaugh-
ter of the men you love?*

(15) In *The Westminster Review* of July, 1907, is the
following suggestion of a topic suitable for discussion in
women's societies and newspapers:

"There is another insidious form of Militarism that is very
widespread and popular. I refer to the Lads' Brigades [in England]
which are attached to so many churches of different denominations.
Under pretext of giving them physical training, boys are taught
the spirit of submission to another's will, and to love the trappings
of Militarism. . . . This coupling together of military training with
religion has been well described by the Rev. Dr. Aked of Liver-
pool [now of New York], as 'preaching heaven and practicing hell.' "

The American mother can not solace herself with the
thought that what Dr. Aked referred to was a practice in far-
away England and does not much concern her. For this new
crucifixion of Jesus and the degradation of the little boys,
a strong society exists in the United States. The United
Boys' Brigade is an organization for training the trigger-
fingers and the blood-lusts of boys nine years and upward in
the basement rooms of Christian churches. "The object of
the organization," as announced in the monthly magazine of
the organization, *The American Brigadier,* is "to . . . promote reverence and discipline . . . to create in them a love
for their country . . . and while the boys are *thoroughly
drilled in military discipline and tactics,* it only serves to
make them true Christian *soldiers.** *The American Brigadier*
announces officially that "there is nothing equal to it in
drawing them into the Sabbath School." Thus the church
is to be made like a prize-fighting ring in order to make it
look good to the little boys. *The American Brigadier,* of
December, 1907, gives away its secret in a lengthy account,
headed, "Securing a New Recruit," as follows:

(One boy says to another): "We go to Bible drill every Satur-
day night and have setting-up exercises and Bible drill, and sometimes we visit other companies. Gee! but our company can show
them how to drill. And we go camping in summer, and we have a

---

* Italics mine. G. R. K.

bully time. . . . Bible drill? . . . Gee! but there are some bully stories in the Bible. . . . We read about Samson, the strong man that beat Sandow all hollow, and King David, the siege of Jericho, and last week we read about a shepherd boy killing a giant with a sling-shot. . . ."

In *The Brigadier* of November, 1907, is an article, "What it Means to be a Soldier," in which is the following:

"There is but one word that covers all, and that is obedience: obedience to orders and strict discipline. The foundation of all military organizations rests upon this one basis."

Precisely: *obedience.*

That is to say, an innocent little fellow who has been drilled thus for several years to forget that *he* has a brain and a will of *his own,* drilled to obey *all* orders *instantly*—such a boy at the age of twenty will, of course, *automatically* and stupidly obey *any* order—*no matter how vile*—even the order: "Fire! Charge!"—though "the enemy," the target, be little silk-mill wage-slave girls ten or twelve years old who must toil a whole week for $1.60, and are out on strike for a dime more per week, and while out on strike are *starved* into being "riotous."

Armed rowdies—with riot guns—for starving, "rioting" children!

The American Brigadier is primarily a religious magazine, so they say; but it offers a breech-loading Springfield rifle as a premium to the boy who will send in the most subscribers. Imagine Christ making his cause popular with little boys by offering them a weapon with which to murder! *The Brigadier* wins the boys to Jesus by seductively baiting the savage that still lurks in the "civilized" breast; the magazine gives pictures of armories, battle monuments, gun drills, military parades, camp life, gay military uniforms, little boys with guns, swords, tents, banners, cannon, pictures also of pompous-looking, gilt-braided "big men," famous professional human butchers. The magazine prints alluring stories of army-and-navy life; and makes a specialty of advertising military arms, military clothing, West Point story books, and so forth.

This organization works in and through the church. It is strong and is gaining ground. It boasts of having branches in many states. In the "City of Churches," Brooklyn, N. Y., the society is specially strong. Much of the military drill work is done openly in the streets, when the weather permits. Many pastors, "in the name of Jesus," of course, are energetically—and patriotically—hustling for the movement, some of them proudly (and craftily) having their pictures taken with the training companies. The pastors' poses in these pictures make the pastors look like valuable assets to the capitalists of their churches, but the poses somehow do not suggest the quiet and gentle Jesus. "Put up thy sword" is out of date with these kerosened procurers political.*

There are many thousands of innocent little church boys thus in training. October 5, 1907, twenty-five hundred of these little fellows marched on Fifth Avenue, New York City, carrying guns and swords, four of the betrayed children dragging a light cannon.

The Federal Government at Washington, by a "judicious mingling" of winks and smiles, is heartily encouraging this "Christian soldier" enterprise. Says the Commander-in-Chief, H. B. Pope, in his Report:†

"In general . . . it can be said that in the quarters where we have desired to obtain recognition, our influence is greater, and the respect tendered to us is much more cordial than ever before. Our own Government has paid special attention in several directions to the work of this organization . . . and our development [is] carefully followed by those highest in authority, who appreciate the possibilities of the splendid soldiery which the organization is making, should the necessity ever arise when this body might be needed [in a strike for example]. . . . Drill should never be allowed to take the place of religious exercises. At the same time a judicious mingling of both constitutes means through which we can obtain highest results."

And the following is from a report on a meeting of the organization held in Calvary Methodist Episcopal Church, New York City, May 13, 1907:

---

* See Chapters Nine and Eleven.
† *American Brigadier*, November, 1907.

"There were also present a number of Army Officers, National Guard officers and veterans of the Civil War. . . . The Church was beautifully decorated with flags. . . . General Campbell presided and presented messages of good will and good wishes from the President of the United States, from Colonel Fred Grant . . . and from many other influential men."

How interestingly consistent—"Good will and good wishes" from the presidential chairman of the executive committee of the capitalist class in America; that is, the National Government,—"good will and good wishes" to the seducers of small boys to serve as fist and tusk for the ruling class.

The "Boy Scout" movement is the latest manifestation of this christened and kerosened cunning to seduce the innocent small boys for the blood-and-iron embrace of Mars and Mammon. Mothers, take notice. Be warned. *Defend yourselves.*

President Roosevelt (international mentor) also furnished bewildering flattery to the boys themselves who show skill in the use of the deadly rifle. The Philadelphia *Public Ledger,* and many other newspapers about the same date, July 16, 1907, printed the following cunning letter written by President Roosevelt to a Brooklyn school boy. The news item with the letter runs thus:

"Oyster Bay, July 17. President Roosevelt has put his hearty approval on public school rifle practice. In a letter of congratulation to Ambrose Scharfenberg, of Brooklyn, winner of the shooting trophy of the Public School Athletic League, he takes occasion to encourage the system of rifle practice inaugurated by General George B. Wingate, retired.

"That the letter to young Scharfenberg may have as far-reaching influence as possible, it was made public at the President's direction today. It is as follows:

" 'My Dear Young Friend:—I heartily congratulate you upon being declared by the Public School Athletic League to stand first in rifle shooting among all the boys of the High Schools of New York City who have tried during the last year. Many a grown man who regards himself as a crack rifle shot would be proud of such a score. Your skill is a credit to you, and also to your principal, your teachers, and to all connected with the manual training school which you attend, and I know them all. [The usual diffident confession of omniscience.]

" 'Practice in rifle shooting is of value in developing not only muscles, but nerves. . . . It is a prime necessity that the volunteer should already know how to shoot. . . . The graduates from our schools and colleges should be thus trained so as to be good shots with the military rifle. When so trained they constitute a great addition to our national strength and great assurance for the peace of the country.' "

That is to say: Tho' the capitalists should refuse to employ 5,000,000 men and virtually spit in their faces and order these willing-to-work men out of the factories and mines to shiver and starve in rags, and thus infinitely humiliate millions of working class wives and daughters with the terrors of poverty—no matter, the rifle-practiced graduates of high schools, colleges and universities will be "ready for use," ready to crush the unemployed if they loudly protest, ready to help the master class thrust all the injustices of a *class*-labor system into the lives of the working class, ready to thrust bayonets into the out-of-work wage-slaves who cry aloud for work, for bread, for justice in the industrial civil war of capitalism.

Bright and early every school day, in New York City, about 600,000 children are *compelled* to salute the flag and recite some mocking lies about the "glorious freedom they have" and the "bounteous blessings they enjoy"—under the "friendly folds of the Stars and Stripes"—tho' a whole half million of the children *have no homes of their own and in a hundred ways are stung with the lash of poverty.*

(**17**) Many additional instructors in military tactics have in recent years been appointed to service in high schools, colleges and universities. United States Army officers are now in ninety-three universities, colleges and schools, drilling 22,910 students in "military departments."

Improved rifles, riot cartridges, and killing equipment are being distributed among the State militia forces; local armories are being improved and made attractive,—all made "ready for use" when needed to pacify the out-of-work wage-earners. Recently in one State, Colorado, military training was being systematically taught in the high schools of six of the largest cities. The Secretary of War in 1909 reported

forty-four schoolboy rifle clubs. In the newspapers and magazines, in the sermons and speeches and especially in the
public school,—by all such means—the size and perfection
of rifles, cannon, battleships and the like, are held up to the
children for their admiration and as evidences of our superiority and of our "splendid civilization." The children are
taught to clap their hands for our readiness to engage in
some great international butchering contest. But the children are *not* taught what arsenals, armories, cannon, rifles,
soldiers, militia, riot guns and riot cartridges—what all these
things mean and what war means for the *working* class.
Never!

(**18**) Let a philosopher speak to the mother and her
children in plain language:

"Europe is still in arms: each nation watching every other
with suspicion, jealousy, or menace. . . . And what is the result?
Russia overwhelmed with a military cancer, a prey to social confusion such as has not been seen in this century. Germany, with
her intelligence and industry, bound in the fetters of military
service, governed as if she were a camp, as if the sole object of
peace were to prepare for war. France staggering. . . . Italy
weighted with a useless army, uneasy, intriguing, restless. . . .
Spain weak from the drain of a series of wars. . . . England uncertain, divided in action, continually distracted and dishonored by an
endless succession of miserable wars in every quarter of the globe.

"Such is the picture of Europe after a generation of imperialism and aggressive war.

"Who is the gainer? Is the poor Russian moujic, torn from
his home to die in Central Asia or on the passes of the Balkans,
doomed to a government of ever deepening corruption and tyranny?
Is the workman of Berlin the better, crushed by military op-
pression and industrial recklessness? Who is the gainer—the ruler
or the ruled? Is the French peasant the gainer now that Alsace
and Lorraine are gone, and nothing exists of the empire but its
debt, its conspirators, and its legacy of confusions?

". . . Who is the gainer by this career of bloodshed and ambition? . . . We hear the groans of the millions—the working, suffering millions—who are yearning to replace this cruel system,
none of their making, none of their choice, by which they gain
nothing, from which they hope nothing."[*]

---

[*] Frederic Harrison: *National and Social Problems*, pp. 237-40.
Written in 1880.

Who indeed is the gainer? The workers lose; and the mothers lose most of all—their children. Yet everywhere complete contempt for the working class mothers of the whole world, absolute scorn for the blood of men and the tears of women—of the *working* class.

What magnificent protest will roll round this world when the working class is roused to think of these things!

(**19**) In the dollar-hunting spirit of the age it may be inquired: Doesn't war make business brisk, and thus furnish work for the wage-earners?

Yes, certainly. But so also would a lunatic in the streets armed with a repeating shotgun shooting down the children at play: he would make business brisk for the coffin trust, the undertakers and their employees—and the grave-digger.

(**20**) Following are several special suggestions for the mothers and fathers of the working class:

(1) Teach the children anti-war recitations and declamations.

Faithfully and patiently help the boys and girls master a half dozen or more passages of the strongest prose and poetry to be found against war; help them in this work till they understand—till their eyes kindle, till their hearts burn, till their imagination is aflame with disgust and detestation for war and for the foul rôle of the armed guard of the ruling class.

(2) Teach the children the pledge on the first page of Chapter One of the present volume. Teach them to teach that pledge, or some similar pledge, to other children.

(3) Teach the boys and girls the *historical origin* of the working class. (See Chapter Eleven.)

(4) Explain to the boys and girls, page by page, all of Chapter Ten, and *urge them to explain the matter to other children.*

(5) Patiently and clearly explain the meaning and the purpose of the local militia and the army.

(6) Interest the children in a circulating anti-war library, and *co-operate with them in promoting the enterprise.*

(7) A Ten-Dollar Cash Prize for the best definition of

a militiaman who is willing to shoot the fathers and brothers of the little working class children of his neighborhood when those fathers and brothers are on strike struggling to better the condition of the mothers and the children—such a prize contest would induce a great amount of helpful thoughtfulness and discussion.

(8) Further suggestions will be found at the opening of Chapter Twelve. See also Index: "Suggestions."

(**21**) Following are several passages suitable for children as declamations. Also see Index, "Declamations."

(**A**) The Soldier's Creed:*

"Captain, what do you think," I asked,
"Of the part your soldiers play?"
But the captain answered, "I do not think;
"I do not think, I obey!"

"Do you think you should shoot a patriot down,
"Or help a tyrant slay?"
But the captain answered, "I do not think;
"I do not think, I obey!"

"Do you think your conscience was made to die,
"And your brain to rot away?"
But the captain answered, "I do not think;
"I do not think, I obey!"

"Then if this is your soldier's creed," I cried,
"You're a mean unmanly crew;
"And for all your feathers and gilt and braid,
"I am more of a man than you!

"For whatever my place in life may be,
"And whether I swim or sink,
"I can say with pride, 'I do not obey;
"'I do not obey, I *think!*'"

(**B**) ROBERT G. INGERSOLL'S MUSINGS AT THE TOMB OF NAPOLEON :†

"A little while ago I stood by the grave of the old Na-

---

* Ernest Crosby: *Swords and Ploughshares.* Published by Funk and Wagnalls, New York.

† See *Prose-Poems and Selections from the Writings and Sayings of Robert G. Ingersoll.* Published by C. P. Farrell, New York.

poleon—a magnificent tomb of gilt and gold, fit almost for a deity dead—and gazed upon the sarcophagus of rare and nameless marble, where rest at last the ashes of that restless man.   I leaned over the balustrade and thought about the career of the greatest soldier of the modern world.

"I saw him walking upon the banks of the Seine, contemplating suicide.   I saw him at Toulon—I saw him putting down the mob in the streets of Paris—I saw him at the head of the army of Italy—I saw him crossing the bridge of Lodi with the tricolor in his hand—I saw him in Egypt in the shadows of the pyramids—I saw him conquer the Alps and mingle the eagles of France with the eagles of the crags.   I saw him at Marengo—at Ulm and Austerlitz.   I saw him in Russia, where the infantry of the snow and the cavalry of the wild blast scattered his legions like winter's withered leaves.   I saw him at Leipsic in defeat and disaster—driven by a million bayonets back upon Paris—clutched like a wild beast —banished to Elba.   I saw him escape and retake an empire by the force of his genius.   I saw him upon the frightful field of Waterloo, where Chance and Fate combined to wreck the fortunes of their former king.   And I saw him at St. Helena, with his hands crossed behind him, gazing out upon the sad and solemn sea.

"I thought of the orphans and widows he had made—of the tears that had been shed for his glory, and of the only woman who had ever loved him, pushed from his heart by the cold hand of ambition.   And I said, I would rather have been a French peasant and worn wooden shoes.   I would rather have lived in a hut with a vine growing over the door, and the grapes growing purple in the amorous kisses of the autumn sun.   I would rather have been that poor peasant, with my loving wife by my side, knitting as the day died out of the sky—with my children upon my knee and their arms about me—I would rather have been that man, and gone down to the tongueless silence of the dreamless dust, than to have been that imperial impersonation of force and murder, known as Napoleon the Great."

(C) VICTOR HUGO'S REFLECTIONS ON WAR:*

"The antique violence of the few against all, called right divine, is nearing its end. . . . A stammering, which tomorrow will be speech, and the day after tomorrow a gospel, proceeds from the bruised lips of the serf, of the vassal, of the laboring man, of the pariah. The gag is breaking between the teeth of the human race. The patient human race has had enough of the path of sorrow, and refuses to go farther. . . . Glory advertised by drumbeats is met with a shrug of the shoulder. These sonorous heroes have, up to the present day, deafened human reason, which begins to be fatigued by this majestic uproar. Reason stops eyes and ears before those authorized butcheries called battles. The sublime cut-throats have had their day. . . . Humanity, having grown older, asks to be relieved of them. The cannon's prey has begun to think, and, thinking twice, loses its admiration for being made a target."

* * * * * * * * * * * * *

"Whoever says today, 'might makes right,' performs an act of the Middle Ages, and speaks to men a hundred years behind their times. Gentlemen, the nineteenth century glorifies the eighteenth century. The eighteenth proposed, the nineteenth concludes. And my last word shall be a declaration, tranquil but inflexible, of progress.

"The time has come. Right has found its formula:—human federation.

"Today force is called violence, and begins to be judged; war is arraigned. Civilization, upon the complaint of the human race, orders the trial, and draws up the great criminal indictment of conquerors and captains. The Witness, History, is summoned. The reality appears. The fictitious brilliancy is dissipated. In many cases, the hero is a species of assassin. The people begin to comprehend that increasing the magnitude of a crime can not be its diminution; that, if to kill is a crime, to kill much can not be an extenuating circumstance; that if to steal is a shame, to invade can not be a glory; that Te Deums do not count for much in this matter; that homicide is homicide; that blood-shed is blood-shed;

---

* See *William Shakespeare*, Part Third, Book III; M. B. Anderson's Translation. Published by A. C. McClurg and Company, Chicago; and *An Oration on Voltaire*, delivered in Paris, May 30, 1878. It is worthy of remark that the orator was repeatedly applauded while delivering the oration, and at the close the entire audience rose and wildly cheered. In the declamation, as here arranged in two parts (to be given together, if desired), the excerpt from the oration begins, "Whoever says today."

that it serves nothing to call one's self Caesar or Napoleon; and that in the eyes of the eternal God, the figure of a murderer is not changed because, instead of a gallow's cap, there is placed upon the head an Emperor's crown.

"Ah! let us proclaim absolute truths. Let us dishonor war. No; glorious war does not exist. No; it is not good, and it is not useful, to make corpses. No; it can not be that life travails for death. No; O, mothers who surround me, it can not be that war, the robber, should continue to take from you your children. No; it can not be that women should bear children in pain, that men should be born, that people should plow and sow, that the farmer should fertilize the fields, and the workmen enrich the city, that industry should produce marvels, that genius should produce prodigies, that the vast human activity should, in the presence of the starry sky, multiply efforts and creations, all to result in that frightful international exposition called war."

(D) INGERSOLL'S VISION OF WAR :*

"The past rises before me like a dream. . . . We hear the sound of preparation, the music of boisterous drums—the silver voices of heroic bugles. We see thousands of assemblages, and hear the appeals of orators. We see the pale cheeks of women, and the flushed faces of men, and in those assemblages we see all the dead whose dust we have covered with flowers. We lose sight of them no more. . . . We see them part with those they love. Some are walking for the last time in quiet, woody places, with maidens they adore. We hear the whisperings and the sweet vows of eternal love as they lingeringly part forever. Others are bending over cradles, kissing the babes that are asleep. Some are receiving the blessings of old men. Some are parting with mothers who hold them and press them to their hearts again and again, and say nothing. Kisses and tears, tears and kisses—the divine mingling of agony and love! And some are talking with wives, and endeavoring with brave words, spoken in the old tones, to drive from their hearts the awful fear. We see them part. We see the wife standing in the door with the babe in her arms—standing in the sunlight sobbing. At the turn of the road a hand waves—and she answers by holding high in her loving arms the child. He is gone,—and forever. . . .

"We go with them, one and all. We are by their side on all the gory fields—in all the hospitals of pain—on all the weary marches. We stand guard with them in the wild storm and under

---

* Slightly abbreviated excerpt from an Oration at the Soldiers and Sailors' Reunion, Indianapolis, September 21, 1876. Reprinted from *Prose-Poems and Selections from Writings and Sayings of Robert G. Ingersoll.* Published by C. P. Farrell, New York.

FOUR VICTIMS OF CHEAP PATRIOTISM

the quiet stars. We are with them in ravines running with blood
—in the furrows of old fields. . . . We see them pierced by balls
and torn with shell, in the trenches, by the forts, and in the
whirlwind of the charge. . . .

"We are at home when the news comes that they are dead.
We see the maiden in the shadow of her first sorrow. We see the
silvered head of the old man bowed with the last grief. . . .

"They sleep . . . under the solemn pines, the sad hemlocks, the
tearful willow and the embracing vines. They sleep beneath the
shadows of the clouds, careless alike of sunshine or storm, each in
the windowless Palace of Rest. . . ."

(E) INGERSOLL'S VISION OF THE FUTURE.*

"A vision of the future rises: . . . I see a world where thrones
have crumbled and where kings are dust. The aristocracy of idleness has perished from the earth.

"I see a world without a slave. Man at last is free. Nature's
forces have by science been enslaved. Lightning and light, wind
and wave, frost and flame, and all the secret subtle powers of the
earth and air are the tireless toilers for the human race.

"I see a world at peace, adorned with every form of art, with
music's myriad voices thrilled, while lips are rich with words of
love and truth; a world in which no exile sighs, no prisoner
mourns; a world on which the gibbet's shadow does not fall; a
world where labor reaps its full reward, where work and worth go
hand in hand, where the poor girl, trying to win bread with a needle
—the needle that has been called 'the asp for the breast of the poor,'
—is not driven to the desperate choice of crime or death, of suicide or shame.

"I see a world without the beggar's outstretched palm, the
miser's heartless, stony stare, the piteous wail of want, the livid
lips of lies, the cruel eyes of scorn.

"I see a race without disease of flesh or brain—shapely and
fair, married harmony of form and function, and, as I look, life
lengthens, joy deepens, love canopies the earth; and over all in
the great dome, shines the eternal star of human hope."

These golden words, these words of immortal beauty, are,
"like love, wine for the heart and brain." They fire the soul,
especially the mother's soul, with a glorious joy, a splendid

---

* Very slightly abbreviated excerpt from a Decoration Day
Oration, delivered at the Metropolitan Opera House, New York
City, May 30, 1888. Reprinted from Vol. IX., p. 453, Dresden
Edition of *Ingersoll's Complete Works.* Published by C. P. Farrell,
New York.

vision of unstained, untroubled pleasure: Mankind at Peace
—Socialized. The children safe. The future vast and beautiful and kind for her and for those that call her Mother.

But again and yet again the cannon's roar will banish the
vision. The future holds agony for the mother, especially for
the humble mother in the working class. Her husband and
her older sons will go to war. They will even thoughtlessly
sink to the level of joining the local militia for local war—
for strike service. The men she loves have been poisoned—
poisoned with the base teaching that brutality is bravery, that
the drawn sword marks the patriot. They are ready, ready
now, at the word of command from a cheap commander to
murder the men of their own class, and break the hearts and
mock the tears of the wage-slave mothers of the world.

These mothers must defend themselves—for the present.

These mothers can defend themselves only through their
younger sons and daughters—by teaching them a class loyalty
which is a new patriotism that will close the local armory,
shame the assassin back to the factory, to the farm, to the
mine, and silence all the cannon on all the earth.

CHAPTER NINE.

The Cross, the Cannon, and the Cash-Register.

"Never land long lease of empire won whose sons sat silent while base deeds were done."—James Russell Lowell.

Speak! Speak!—you leaders of the toil-stained multitude whom the Great Christ of Peace so boldly defended.

Speak!

Rebuke the brutes who betray Christ's humble followers!

Speak! There is no excuse for silence—on your part.

Speak defiantly—and *clearly.*

You have for nearly two thousand years held the brain of vast portions of the human race in your hands. Have you taught peace—*effectively?*

Look—see that gaping war-stab in the breast of the working class.

THE CASH COST OF MILITARISM IN THE WORLD FOR FORTY-EIGHT HOURS WOULD BE SUFFICIENT TO PROVIDE A 150-PAGE BOOK AGAINST WAR FOR EVERY PERSON ON EARTH WHO CAN READ.* THREE SERMONS PER YEAR AGAINST WAR IN EVERY ONE OF 160,000 CHURCHES OF THE UNITED STATES COULD BE PAID FOR, AT THE RATE OF $50 PER SERMON, WITH LESS THAN THE COST OF TWO FIRST-CLASS BATTLESHIPS.

"Nothing can be clearer than that the leaders of Christianity immediately succeeding Christ, from whom authentic expressions of doctrines have come down to us, were well assured that their Master had forbidden the Christians the killing of men in war or enlisting in the legions. One of the chief differences which separated Roman non-Christians and Christians was the refusal of the latter to enlist in the legions and be thus bound to kill their fellows as directed."†

---

* See Chapter Four, Section Two, "The Cost of War in Cash."

† "Documents of the American Association for International Conciliation," 1907-08.

IN MY NAME! AFTER NINETEEN HUNDRED YEARS!

Eagerly we search the world for relief from the hell's horror of war.

There! There is the Church—the Church with her vast influence!—and she breathes, "Peace, good will to all men."

The Church?

Will the Church save us from war?

We shall see.

Reader, let us always open wide our souls to every man and to every influence great enough to make us socially wholesomer.

Sincerely, I admire every great Priest, every great Rabbi, and every great Preacher of our time who is too fine, too proud, too nobly social and international to rent his eloquent voice to the captains of industry for the blood-spilling business of conquering the markets of the world with sword and cannon and for the equally brutal business of benevolently stealing large sections of the earth to be swinishly exploited by money-greedy capitalists.

These men are masculine—unafraid. Let us salute them: "Good cheer, noble friends!"

Boldly these greater Priests refuse to toady to industrial and political masters and thus refuse to scream for war.

Defiantly these greater Rabbis refuse to inflame the tiger lurking in every human breast and thus refuse to prepare men for war.

Nobly these greater Preachers refuse Caesar and Shylock, and thus they stand by the Man of Peace and abhor war.

But, unfortunately, these grand bold souls are in helpless minority—at present.

And thus again we find the following question burning for an answer:

Which way shall the working class turn for deliverance from the curse of war?

Who will rescue the working class from these cyclones of lead and steel?

The Church? The Clergy?

Let us study this matter.

Long ago when the deluded soldiers of an "established"

church "patriotically" murdered the Great Carpenter, the "established" church of his locality hypocritically stood by the pagan Roman government, lending assistance to the pagan government and urging the pagan soldiers to slay Jesus Christ. And today the Christian church flatters the soldiers, "stands by the government,"—any and all "Christian" governments,—in any and all wars, and thus refuses to protect the working class from the sword and cannon; refuses to draw the bayonet from the breast of the humble working man; refuses to defend the working class woman from the blood and tears of war; refuses to shield the faces of the little children of the working class from the steel-shod hoofs of the galloping war horse.

This Chapter is a discussion of one of mankind's *misfortunes,* to show the despotism of the dollar,—TO SHOW THE TYRANNY OF THE ECONOMIC ELEMENT OF HUMAN LIFE; and let me here give most sincere assurance that this Chapter is written with not even the slightest degree of malice toward the Church. However, the Church taught me: *"Speak the truth."*

Well, here is a truth, a truth to be stripped naked and expressed because it is so vitally important to hundreds of millions who toil:—

The three mighty hosts of the Peace-Preaching Christ, the Greek Catholic Church, the Roman Catholic Church and the Protestant Church, these, bitterly at war with one another and defending the industrial despotism called capitalism,—refuse, flatly refuse, to *unite* their powerful voices in a defiant and *effective* declaration against war; refuse thus to help lift the huge burden and curse of war from the toil-bent shoulders of the working class; refuse to remove the thorn-crown of war from the brow of labor. The working class, millions of them loving Christ sincerely as I do, must learn and face the fact that the Church of the Great Carpenter Christ refuses to save the working class from the periodic baptisms of blood and fire called war.

"Put up thy sword," said Christ.

"Business is business! There is no sentiment in business! We must conquer the markets of the world," say the capitalists.

And there is the parting of the ways for toads and men, for the time-server and the prophet, for the emasculate and the masculine.

In 1898 a certain man lived in a small western "city"— and took notes. A local company of working class volunteers was organized to go to Cuba to slaughter the working men in the Spanish army and thus secure greater opportunity for American capitalists. On the day of departure of the volunteer company the people, thousands of them, assembled on a wide public square, surrounding the local volunteers. Suddenly, when interest was intense, a high table was rushed to the center of the square, a banker thoughtfully assisting. Hastily a meek and lowly follower of the Peaceful Jesus— a preacher—took his place upon this table, his eyes flashing hate and his chest bulging heroically. All hats were off. All heads, but two, were bowed in prayer. With head erect and eyes open the preacher, in prayer, addressed—the audience. With his eyes to the sky, the preacher, praying, used the name of God and the ears of the people. There was no "praying in secret" about that "eloquent effort." The prayer was "powerful." That prayer was an assault—an assault upon the finest sentiments that bloom in the human heart, the sentiments of the brotherhood of man.

But what of that? "Business is business."

That eloquent prayer electrified the vast audience. The preacher became an incendiary—he committed arson. His ferocious rhetoric set on fire the gullible souls of young men, humble women, innocent small boys and tender little girls. With crafty eloquence he petted the working class volunteers till they stood more erect in manly pride and licked their lips for the blood of almost equally ignorant Spanish working men; with flattering phrases he seductively praised the plain women who bore these "brave boys" now ready to butcher, praised them till these gentle, humble mothers were warm with an elation known only to mothers of strong men, praised them till they were keen with a savage gladness that they had borne these men now burning to slaughter humble toilers from the working class homes in Spain. With artful power of phrase and voice the preacher praised the small boys present, praying for "more brave boys in future years to stand by the flag"—caressed them thus till the poor little fellows longed to be men in order that they too might rend the flesh of humble working-class men in war—somewhere, anywhere, somehow, sometime. And then with cunning suggestiveness and with vulgar boldness this handsome panderer to capitalist masters rudely invaded the holy of holies, the innocent imagination of tender little girls present, brutally outraged the sacred instincts of kindness natural to these dainty little maids till these young doll-lovers were half excited with a dim but horrible hope, till their faces flushed in anticipation of the patriotic part they too in future years might have in sending their assassin sons to the front.

The prayer ended. The preacher rolled his fine dark eyes and fervently bellowed, "Amen!"

He had done *his* work. He had played *his* part. Souls had been branded. Human brotherhood had been suffocated in the hearts of gullible working men—strangled with elegant (and pious) eloquence.

Then the thousands of humble working class people moved off, "hoofing it," marching behind the soldiers to the railway station. A half dozen bankers, a dozen lawyers, and many other "leading business men" lingered, left their carriages, surrounded the preacher and congratulated him on his "splendid effort";—and that was part of his pay for his eloquent ferocity. Well-dressed women of the "best families in the city" gave the preacher their gloved right hands and practically embraced him with the virtuous and caressing fondness in their eyes;—and that was part of his pay for scarring the souls of men, women, and little children with the branding-iron of Old Testament ferocity. That savage prayer made him more popular in the city;—and that was part of his pay for his noble ferocity. He was now more secure in his job;—and that was part of his pay for his ecclesiastical buncombe and flap-doodle,—for his jungle growl

of civilized ferocity. The collections were for some time
larger in his church;—and that, yea, that also, was part of
his pay for serving the cash-register and thus playing the
rôle of betrayer of the Prince of Peace.

The handsome preacher had performed a miracle. He
had so fixedly riveted the attention of the "brave boys" upon
the Spaniards that the gullible volunteers noticed nothing
strange in the fact that strong, healthy bankers, lawyers, merchants and preachers (patriots all of them of course)—with
the stealthy quiet of a cat on a carpet—remained at home
just at the very time when "great deeds of glory and patriotism" and manly heroism were to be done.

Doubtless many a shot-torn boy soldier wallowing in his own
blood, his chest half crushed with the hoofs of galloping
cavalry horses, his splintered bones grinding together at every
move, the roar of cannon and the din of curses, prayers,
yells, sobs and groans of dying comrades crowding into his
ears—thinks of his well-fed, soft-voiced pastor at home far
away (and safe), the *good* man, the *nice* man, who fired
his and his fellow-fighters' hearts with "lust of death and
vulgar slaughter," who helped betray him and his fellows to
the human butchering field. No doubt many working class
people fondly hope that the ministers of the Christ of Peace
will presently *combine* and use their vast influence against
war—to drive the red demon from the earth that it may no
longer desolate the homes of the humble.

Vain hope.

Long ago the cynical, shrewd (and carefully baptized)
Napoleon Bonaparte remarked, with biting irony, "God is
always on the side of the heaviest battalions."

Today it is easy to see that not Christ,* but the Church
of Christ, is on the side of the business man and the politician concerning war.

And thus the bayonet still sticks in the breast of the
working class.

Thus the Cross dips to the cannon.

---

* See Chapter Eight, Section 13 and 14.

Really, will not the followers of the gentle Christ of Peace presently sweep war from the world?

They most certainly will do nothing of the kind—as long as war is profitable for the "leading citizens."

"Leading citizens" actually lead. They are the capitalists. Industrially and politically the capitalists have the world by the throat. They force their ambitions, their purposes, and their policies upon both the preacher and the wage-earner. Their purpose is: profits, more profits and still more profits. Their policy is: more markets and more territory—for more profits, at all hazard, in absolute defiance of Confucius, in defiance of Buddha, in defiance of Christ, in shameless defiance of the sacredness of human blood. They will, if need be,—that is, if business, commercial exigencies, require it—they will order the high-salaried generals to wash the earth with the blood of the socially despised working class, while safe in their palatial homes these "leading citizens" will masquerade as patriots, and on the "holy Sabbath day" they will virtually force their salaried pastors to pray and shout for blood-dripping victory.

This is the industrial rulers' history.

This is the industrial rulers' present politics.

This is the industrial rulers' future program.

And the preacher must therefore salute the cash-register and baptize the cannon—or *lose his job just like any other hired man* who fails to please his *economic* master.

"Business is business,"—*that* is "the law and the gospel" of capitalism.

Let us study the matter a little further.

When a war is on the world's stage the bright lights are so confusing that it is difficult to see the "leading citizens" in the background, "in the wings," so to speak. For example:

The American people are still clapping their hands and hurrahing for "our noble Christian President" for his part in bringing about peace between Russia and Japan. But why —just why—did not the "noble Christian President" nobly interfere many months before he did interfere? The blood of tens of thousands of humble working-class soldiers in both

armies was running down the hillsides in Manchuria in
streams—months before.   But no interference by the "noble
Christian   President" (recently so boisterously boastful of
"his" own noble slaughtering on San Juan Hill).

Let us understand.

For many months it seemed that Christian Russia would
surely win the war and still be able to pay interest and
principal of *American investments in Russia.*   Later the Russian Government and Russian credit became very unsteady. Immediately the capitalist actors in the background, with money
invested in Russian enterprises, put on the pressure, applied
"influence," to our government, and then, and not till then,
did President Roosevelt rush to the footlights of the world's
stage and whine and scream for peace.

For many months, while the blood of Japanese and Russian working class men was gushing from a million wounds,
while the humble wives and children of these "common" men
were wild with grief—all the while "our noble Christian
President," *like all other Christian rulers,* was as silent as a
fish; but when principal and interest of American parasites
got in danger, our "noble Christian President" promptly became nobly noisy and craftily pious and peaceful.

And that is a fair sample of a "Christian government's"
influence for peace.

At no time did the Church urge or demand peace,
and at no time did the Church throw its powerful influence
upon our President or upon the head of any other government to bring about peace.*

---

* It is mildly encouraging to reflect that very heavy and very
general international investments in national and industrial bonds
would have at least some tendency to dampen the bond-buying capitalists' enthusiasm for war; because, in some cases, a disastrous war
might result in the repudiation of bonds and, in most cases, might
easily result in a great temporary reduction of dividends from industrial investments.   Another thing to be noted here is that sometimes
the investors in the bonds of an unstable nation about to go to
war, may regret the threatening war and urge against it and even
decline to buy war bonds, *before the war is declared,* in order to protect their investments already made.   But after the war is once

Our gentle Christian President, Mr. Roosevelt, head of the greatest Christian republic on earth, said recently to a hand-clapping Christian audience, "I want for soldiers young men not only willing but *anxious* to fight"; that is, anxious to murder. That foul sentiment should have been drowned with hisses. The ferocious Christian Tsars of Russia, the blood-thirsting Caesars of the ancient pagan Roman Empire, the chiefs of savage tribes and modern republics,—all the ancient and modern, savage and civilized hero rulers who have sat on thrones and stood on the necks of nations—all these bullies have always been eager to have for soldiers "young men not only willing but anxious to fight"—that is, willing and anxious to cut the throats of their fellowmen in an intertribal or international festival of blood called a patriotic war.

And always, since society was first organized on a *class*-labor plan, the organized "spiritual guides" of society have "stood by the government," leagued with the hero ruler for the ruling class.

Mr. Roosevelt, for the moral improvement and spiritual guidance of small boys who may read his heroic record as a patriotic warrior, sets it down with evident pride that he shot a Spanish soldier (probably a humble workingman) in the back as the poor, ignorant, frightened fellow fled from the bloody field.* Mr. Roosevelt, as related in Chapter Eight, Section 16, urged in an Annual Message that rifle-practice ranges be provided in the public schools for young school boys —presumably that the little fellows may become "not only willing but anxious to fight." And the Church of the Peaceful Christ did not dare rebuke the "great Christian President"

---

entered upon these same regretful investors feel almost compelled to purchase the new issue of war-bonds in order to make victory more certain for the nation whose bonds they already hold, and thus protect the market value of their original investments. French investors in Russian bonds and enterprises to the extent of more than a billion dollars found themselves in this predicament in the case of the recent Russian-Japanese war. See Index: "Bankruptcy, Danger of."

* See Chapter Seven, Section 17.

for urging such a barbarous outrage upon the schoolboys'
dawning social consciousness and their finer sentiments of the
brotherhood of man.

Recently a school teacher in the city of Washington, where
this swaggering-bull-pup patriotism has been most effectively
suggested, asked her school children: "What is patriotism?"
She got the answer: "Killing Spaniards!" Thus have the
little people been outraged with befouling suggestions that
cheap race-hatred is patriotism. But the Church does not
dare cry out, in defense of "these little ones": "Stop that!
You noisy betrayer! Cease pouring venom into the hearts
of these helpless little children!"

> "With a hero at head and a nation
>   Well gagged and well-drilled and well cowed,
> And a gospel of war and damnation,
>   Has not an empire a right to be proud?"*

Quite naturally no protest is made.

The working man wonders why,

The working woman wonders why,

The children wonder why—

Why do not the Christian emperors, and Christian kings,
the Christian tsars and Christian presidents, the Christian
Parliaments, congresses, diets and cabinets of the whole Christian world promptly call a world convention of the Christian
rulers of the Christian world, and in this convention declare at once that never, never again, *under any circumstances,*
shall there be a war between Christian nations?

Yes, indeed, why not?†

For this reason:—The Christian nations are capitalist
nations managed for the capitalist class. Each great Christian nation knows that it must find a foreign market for the
EMBARRASSINGLY LARGE SURPLUS of goods which its capitalists do not consume or invest and its working class is, by the
wage-system, not permitted to consume. Each and all these
nations know that this FOREIGN MARKET MUST BE FOUND
OPENED AND PROTECTED—with Christian sword and cannon

---

* Swinburne: "A Word for the Country."

† See Index: "The Hague Peace Conference."

if need be—in order that the capitalists of these countries may make more profits. Indeed, when markets must thus be had, Christians, Jews, Mohammedans, Buddhists, Confucians—with lust for profits—trample down all things fine, sand-bag everything noble, spit in the face of every man of peace, and shout, "Stand back! Stand back! Bring on the cannon! Business is business! There is no sentiment in business! To hell with the mollycoddles! We are in business for *profits!*"

With noble exceptions, at such times Christian preachers, priests, and bishops of the warring nations, with the swagger and pomp of cheap "fighting parsons," step briskly to the front of the stage, consecrate the cannon, "bless" the sword, baptize the butcher, and, on both sides, with pious savagery scream to the "God of battles," also to the "God of peace," for victory "in this *righteous* war," for victory in this "armed *crusade for Christ,*" for victory in this "glorious effort to *advance His kingdom,*"—always, always, of course, some lofty name, some swelling phrase, to veil the huge and pious murder.

Sacred wholesale assassinations—for the Peaceful Jesus' sake!

Even every massacre of the peaceful Jews in Russia is sanctioned by the Greek Christian Church,—and the Roman and the Protestant churches and the Christian governments of the world do *not* unite and demand peace for the peaceful Jews.

"God moves in a *mysterious* way his wonders to perform," we are piously taught.

Mysterious. Very.

But it is *not* mysterious why pro-war preachers, priests, and bishops are not slaughtered on the battleline and then eaten by buzzards when the cannon's feast is finished. These men are too intelligent—too cunning—for the buzzards' banquet.

Every distinguished professional butcher in modern times has been a "member in good standing" in his denomination and his blood-stenched fame is recited with pride.

That mysterious?

All soldiers are blessed as they march away to "Death's feast."

The preacher consecrates the cut-throat.

The bayonet is prepared—with prayer—to be thrust into the bowels of the toilers.

All wars are somehow pronounced "mysteriously the will of God"; and the cannoneers who hurl shot and shell into a city or village and cannonade helpless women and children —these are "the servants of the Lord"—mysteriously.

And thus to the appalling music of the cannon's roar the Cross is dragged down into the bloody mire where men die cursing the preachers safe at home who helped trick them to the hell called war. And thus, too, the spirit of the great fraternal Christ is banished from the lives of the be- trayers and the betrayed—and Christ is crucified anew.

Because it is profitable.

Thus in all Christian nations the Cross dips obsequiously to the red-throated cannon—and to the cash-register.

Business is business; the rulers rule; and gold is God.

That is, under capitalism.

Reader, name one "civil" war or one international war of modern times powerfully, effectively hindered by the Church of the Man of Peace.*

Just one.

But no matter! Since long before the slaughter of the Carpenter our brothers of the working class have furnished the blood and tears—cheap blood, cheap tears,—about forty cents a day for American "regulars" in the "year of our Lord" 1910.

Learn this, you toilers: The capitalists have the preacher cornered and shackled. The working class must be their own saviors from the horrors of war. In Chapter Ten I shall explain how this can be done and even now begins to be done by the working class.

---

* See Chapter Four, Section One.

But the workers should learn from history and keep distinctly in mind this great lesson: With noble individual exceptions the ministry, the religious leaders, have in times past *defended chattel slavery* with its unspeakable horrors for the *working* class; and have *defended serfdom* with its hell for the *working* class; and have ignobly defended all Christian national and international wars of modern capitalism praying on both sides to the "God of battles" for "glorious victory" regardless of the blood spurting from a million wounds in the torn breast of the *working* class.

The path of human progress in modern times is steep and slippery with the carcasses and blood of the socially despised working men—and the Church has not *defied* the cash-register idolater and *demanded* peace.

Unrebuked, right proudly the cash-register devotee, the business man, blurts out: *"There is no sentiment in business."*

That proposition, "No sentiment," is enough to make a cannibal blush. Yet that doctrine is at the heart of capitalism.

If there is no sentiment in business, then there is no brotherhood in business, for brotherhood is a sublime and beautiful sentiment.

And if there is no brotherhood in business there can not be Christian fellowship in business.

Thus business banishes Christ and the Cross retreats before the onslaughts of the cash-register.

But it is actually and sadly *true* that business, competitive business, is too little and belittling, too wolfishly fierce, for deep and loyal brotherhood. This is also true of the great *class* competition, the *class struggle,* the embittering clash of *industrial class interests.*

And where there is no deep and loyal brotherhood, no great *socializing unity of interest* stretching from the centre to the rim of society, including all, *peace is impossible.*

Thus it is that in the great competitive business world, like quarrelsome dogs, every business man's hand is against every other business man's hand competing in the "same line," to "put him out of business" and thus "get more business."

Thus local neighbors are at war in a Christless scramble for business.

Thus nations also, fiercely struggling for markets and territory, are at war—commercial war—sometimes needing sword and cannon. (See pp. 40-41.)

Now, notice: Christian business men in this brotherless, Christless scramble called business *must have the scramble made "respectable."* For this purpose the minister is most serviceable. The business men need the minister—"need him in their business"—to consecrate and sanctify the ways and means, even the sword, the cannon and the vast human slaughterings called war.

"Put up thy sword," said Christ.

"Business is business! Bless the butcher! Grind sharp the sword," commands the business man.

But "no man can serve two masters."

Here the minister, just like the "common working man," is face to face with the MOST DOMINEERING FACT AND FORCE IN HUMAN LIFE; namely, ECONOMIC NECESSITY. The preacher and the plumber, the rabbi and the sweat-shop tailor, the priest and the hod-carrier—these must *live;* they must *"get a living."* But the capitalist controls the opportunities to "get a living." The "common working man" is embarrassed. The minister is also embarrassed—*tho he may be—and very often is—one of the noblest men in the world, he is embarrassed.* This ECONOMIC force grips them both like a vise. They must live. To live they must kneel before the king—the kings in industry.

OBEY OR STARVE.

The inevitable follows:

The plain common working man and the haughty and cultivated minister—both of them—bow their heads and submit their necks to the cruel yoke, the yoke of capitalism.

The rulers rule.

Capitalism, internationally, is—for capitalists—a struggle for a strangle hold among jealously competing, unneighborly neighbors, a struggle for business.

Capitalism thus becomes a stupid snarl of "foreigners"—to each nation all other nations are "foreigners."

And thus the world is petty, unsocial, "foreign,"—a war always possible and threatening between "foreigners,"—the unfortunate ministers, most of them, not to the contrary.

BUT, READER, THERE ARE NO "FOREIGNERS"—FOR ME AND MY INTERNATIONAL FRIEND CHRIST AND MY INTERNATIONAL COMRADES.

Then why should a group of Christless, plutocratic political crooks and flunky-champagne-guzzlers in Paris or Tokio, in Berlin or London, in Madrid or Washington—why should any such group of political bunco-steerers by a pompous declaration of assassination officially decide for you and me and our brothers of some so-called "foreign nation"—that we working class brothers are "enemies" and that we must lay down the instruments of production and take up the weapons of destruction and butcher ourselves by the tens of thousands?

Why should we permit a band of cheap "statesmen" to order us to tear one another's throats like dogs?

Why should *we* fight?

We have no quarrels.

The thing is ridiculous—utterly ridiculous, is it not?

And an equally important question is:—Why should we working class brothers of all the world ever permit any ecclesiastical savages to fan the flames of international hatred in our souls by means of pious prayers and sermons in favor of war?

Even more ridiculous, isn't it?

Let us refuse to murder. The blood-spilling business is too small for brothers, too savage for socialized men, no matter what their religious faith may be.

Perhaps, brother, you and I do not agree on Christ. But we can be good friends any way, can't we?

Now, I will tell you frankly, the Peaceful Christ seems to me to be so much grander than a war-preaching preacher, so much nobler than a flunky "fighting parson," that he gains my sincere admiration. Such a great brave brother he was.

Christ was the most defiant preacher that ever walked the earth or flashed as a character conception in the human brain.

Christ, the historical revolutionary Christ, or Christ, splendid creation of imagination, or Christ divine—whichever or whatever he was—he wins and compels my gratitude:

Because he was neither an automaton nor a tool;

Because official ruffians even before his mockery of a trial viciously pronounced him an "undesirable citizen";

Because "leading citizens" could not use him, could not rent his influence;

Because he scorned the opportunity to become "successful in life" in the contemptible rôle of intellectual prostitute;

Because he despised the lusting devotees of Mammon;

Because he forgave the "duly convicted" crucified thieves and whipped the unconvicted bankers from the temple;

Because with stinging words he lashed the whited sepulchres called "the very *best* people";

Because he was so fine and great he promptly became extremely unpopular with coarse and savage little "prominent people";

Because he was so gentle and terrible that the noisy and cruel "law-abiding leading citizens" in their swaggering ignorance and malignance decided he was an anarchist and proceeded to shut off his free speech;

Because he was neither narrow enough to be national nor ignorant enough to be orthodox;

Because on the last morning of his life he so proudly despised the official political bull-pups who teased him and insulted him—and could not understand him;

Because, on the same morning, he so finely scorned the bigoted little orthodox holy bullies who hindered him and wolfishly screamed for the Carpenter's blood;

Because children charmed him;

Because the humble "common people" swarmed around him and loved him—in spite of their pious and orthodox "spiritual advisers";

Because he scorned the "dignity" of some men and saw the Dignity of Man;

Because he came from the bottom up and never forgot— *never hesitated to defend*—"even the least of these," including his sad, shamed, outlawed sister;

Because he did not whimper and cringe when certain religiously eminent small souls spat in the face of the World Soul;

Because the great wholesome brother was a true Social Soul, loving all mankind;

Because, especially because, he so finely forgave the thoughtless working class soldiers who mocked him, forced a thorn crown upon his head, drove nails through his flesh, sneered at his agonies, and thrust a spear into their working class Brother Carpenter;

Because he said, "Put up thy sword," regarded no man as "foreigner," and died for International Fraternalism.

A Social Man.

A Sample.

I love him.

Let us, too, brother, be social and international.

Let us bury the hatchet, break the rifle, spike the cannon, despise the sword, accept the Sermon on the Mount for its spirit of peace, and scorn any sermon that urges us to war against our own class brothers. Let us detest any sermon that stirs and fosters the tiger within us and arrests our social development.

Social development.

"Social development," did I say? Yes, reader, that is what we need, social development.

Man on his long march upward—up from the jungle— has been impeded by a heavy burden—in his blood. He has carried the menagerie—in his veins.

Here permit me to use a very homely metaphor, a figure of speech neither to your taste nor to mine, yet needed and defensible:

In its social development the world is hindered by too much bull-pup.

A bull-pup is at a disadvantage—socially. His social development is stunted. The malignant wrinkles of his prize-fighter face obstruct his vision. His outlook is restricted. Thus his notion of the world is small. Hence the bull-pup is narrow, local and unsocial. Being socially local and mean —and therefore petty and pugnacious—he enjoys a fight. In the world of dogs he is a tough, a "rough-rider" and a "war-lord." All other dogs are "foreigners," "guilty," and "undesirable citizens."

Peace is too large and fine for the bull-pup. War is "dee-lightful," "just bully"—for the bull-pup.

Thus even the humble dog world is worried and hindered by the socially narrow and pugnaciously strenuous bull-pups —"great" and "successful," in their estimation.

Thus littleness and localism hinder even brutes in their social development.

And it is thus in the human world also.

Confucius was a great man.

But Confucius is hindered—hindered by littleness—little Confucians.

Christ? Christ is great, fascinatingly, commandingly great.

But Christ is hindered—hindered by the pettiness of pugnacity, hindered by littleness, little Christians.

Let us be brothers? Let us have peace?

Not yet. We can't. We must wait. Strange, but true, we must wait for the most reasonable thing in the world.—peace.

Peace is on the program—next number.

From the warring tribes of the long, long ago, up, up, upward to the federated races of the world,—that is the first number on the program—a long steep climb for the human mind, up, up through the hundreds of centuries, a half million years consumed in expanding the human heart, in refining the human affections, in strengthening the social vision to see all the way 'round the world, in widening the diameter of Society, in creating, revising, and re-creating a definition of "Brother,"—the race generating the Social Man, the World Patriot, the International Citizen.

The arithmetic of history—Given: Life. To find, or produce, or deduce, the god, the god of aspiring intelligence, the god of a socialized race. A puzzling problem—how to subtract the brute, add the brother and multiply the brains; how to proceed to the next number on the program—Peace; how to move our bruised lips to say: "Put up thy sword. We are of one blood."

We are hindered.

Brotherhood and peace—divinely high thought!

But, alas! the thought is too high for low-browed strenuosity of the tough-rider type; the thought is too large and fine for the poor brain of a bull-dog or a human bully or a socially blunted holy man or any other breed of stunted runts.

The strutting, thin-brained rooster in the farmyard crows, "Hurrah for this our very own dunghill, the finest filth pile on earth." Thus this spurred and feathered patriot virtuously cultivates his vanity by boisterously challenging "the enemy" in the neighboring farmyards.

"Hurrah for our tribe," screams the savage—patriotically.

"Hurrah for our village of Squeedunk," yells the local human shrimp. More patriotism.

"Hurrah for our great city!" squeals the boastfully "metropolitan" small man sweltering in unspeakable corruptions.

"Hurrah for the nation—right or wrong!" yelps the patriotic national mongrel.

And thus these socially puny creatures, these social runts, stand ready, as it were, to "patriotically" throw carbolic acid at their national and international neighbors.

"Hurrah for Mankind, hurrah for Life!" finely calls the socially developed man, the Increasing International Man.

Really, reader, the narrow-visioned provincial, the local sniveling, the social shrimp, the pugnacious nationalist, the racial bigot, and the stunted, sacerdotal manlet—really, these unsocial people are, as yet, too local and little and narrow for a federated world, for an internationally social Christ.

Really, these unsocial human runts can not sincerely and effectively carry "to all the world" any magnificent social gospel of "peace on earth, good will toward all men," and "make of one blood all nations"—even tho' they be baptized.

Now please do not misunderstand me. I do not belittle the rite of baptism.

But baptism has no effect on a declaration of war by an extremely narrow local bull-dog, whether he be a humble canine wearing a brass collar, or a strutting puny human being wearing a "Prince Albert," or a lard-and-tallow millionaire worshipping a cash-register. None of these is emotionally and socially fine. As usual, the world is embarrassed when trying to make a silk purse of a sow's ear.

A Christian assassin mounted on the throne of Russia remains an assassin—in spite of his baptism.

A Christian bully elevated to the throne of the German Empire or to American presidential distinctions, remains a pugnacious ruffian, spoiling for trouble, always "not only willing but anxious to fight."

Sacerdotal ceremonies have no effect on a leopard's spots, a tiger's stripes, a bull-pup disposition, or a cash-register ambition.

War among brothers is civil war.

All men are brothers.

Therefore all war is civil war.

But peace is hindered by local littleness—especially by the belittling, localizing effects of the sacred cash-register and its smaller unsocial time-servers.

The Confucian capitalist, the Christian capitalist, and all other kinds of capitalists of the whole world stand behind their blessed and belittling cash-registers, plot in their Wall Street dens, cheating, cheating, cheating—and snarling at one another. And this unsocial snarling is called business, and this Christless business is morally legitimated, "made respectable," by too many unsocialized "spiritual advisers." Some of the holy men are finely social, nobly large, splendidly fearless; and these great social souls refuse, proudly refuse, to "sic" or urge the "dogs of war." But unfortunately these truly greater holy men are too few and they are threatened and bullied by the over-fed, fat-pursed industrial Caesars in the best pews of the house of God; and, moreover, these greater holy men are abused and outvoted in the church conventions by their less developed brethren, if they oppose a war—especially if there is a "national crisis."

And there is always a "national crisis" imminent when greater markets must be had and new territory is to be scrambled for by the capitalists of the world.

Whenever there is a "crisis on," whenever the cash-register captains, the politicians and unsocial "spiritual leaders" believe, or announce, that there is a "crisis upon us,"—at such times Christ, the peaceful, nobly social Christ, is thrust to the rear of the stage and forced to be silent, while the "fighting parsons" and the politicians and the money-mongers and some glory-hunting buccaneers rush to the front of the stage and scream for war—a "patriotic war."

And more and more the actual necessity for a larger foreign market produces a "crisis."

It is coming—another war.*

Then for brotherhood—a sneer.

Then for the man of peace—a scornful "Mollycoddle!"

Then for Christ—coarse jeers.

Then for markets, for profits—blood and tears.

Then will the malignant manikins patriotically and profitably shout for "national honor."

Then Christ must wait.

Peace must wait.

Brotherhood must wait.

International federation, social grandeur, the human race, must wait.

All these must wait for the poor little fellows to get the emotions of the prize-fighter and the savage heat and hate of the bull-pup out of their veins; all these must wait, too, while the cash-register devotee and his man Friday get the money—and "divide up."

---

* See Index: "Another War."

Possibly, reader, some of these paragraphs seem unfair.

Very well; perhaps it will seem fair to let a *clergyman* speak with frankness on this matter. Here following are some paragraphs from a powerful book, *The Moral Damage of War,* by the fearless Dr. Walter Walsh, a distinguished and eloquent clergyman of Dundee, Scotland.* In the chapter, "The Moral Damage of War to the Preacher," Dr. Walsh speaks to his clerical brethren with the courage and directness of the ancient Jewish prophets. Here are some illustrative paragraphs (reprinted with kind permission of publishers):

"The belief that Christianity is incompatible with war, was designed to abolish war . . . was held by all the Christians of the first three centuries. . . . Christianity is the religion of peace. How then is Christendom still at war? We naturally turn to the professional teachers of religion for an answer.

"The paid teachers of Christendom are numbered by hundreds of thousands: Priests, bishops, ministers, catechists and so on,— while their lay helpers—deacons, church-wardens, elders, Sunday-school teachers, missioners, lay preachers—may be counted by the million and *it is incomprehensible that war should continue to exist in Christendom unless by first demoralizing these formers of religious opinion.* The fact also that all Christian countries alike compete in the equipment and spoils of war can be understood only as a proof of a corrupt or undeveloped conscience. The reason why Christendom is today in such straits and that so many countries wallow in debt, waste, ignorance, covetousness, poverty and misery unspeakable, is chiefly that the paid teachers of Christianity with their hosts of unpaid assistants have capitulated to the war god. . . . War is never pure, but is hell; and it can never be permissible to inaugurate heaven by the help of hell. . . . Here and there a smaller Elijah refuses to bow the knee to the military Baal, a faithful Micaiah, tho' smitten on the mouth, continues to bear his testimony to the true significance of the gospel. . . . 'For centuries the church met the hostility of a pagan and unscrupulous world and never flinched. . . . No revenge or bitterness marred the security of her soul.' . . . The appalling nature of the preacher's defection is seen by the contrast with the magnificent opportunity war time affords him, than which prophet or apostle never had a greater. . . . *A trial of strength between conflicting nations is also a trial of the preacher's moral character;* the height of noble opportunity to

---

* Published by Ginn and Company, New York.

which it lifts him has its counterpart in the base opportunism to which he may descend. He may temporize like a politician. . . . He may accept the carnal policies of the parliament as limitations of his gospel and hang his head like a dumb dog when statesmen fling Christianity incontinently out of the house of legislation. He may soothe his conscience with the lie that war is a matter of politics, having nothing to do with the preaching of the gospel, and slide gently down into the dastard, blind equally to *the humor and the atheism of his position.* Between the churches which cry, "No politics in the gospel!" and parliaments which cry, "No gospel in politics!" the Son of Man is hard put to it to maintain a footing in modern affairs. . . . Few invocations to the Prince of Peace are heard [in time of war], but many to the God of battles. . . . The conscience [of ecclesiasticism] lies limp and voiceless before the uplifted sword, bribed by gold, paralyzed by fear . . . shielding itself. . . . The federated tribes of Israel slink to their tents, murmuring some safe platitudes about peace and prayer meetings whilst the world triumphs, the flesh riots and the devil grins with infinite content. . . . It were hard to say which is worse,—the silence of the pulpit or the timidity or wickedness of its speech when it does find tongue. . . . A dumb dog is bad, but a bloodhound baying upon the trail is worse. . . . What is to be said of a preacher, who, when the war spirit and the peace spirit are trembling in the balance, either can not speak or speaks only to blaspheme his own gospel? . . . *It can not be doubted that the church, exerting herself in accordance with her principles, could make all bloodshed impossible, and could have averted every war of recent times;* yet on many such occasions the multitude of ministers stir no finger, preach no sermon, sign no petition, sound no note that the government, willing enough to know the temper of a nation, can interpret as hostile to their project. . . . The appalling truth has to be faced: that the church, contrary to every expectation that might be formed from her principles and the character of the Being she worships, is always, as a whole, for the war of the day. It is true that when peace is the popular cry, the preachers are also for peace. If there is a peace crusade on hand which excites the shallow enthusiasms of the fashionables, the preachers will also catch the excitements of the hour; but when the white banner yields to the red, the pastors beat the drums for the fighters as furiously as they had previously denounced the savagery of armed conflict. . . . Organized Christianity divests herself of her robe of righteousness and her garments of meek humility to clothe herself in khaki. . . . A thousand pulpits are manned by Bible bullies who cite every obsolete and bloody precedent of the wars of the Jews and show themselves destitute of the elementary humanities and of the faculties necessary to discriminate between Judaism two thousand years before Christ and

Christianity two thousand years after him. . . . What can mankind do with a church that peels itself like a pugilist and reveals the murdering pagan instead of the martyred Christian; which for carnal reasons cancels the Sermon [on the Mount], contradicts the Beatitudes, flatly denies the gospel, repudiates every specific Christly ideal, and unseats Jesus in order to elevate Mars to the throne of conscience? . . . At frequent intervals the cross with its suffering victim recedes and out of the blood-red mist emerges the foul idol of war erect on his crimson chariot. . . . The sanctification of revenge is, indeed, the vilest function performed by a war-poisoned, blood-stained church. . . . It is thus that the masses are kept from seeing the degenerate nature of the thing. . . . Their pastors lead them into the blood-red fields of Jahveh when the politicians give the word, and into the green pastures of the Naza-rene only when there is no national scheme of murder and robbery afoot. . . . The churches as they are today can not prevent war. Their palsied lips can not echo, however feebly, the words of the master, 'Put up again thy sword into its place!' There is not spiritual power left in organized Christianity to insure the sub-stitution of reason for brute force. . . . Alas! it has hitherto been impossible to get Christianity to obey Christ."*

That is the language of a brave Christian preacher. In connection with the reverend Doctor Walsh's chastisement of the church in the morning of the twentieth century it is in-teresting to read on the same subject the words of a philos-opher of the eighteenth century, Voltaire.†

"This universal rage which devours the world. . . . The most wonderful part of this infernal enterprise [war] is, that each chief of murderers causes his colors to be blest, and solemnly invokes God before he goes to exterminate his neighbors. . . . A certain number of orators are everywhere paid to celebrate these murderous days. . . . All of them speak for a long time, and quote that which was done of old in Palestine. . . . The rest of the year these people declaim against vices. . . . All the united vices of all ages and places will never equal the evils produced by a single campaign. Miserable physicians of souls! you exclaim for five quarters of an hour on some pricks of a pin, and say nothing on the malady which tears us into a thousand pieces. . . . Can there be anything more horrible throughout nature?"

And now let us get at this matter from the point of view

---

* Italics mine. G. R. K.
† *Voltaire's Philosophical Dictionary.*

of a political economist, a really great economist, John A. Hobson—who puts the case thus:*

"When has a Christian nation ever entered on a war which has not been regarded by the official priesthood as a sacred war? In England the State Church has never permitted the spirit of the Prince of Peace to interfere when statesmen and soldiers appealed to the passions of race-lust, conquest and revenge. Wars, the most insane in origin, the most barbarous in execution, the most fruitless in results have never failed to get the sanction of the Christian Churches. . . . *There is no record of the clergy of any Church having failed to bless a popular war, to find reasons for representing it as a crusade.*"

The following lines from a British philosopher, Frederic Harrison,† are to the point for the workingman's instruction:

"The official priests of the old faiths accept without questioning the authorized judgment of the political government. They are engaged . . . in calling upon their God of Battles (can it be, their God of Mercy?) to keep the British soldiers—the invaders, the burners of villages, the hangmen of [native] priests—in his good and holy keeping. . . . A system of slavery prepares the slave-holding caste for any inhumanity that may seem to defend it. . . . If it hardens our politicians, it degrades our churches. The thirst for rule, the greed of the market, and the saving of souls, all work together in accord. The Churches approve and bless whilst the warriors and the merchants are adding new provinces to empire; they have delivered the heathen to the secular arm. . . . Christianity in practice, as we know it now, for all the Sermon on the Mount, is the religion of aggression, domination, combat. It waits upon the pushing trader and the lawless conqueror; and with obsequious thanksgiving it blesses his enterprise."

Who, indeed, shall deliver us from war?
Our pastors?
Hardly.
The pastors' economic masters will not permit them to do so.
Tho' the machine guns mow down a million of the world's choicest working men, pile up windrows of human carcasses

* *The Psychology of Jingoism*, pp. 41, 133.
† *National and Social Problems*, pp. 252-53.

and desolate the huts, flats, hovels and "homes" of the poor; tho' ten million pairs of calloused hands of agonizing working class women be stretched toward well-fed, comfortable pastors, begging for a *united, effective declaration* against war; tho' these ten million humble working class mothers, their eyes streaming with tears, on their knees beseech the "holy men of God" to unitedly cry aloud against the accursed "Death's feast" where their dear ones are devoured; tho' multitudes of little working class children in mute despair dread the roar of the belching cannon that slay their fathers and brothers; still the pastors (most of them) will "stand by the administration" in any and all wars, as usual.

"The administration," "the government," under capitalism, is simply the *executive committee of the capitalist class.*

The capitalist class are internationally struggling for the world market.

In these international struggles the capitalists need the support of public opinion.

Public opinion can be created and controlled by the pastor.

The pastor must therefore be controlled by the capitalist.

The campaign begins—to capture the market and the minister.

The soldier goes to war and the capitalist goes to church.

The soldier takes a gun, the capitalist takes gold.

The soldier slays.

The capitalist prays—by proxy.

Being "the will of God" it is, of course, "mysterious."

The capitalist occupies the very best pew in the house of God—and lays beautiful bankbills in the collection plate.

The minister is embarrassed—and impressed.

The pastor and his master divide up.

The war? Isn't *war hell?*

It beats hell.

But it is "all for the best"—mysteriously.

With conscience "seared as with a hot iron" the preacher joins the politician; and the precious pair unite their rented voices in patriotic melody in support of the capitalist class.

Brother,—you of the working class,—Jew, Roman Catholic, Greek Catholic, Protestant, peaceful Buddhist or peaceful Confucian, or what else,—wherever you are, whatever you are in religion, worshipping, searching, groping through the universe for God, worship as you prefer, worship whom you prefer: I do not seek to break your church allegiance. But, sir, to save your life, to save your own wife's tears, to defend your own children, to protect your own working class, I do wish to have you realize *distinctly* that:—

The working class must draw the bayonet from its own breast. So far as *war* is concerned the working class must band together and stand together against war. The working class must themselves protect the working class against the industrial system through which they are *robbed and betrayed.*

The workers of the world need a political party of their own class—and as wide as the world, International, and committed to *justice and therefore to peace.*

Listen to the confession of the editor of a very powerful capitalist newspaper:

"It is significant that the Socialists of different races, and speaking different tongues, strangers in blood and customs, in Germany, France, Great Britain, Austria, and Italy, constitute the *one great peace party of the world.*"*

Listen again—to the best-known and the best loved Christian woman in the United States, Miss Jane Addams, of Hull House, Chicago:†

"The Socialists are making almost the sole attempt to preach a morality *sufficiently all-embracing and international* to keep pace with even the material internationalism which has standardized [even] the threads of screws and the size of bolts, so that machines become interchangeable from one country to another. . . . Existing commerce has long ago reached its international stage, but it has been the result of business aggression and constantly appeals for military defense and for the forcing of new markets."

You, you who are to be tricked and shot at the factory door

---

* The New York *World*, editorial, August 15, 1907. Italics mine. G. R. K.

† *Newer Ideals of Peace*, pp. 114-15. Italics mine. G. R. K.

and on the battlefield, go to your public library and get *Christianity and the Social Order,* and read there the words of a preacher great enough for the City Temple of London, great enough to be the worthy successor of the world-known Joseph Parker, read the Reverend Dr. R. J. Campbell's splendid tribute to the Socialist Party as the only political party in the world today scorning the belittling jealousies of capitalist statesmen and working effectively for international brotherhood.

Reader, you working class reader, a special word here:

Perhaps your working class neighbor's son is at this moment falling into a patriotic trance, gullibly planning to join the local militia or the standing army or the navy, meditating on butcheries. Go to him. With a firm grasp on his mind (if he has one) wake him, rouse him, from that race-cursing dream, rouse him from the spell that for thousands of years has damned his class. Be kind. Be patient. But—wake him. Wake him for the *world* movement for the *working* class. *Wake him for the war*—the war without a sword, the war without a cannon; the war with a printing press, the war with a book. *Teach him that salvation is through information.* Teach him that the "truth will make him free." In his brain kindle a fire, a divine unrest, a desire that can not die, the desire for peace born of justice.

Otherwise, beware lest your neighbor's son be wheedled at any moment into the militia or the standing army or the navy—*ready* to be consecrated, sanctified, blessed,—for wholesale assassination, *ready* as a militiaman, as a Cossack, as a soldier, to stain his consecrated sword with the blood of his neighbors and brutally—patriotically—laugh at the tears of women and children.

Read to your neighbor the next Chapter: "Now, What Shall We Do About It?"

CHAPTER TEN.

Now What Shall We Do About It?

"No people will toil and sweat to keep a class in idleness unless *cajoled* or *compelled* to do so. . . . There are various devices by means of which a body of persons may sink their fangs into their fellows and subsist upon them. Slavery . . . is the primary form of the parasitic relation. By modifying this into serfdom the parasitic class, without the least abating its power of securing its nourishment from others, places itself in a position more convenient to it and less irritating to the exploited. . . . Finally, the institution of property is so shaped as to permit a slanting exploitation under which a class is able to live in idleness. The parasitic class is always a ruling class, and utilizes as many as it can of the means of control."—Professor Edward A. Ross, Department of Sociology, University of Wisconsin.*

"The various institutions, political, ecclesiastical, professional, industrial, etc., including the government, are devices, means, gradually brought into existence, to serve interests that develop within the State."—Professor Albion W. Small, Head of Department of Sociology, University of Chicago.†

"The non-industrial or *parasitic* classes are often the most active. . . . They are wonderfully successful in *creating the belief* that they are the most important of all the social elements."—Dr. Lester F. Ward, Department of Sociology, Brown University.‡

The preceding chapters have, it is hoped, been of some assistance to the reader in realizing in what unqualified contempt the working class are held in our boasted civilized society,—how utterly the working class are tricked and betrayed, brutalized and bled, degraded and despised, robbed, starved and stung,—their flesh torn, their blood spilt, their bodies tossed to the buzzards and grave-worms, and even the widows and orphans insulted with thirty dirty pieces of silver in payment for the life and love and joy lost in war. Having tried to make this, and more, clear, now let me explain "what to do about it."

---

* *Social Control*, pp. 376-79. Italics mine. G. R. K.

† *General Sociology*, p. 233.

‡ *Dynamic Sociology*, Vol. I., p. 582. Italics mine. G. R. K.

What, indeed, shall the working class do to rid themselves of the curse called war?

We can do nothing, absolutely nothing, with sweeping effectiveness, till we understand the industrial structure and purpose of the present order of society, and, as a class, also understand the art of self-defense—political and industrial class-defense.

Repeatedly in preceding chapters I have written of two classes.

Are there indeed two classes?

Get distinctly in mind the three following propositions stating the three largest facts of all concerning the present order of society:

First Proposition: In the present capitalist form society is divided into two classes, two industrial classes: the capitalist class and the working class.

Second Proposition: Industrially, society is organized and managed for the *special* benefit of *part* of society—for one class, the capitalist class.

Third Proposition: Each of these two classes has industrial interests *as a class;* these class interests conflict; and there is, therefore, as a part of and because of the *class* form of society, a constant class conflict, a *class struggle*.

Let me try to make these three propositions clear. Please note carefully the exact wording of the propositions to be explained.

The explanation,—first proposition:

Of course you wish to live and be comfortable. To live and be comfortable you must consume useful things. But before you can consume useful things they must be produced. And since this is true of all the members of society it is readily seen that the FIRST task of society, the primary social function, is production.

Production, industry, is the foundation of society.

Now, in performing this industrial work, in doing this first thing, we use raw materials, mines, forests, fields, mills, factories, tools, machinery, railways, etc., etc.; and these

things are called the MEANS OF PRODUCTION. We make use
of these things, these means of production, in *applying our
labor-power*—that is, in producing the things society wishes
to consume.

But:—

One class privately own the coal mines and iron mines
and buy labor-power;

The other class work in the coal mines and iron mines
and sell labor-power.

One class privately own lumber forests and marble
quarries, and buy labor-power;

The other class work in the lumber forests and marble
quarries, and sell labor-power.

One class privately own cotton mills, steel mills, and
flour mills, etc., and buy labor-power.

The other class work in cotton mills, steel mills, and flour
mills, etc., and sell labor-power.

One class privately own railroads and buy labor-power;

The other class work on railroads and sell labor-power.

Or, to say it briefly,

One class, the *capitalist* class, privately OWN the chief
material means of production—and BUY labor-power.

The other class, the *working* class, USE the chief material
means of production—and SELL labor power.

Surely you can see that there are two *industrial classes.*

There are, under capitalism, not only two industrial classes,
but also two social classes. Industrial classes become social classes.

Johan Kaspar Bluntschli, one of Germany's most eminent writers
on political science, has this to say:

"Classes have very often been founded on the basis of property.
In these constitutions . . . property becomes the determining political
force, and citizens are valued by amount of their income. . . . The
Proletariate . . . consists mainly of the waste of other classes, of
those fractions of the population who, by their isolation and their
poverty, have no place in the established order of society." [That is,
they are in no *commanding relation* to the industrially vital property.]*

---

* See *The Theory of the State,* Bk. II., Chs. 17, 18,

"Conversely, social rank depends on economic conditions; the state is made . . . conservative . . . by the economic interests at its foundation. . . .

"Perhaps its [property's] most important social effect has come to be the fact that the possession of property is so generally the basis of social differentiation. In earlier times, physical force, later, institutions of caste, were the basis of differentiation in society; wealth is the most universally recognized source of power, so that social rank is often determined by the possession of wealth."
—Professor Fairbanks, Yale University.*

And now the *second* proposition: Are these industries and the other industries really operated for the *special benefit* of *part* of society? The answer is clear in the following illustration:

If the profits on all these industries should, during the next twelve months, *rise two billion dollars higher than usual,* would the *wages* of the workers engaged in these industries be *increased* in *that proportion?* Most certainly they would not. You know very well they would not. But why not? Simply because these industries, like all other industries, are, under capitalism, operated for the special benefit of those, the capitalist class, who privately own these industries and buy labor-power, and, by this arrangement, live on profits,—on surplus value.†

And, finally, the third proposition: Do the industrial interests of these two industrial classes fundamentally *conflict?* Perhaps the answer will be clear in the following homely illustration:

If you are selling a horse, you wish to sell him for—say $300. But the buyer of the horse wishes to buy the horse for, say, $150.

Clearly there is a conflict of interests between the buyer of the *horse* and the seller of the *horse.*

A wage-earner selling labor-power wishes to sell, say, eight hours labor-power for $6.

The capitalist employer buying labor-power wishes to buy,

---

* *Introduction to Sociology*, pp. 132-36.
† See Chapter Three, The Explanation.

say, nine hours labor-power for $2.50—in order to get the surplus value—that fascinating *surplus*.

Thus there is a fundamental conflict between the industrial interests of this buyer of labor power and the industrial interests of this seller of labor-power.

And it is just so with the two industrial classes.

There is a fundamental conflict of industrial interests between the employer class buying labor-power and the working class selling labor-power.

Between these two industrial classes there is a struggle, a class struggle—to defend their conflicting industrial interests.

This class struggle takes on many different forms—but it is *always* the same thing down at the bottom—a class struggle *in industry*.

The three propositions explained above are most important. A clear understanding of these three propositions always—always—revolutionizes the *political* thinking of the working class man, or woman, who has not, before, understood them. These three truths destroy old political prejudices and customs, cut the reins by which the political tricksters misguide the workers, clear the air of "hot air," reveal the blind alleys of old party politics, point the road to power and freedom for the working class, and make a rock-bottom foundation for a working class political philosophy and policy and tactics.

The capitalist class (who rule and ruin the toilers) regard these three truths as more dangerous than any other, or all other, teachings that ever reach the working class mind. It is to the capitalists' interest that the workers should not learn these three truths. But it is to the interest of the working class that the working class should learn these three truths.

With these three primary facts of present society clearly in mind let us proceed.

In addition to their powerful position as capitalist OWNERS OF THE MEANS OF PRODUCTION, the capitalist class have three *special advantages* over the working class in this class struggle:

(1)   The capitalist class are more *class conscious* than the working class are—at present.   That is, the capitalists more *distinctly realize* that, as capitalists, they *constitute a class*—with *class interests* to defend.

(2)   The capitalists, because they are more class conscious, are, naturally, more *class loyal* than the working class are—at present.   In obedience to the *biological law of self-preservation,* a *class,* as well as an individual, will defend themselves, as a class—that is, will be class loyal—in proportion as they are class conscious, or in proportion as they are aware of and understand the interests of their class.   Tho' the capitalists understand that they are a class with class interests, they are always cooing softly to all workers who are ignorant enough to listen, cooing sweetly about "no classes," "all in the same boat," "harmony of interests," "Capital and Labor are brothers," etc.

(3)   The capitalists *study* tactics of class warfare—tactics of industrial struggle, far more than the working class do—at present.   Being more class conscious and therefore more class loyal and consequently more eager, as a class, for self-defense, the capitalist class naturally study more patiently the ways and means for their own class defense.   And *because they do study more they really know more*—at present —about politics, about the game called the class struggle, about the art of self-defense, *class defense in industry.**

In all the modern forms of this unhappy class struggle, one phase of which is called war, the capitalist class are awake and watchful, united and victorious—seated in the saddle of power at the head of the procession; and the working class are drowsy and confused, divided and defeated—limp-

---

* "Classes differ in readiness to twist social control to their own advantage. . . . In general, the more distinct, knit together, and self-conscious the influential minority, the more likely is social control to be colored with class selfishness."—Professor E. A. Ross, Department of Sociology, University of Wisconsin, *Social Control,* p. 86.

ing afoot and ridiculous at the tail end of the grand march of the world's affairs.

All great military leaders in all wars—in all struggles—in all time have always used the two following tactics:

FIRST: Divide the enemy, if possible, and have them crush one another; or,

SECOND: If circumstances hinder the first tactics, then divide the enemy and crush them one part at a time.

And the captains of industry, the capitalists, right now employ these tactics with success. They themselves band together, but they divide and rule the working class. More class conscious, more class loyal and more studious of the ways and means of struggle than the working class are, the capitalist class proceed as follows:

(A) On the Economic Field the capitalists divide the working class and have them fight one another; and thus the capitalist class are easily able to defeat and fleece the workers all the time, everywhere. The workers, having no part in the ownership of the means of production and being thus divorced from a commanding relation to the economic foundations of society, craftily fooled with false teaching of "capital-and-labor-harmony-of-interests," sore and humble with disappointment, whipped with the lash of hunger, stung to desperation, confused and traduced by bribed pets, spies and traitors,—the workers angrily, blindly, split up into jealous groups, shamefully turn against one another, fight one another, under-bid one another, "scab" on one another, desert one another,—defeat one another. Moreover one part of the working class is flattered and cheaply bribed into volunteering to organize and arm themselves and proudly stand guard over their brothers and against their brothers; and thus the workers spy and inform on one another, arrest one another, jail one another, "bull pen" one another, bayonet one another and shoot one another—under the capitalist system—the present class-labor system.

The working class, of course, are thus easily defeated and robbed industrially.

The busy human bees sting themselves—and lose the honey of their own industry.

And all this is entirely satisfactory to the industrial masters—great and small. (See page 175, [5].)

The rulers rule.

(B) On the Political Field the capitalist class divide the working class into two or more groups and have them politically antagonize themselves, have all the workers all the time politically sting and defeat one another—that is,—have them cancel the political *class*-power of the working class.

One part of the working class vote one capitalist class party ticket, another part of the working class vote another capitalist class party ticket, another another, and so on. Thus millions of the confused working class politically defeat the working class and politically support their industrial masters by politically supporting *political parties* (variously and craftily labeled) *which unanimously stand for the capitalist system.*

Thus the confused working class are easily defeated *politically*—which makes it far easier to rob them *industrially.*

By electing to political power *any* political party standing for *any* form of the capitalist *class*-labor system the working class give the *capitalist class complete control* not only of all the political institutions, but also of all other institutions useable by a class in self-defense; because *the control of political institutions carries with it the legal right to control all other institutions.* In this political confusion, division and eclipse, the working class are as helpless as sheep, and, like sheep, are shorn by their political and industrial shepherds.

And this also is entirely satisfactory to the masters of industry—both great and small.

The rulers rule.

We must learn this: Everywhere, always and under all circumstances the working class must *stand together* in the use of *all* forms of power we have in defense of our *class.*

Having distinctly in mind, then, these important preliminaries,—and especially the fact that whatever we do in self-defense we must do *as a class banded together,* let us consider still further the source—the fountain-head—of the trouble called the class struggle, one form of which is commonly called war.

Society has many functions to perform. In order to perform these functions society must be organized.

Always, it is most important to note, society is organized primarily with respect to the function of wealth production, because the production of things to live on comes before every other social function.

For the performance of this function of wealth production society, developed beyond tribal communism, can be organized in two ways and only two ways:

First Possible Form of Social Organization: On the **Plan of Mutualism**—under which the INDUSTRIAL FOUNDATIONS of society are PUBLIC PROPERTY.

Society can be organized for the performance of this great industrial function of production on the plan of mutualism— *all* of the people having joint-ownership and joint-control of the *chief material means of production,* all of the people of proper age and condition of health performing useful, necessary social service,—there being no industrial master class and no industrial dependent class,—the industrial independence of all the members of society being due to the fact that each is an owner, a joint owner, of the chief material means of production. Every one is thus *commandingly related* to the absolutely necessary *means of life.* With equality in ownership and equality in control of *the things used in getting a living* the people become *equals in opportunity* to get a living,—that is, industrially free. The dominant institution would be the institution of public property in the dominant means used in performing the dominant social function. This would render impossible the domination of society by a *group* or *class* within society—ALL the members of society *would have their feet firmly planted upon the foundations of life,* the means of life, the means of production; and *could not be crowded off the foundations* and robbed by private owners of these foundations.

This form of society may properly be called an industrial democracy.

The *purpose* of this form of society is the *welfare of all* the members of society.

Under this form of society there would be no industrial classes; and therefore, class robbery would *not* be and could *not* be organized, legalized and easy.

Second Possible Form of Social Organization: On the **Plan of Antagonism**—that is, with a *Class*-Labor System —under which the INDUSTRIAL FOUNDATIONS of society are PRIVATE PROPERTY,—privately owned by one class and productively used by the other class.

Society can, indeed, be organized for the performance of this great industrial function of production on the plan of a class-labor system—one part of society being in the strategic position of industrial masters, a ruling class, their mastery being due to the fact that they own as private property the *chief material means of production;*—the other part of society being in the helpless position of industrial dependents, a working class,—their industrial dependence being due to the fact that they have no effective share in the ownership and control of the chief material means of production.

This form of society we may properly call an industrial despotism.

The *purpose* of this form of society is the *special welfare of part* of the members of society.

Under this class-labor form of society, class robbery is *organized, legalized, and easy.*

The *foundation institution of all despotism* is the institution of private property in the economic foundations of society—that is, in the means of production. This is the rock-bottom of organized, legalized and easy robbery of the workers by the shirkers.

Historically society has been organized in a class-labor form in three different ways,—as follows:

(1) CHATTEL SLAVERY, instituted thousands of years ago, was a *class*-labor system,—an organized, legalized opportunity for wholesale class robbery; and under that form of class-labor system, with class robbery legally *arranged* for, class robbery was, of course, respectable, profitable and easy— and therefore inevitable.

Peace was impossible.

The *purpose* of this form of society was *unsocial*.

Under this form of society the masters were in legal possession of the means of production and also of the forts, courts, and legislatures (such as existed); and were thus *in perfect position* to defend and extend their industrial robbery.

The chattel slave owners were thus parasites, aggressive social parasites.

That is admitted.*

(**2**) SERFDOM, common in Europe only a hundred years ago, was also a class-labor system—an organized, legalized opportunity for wholesale class robbery; and under that form of class-labor system, with class robbery legally arranged for, class robbery was, of course respectable, profitable and easy —and therefore inevitable.

Peace was impossible.

The *purpose* of this form of society was *unsocial*.

Under this form the masters were still in legal possession of the means of production and also of the forts, courts and legislatures, and were thus *in perfect position* to defend and extend their industrial robbery.

The landlords-and-masters of the ancient serfs were thus also parasites, aggressive social parasites.

That is admitted.

(**3**) CAPITALISM, the present system, is also a class-labor system, an organized, legalized opportunity for wholesale class robbery; and under this form of class-labor system, with class robbery legally arranged for, class robbery is to-day, of course, altogether respectable, abundantly profitable and temptingly easy—and therefore, naturally, inevitable.

The purpose of the present capitalist form of society is

* See Chapter Eleven for suggestions on the origin of large-scale parasitic aggression; and on the origin and history of the working class and of the class-labor form of society.

the special welfare of only a part of society, the capitalist class, and is, therefore, an unsocial purpose.

Peace is impossible—while capitalism lasts.

Under this form of society the masters, the capitalist class, are in possession of the means of production; that is, in legal possession of the industrial foundations of society, and also in legal control of the arsenals, cannon, soldiers, forts, courts and legislatures, and are thus *in perfect position* to defend and extend their industrial robbery.

The capitalists (*so far as they receive social incomes without rendering equivalent social service*) are thus parasites, aggressive social parasites. (See footnote, pages 298-99.)

That is admitted. That is admitted, explained and condemned even by the President of the American Sociological Society, Dr. Lester F. Ward, Professor of Sociology in Brown University.*

---

* See *Dynamic Sociology*, Vol. I., pp. 581-97; *Psychic Factors in Civilization*, Chapter 24.

Note carefully the quotation on methods of social parasites at the head of the present chapter from Dr. Ross's *Social Control.* Professor Ross is generally recognized as one of the most profound and brilliant writers on Sociology.

It is important to consider, too, that, as a Socialist, Dr. Franklin H. Giddings, Head of Department of Sociology in Columbia University, recognizes the capitalist class's parasitic relation to society. Dr. Giddings is recognized in all the universities of the world as having few equals as a sociologist.

The social parasites of the world will never forgive the learned Socialist, Dr. Thorstein Veblen, recently of the University of Chicago, for writing his bold and astonishing book, *The Theory of the Leisure Class.* The screaming mockeries and glittering pretentions of the "princely-fortune" parasites of capitalism are mercilessly explained by him.

It is noteworthy too that the Editor-in-Chief of the American Journal of Sociology, and Head of the Department of Sociology in the University of Chicago, Dr. Albion W. Small, has for many years been calling attention, in lectures, to the parasitic nature of *one* of the forms of capitalist income, thus: "There is no moral justification for the taking of interest incomes." In his *General Sociology*, pp. 268-69, Dr. Small says: "In the first place, capital produces nothing. It earns nothing." See also his suggestions on

This parasitism of capitalism is easily seen in this way: Wealth equivalent to three hundred and sixty-nine tons of gold ($200,000,000) was given by inheritance to William H. Vanderbilt's eight children.*

If the daughter of John D. Rockefeller, senior, should by inheritance receive one-half of the present six-hundred-million-dollar fortune, she would receive, without rendering any service whatever, wealth equivalent to five hundred and fifty-three tons of gold.

Billions of dollars' worth of mines, railways, factories, forests and other means of production, will, *by inheritance, without function,*—that is, without service—legally fall into the hands of the children of the present capitalist class, whether those children are intelligent, virtuous and industrious, or stupid, vicious and lazy. And thus, like the children of kings and nobles, they will be *in position to win the race of life without running,* in position to *prey upon others* in the struggle for existence, in legal position to procure *substance without service.*

This whole vast scheme of robbery—social parasitism—is "correct" and "proper,"—that is, the process is ELABORATELY LEGALIZED.

Parasitism is robbery.

Parasitism does not cease to be parasitism, nor does robbery cease to be robbery, when, like chattel slavery, it shrewdly gets itself organized, baptized and legalized as an "eminently respectable" and profitable righteous institution for committing perpetual grand larceny.†

Thus at present, as in the past under slavery, as in the past under serfdom, the ruling class, as intelligent parasites, prepare for·class aggression, prepare for class robbery. They

social parasites on page 266, where he is clearly in considerable degree in agreement with Dr. Ward.

Gustavus Myers' *History of Great American Fortunes* is here again commended as an extraordinary record of remarkable social parasitism in American history.

* See *Twenty-Eight Years in Wall Street,* p. 388; by Henry Clews, a very well known banker of Wall Street.

† See Chapter Three, "Explanation"—Surplus.

as a class create and secure their opportunity for legally robbing the producing class by arranging to *control the industrial
structure* of society and thus control the *performance* of the
industrial function—that is, the fundamental function, the
first function, of society.

The ruled and robbed working class must get it in mind
distinctly and unforgetably that the foundation of all class-
labor forms of society, that which gives to *part* of society the
control of society, the foundation upon which industrial parasitism rests, the substructure of all despotism—is the *institution of private* property in the *chief material means of
production.* This institution SPLITS SOCIETY INTO TWO
CLASSES, namely, the producers and the parasites. Political
parties do not create classes. Political parties are a *consequence* of industrial classes and are intended to *defend* industrial classes. Sometimes, to make sure of victory, the
capitalist class have several political parties in the field—
under shrewdly *confusing names.*

A class-labor system, any class-labor system, all class-
labor systems—*provide, by means of institutions,* the LEGAL
conditions and opportunities at the industrial foundations of
society for part of society, a class, to act directly or indirectly as parasites; and it is *entirely natural* that that part
of society, in pursuing their own interests, should use their
opportunity to act like parasites. And it is *entirely natural*
also that there should be resistance by the producers, and
therefore class struggle, class war. Indeed all class-labor
forms of society are industrially so *brutally unjust and therefore so irritating* that the *largest* fact in such societies is an
eternal, internal, infernal conflict of industrial class interests
—an endless civil war in industry, a class war, a class
struggle, *around and around the industrial foundations of
society.* (See pages 167-70.)

Antagonism is thus in the *Structure* of *class*-form society.

This helps to an understanding of past and present conflicts.

It becomes evident that the source of war is to be found
at the industrial foundations of society.

War — war broadly considered — the class struggle, throughout the history of civilized society is no more and no less than the natural aggressive robbery by a part of society provided with an opportunity to rob and the natural resistance of the class that is robbed.

WAR, THE WAR, IS AGGRESSION AND RESISTANCE—ROBBERY AND RESISTANCE—PLUNDER AND PROTEST :—

(1)   The aggressive industrial robbery by one class, and

(2)   The resistance to industrial robbery by the other class.

Not only in the history of civilized peoples everywhere for thousands of years, but also in our own present-day capitalist society everywhere, we see this natural aggression and natural resistance.

The result to-day—as in the past—is struggle, war, class war—between the parasites and the producers.

The war is the *class* war.

Modern "foreign" wars are simply contests between different groups of capitalists (the workers of course doing the fighting and bleeding) *to extend the area of opportunity for industrial class robbery,* and are thus simply *phases* and *extensions* of the class war.

War, then, begins with aggression, continues with aggression; and is at present extended by aggressive foreign wars of industrial or commercial conquest.

To summarize.

(a)   *War, conflict, class aggression and class resistance, are inherent in all class-labor forms of society.*

(b)   *Capitalism is a class-labor form of society.*

(c)   *Therefore, under capitalism there will be, there must be as long as capitalism lasts—class aggression and class resistance, class conflict—class war.*

THE CONCLUSION CANNOT BE DODGED: PEACE IS IMPOSSIBLE—UNDER CAPITALISM.

A million sermons and a million peace talk-fests cannot heal the smarting wounds in the robbed toiler's breast; cannot pull the fangs of the capitalists from the flesh of the toilers, *as long as capitalism lasts.* Organized eloquence can not stop a cannon ball or persuade the rulers to resign.

Under capitalism, as under slavery and serfdom, the employers are in a position *down at the industrial foundations of society* to legally filch their livings from the working class —thus:—the capitalists privately own and privately control the means of production—the things the workers must use in getting a living. Like leeches the capitalist class are thus fastened to the very foundations of society. Here at the industrial foundations of society the industrial blood of society, wealth, is produced. And here are the leeches; and here they are in absolute control of the industrial blood of society. And it is natural, entirely natural, that here, in such position with such opportunity, they should, like leeches, suck this industrial blood, that is, behave like parasites.

The capitalists—with society arranged in this manner— are indeed in position to rob the world wholesale, in position to hold up all the weary producers on all the earth.

This organized, legalized hold-up and the resistance to this hold-up—this is war, *the* war.

The policeman, the militiaman, the cossack and the soldier are all always ready to rush upon the world's stage to serve.

To serve whom?

In all the conflicts due to class-labor forms of society, the ruling class, as already indicated, have always a heavy social fist, a social weapon—an *armed guard,* such as militia, heavy police forces, and standing armies to extend the robbery and to protect the industrial ruling class in their unjust, unsocial position of legalized robbers of the working class. All talk, all hope, all prayer, for peace and quiet and harmony are idle as long as society is unjustly organized—that is, unsocially organized, down at its very foundations, one part of society being in the position of industrial masters, the other part of society being in the position of industrial dependents. The *yawning chasm* in society thus created between the two warring classes—*can never be bridged with wishes, hopes and prayers, nor by peace conferences dominated by profit-stuffed masters and their well-fed intellectual serfs who dare not admit the fundamental cause of war.**

THUS IT BECOMES CLEAR WHAT THE FUTURE HAS FOR THE WORKING CLASS—WHILE CAPITALISM LASTS:

In spite of all the sincere and insincere hopes and prayers for peace there will always be, under capitalism, legalized wholesale plundering of the workers by the capitalist employers—a form of aggressive social parasitism by the employers and *vigorous resistance by the workers in proportion to their realization of the robbery;*—and consequently there will be wage struggles, wage reductions, compulsory under-consumption, "over-production," unemployment, bread lines, soup kitchens, rent riots, evictions, "demand-work" marches,

---

* Andrew Carnegie is a sample of a profit-stuffed tyrant whose parasitic industrial income is tens of millions per year without rendering industrial service, whose legally parasitic heirs, rendering no industrial service, will, like leeches, suck up many millions per year. The audacity of his hypocrisy is typical of his class. In recent international peace congresses Carnegie has been steadily grinning and chattering in the spot light. But study this man for a moment:

(1) In the Homestead industrial civil war, in 1892, Pinkertons received $5 per day and expenses for murdering Carnegie steel workers.

(2) The Carnegie Company furnished the Russian Government steel armor for warships at about one-half the price the same company *patriotically* charged Carnegie's own dear, dear country.

(3) "Our records show that the companies governed by Mr. Carnegie received more rebates [*in anarchistic defiance of his country's laws*] during the time when rebates were given by our road, than any other shipper in any line of business."—First Vice-President Green of the Pennsylvania Railway Company. Quoted in the New York *Independent.*

(4) This same crafty gentleman recently provided enormous old-age pension funds for college and university professors. This will perhaps tightly seal the lips of thousands of teachers on the raging civil war in industry in which war Carnegie is already a blood-stained tzar. Fearing to lose their old age pensions, teachers may find it easier and more "respectable" to desert the working class in its struggle against the capitalist class—Carnegie's class. (See Index: "Hague Peace Conference"; also Chapter Two, pages 24-25.

strikes, picketing, "scabbing," boycotting, lockouts, injunctions, "bull-pens," blacklisting, insterstate kidnapping; and also anti-picket thugs,—policemen, Pinkertons, deputy sheriffs, constabulary, cossacks, militiamen and the "regulars" shooting down underpaid, underfed workers; everywhere the belittled lives and the spilt blood of the working class.*

And there will be increasing opposition to free assemblage, opposition to free speech, opposition to free press—in order to silence discussion and stop the spread of knowledge of what is fundamentally wrong.

Also there will continue to be, from time to time, naturally, under capitalism, wars of conquest to widen the field of exploitation—to enlarge the opportunity for aggressive social parasitism,—wars to open up foreign markets, wars to protect foreign markets for products which the producers' wages will not permit them to consume and the employers are not able to consume;—and everywhere the world will be stormy with the stirring trumpet call, "To arms! To arms!" —stormy with the crafty and confusing cry, "To the front! To the front! The flag!"—stormy with the shrilling fife, the roll of drums, the rattle of musketry, the flash of swords, the booming roar of cannon, burning cities, sinking warships and the thundering tread of galloping cavalry horses,— the class struggle in a thousand visible bitter forms,—and everywhere windrows and ditchfuls of dead men, dead working men, everywhere the torn flesh, the slit veins, the streaming blood and tears of the working class: hell everywhere except in the homes of our "very *best* people" who in times of trouble as in times of peace are always calmly feeding (like leeches

---

* "If, however, there occurs some general industrial disturbance of a serious sort, such as a condition of over-production, . . . it is likely to turn out that these *vocational* groupings will be weakened or even destroyed. In their place the *economic classes* will enter the *political* arena, and carry on the conflict with great energy. . . . It may be that the standard of life of an industrial class may be so seriously threatened that this class struggle will reach the extreme of absolute hostility."—Professor Albion W. Small, Head of Department of Sociology, University of Chicago: *General Sociology*, p. 264. Italics mine. G. R. K.

ever feeding) on the surplus legally filched from the working class.

Thus capitalist society is everywhere cursed with a festering social sore, an unhealable sore, poisoning, withering the best things in society, blasting the finer forms and feelings of brotherhood and peace. Everywhere the lives of the toilers are vulgarized and brutalized and wasted. And all these things will always be natural and unescapable facts and parts of any class-labor form of society, an unsocially organized society, with injustice organized, legalized and easy, down deep in the industrial foundations of society,—ever an endless civil war in industry between the two, the only two, industrial classes.

Now what shall we do about it?

It is as plain as "a, b, c."

War and all the forms of the class struggle are excessive social inflammation.*

(a) Injustice violently inflames society.

(b) Social parasitism is monstrously unjust.

(c) Social parasitism therefore inflames society—and should be destroyed.

(a) Any form of society that produces and protects a class of social parasites will always inflame society, and should therefore be destroyed.

(b) Capitalism produces and protects a class of social parasites, and thus inflames society.

(c) Capitalism must therefore be destroyed.

Justice soothes society.

Society must be organized with justice *in its structure.*

We must search for justice—for a new *social structure.*

We must construct a form of society that will "make it easier to do right and more difficult to do wrong."†

Shall we be non-resistant?

No, emphatically, no.

* Reread first page of Preface.
† William E. Gladstone.

Non-resistance is not natural (especially for the class conscious workers)—for workers who *understand their interests as a class;* and non-resistance is not reasonable, is not safe, and is not possible. Non-resistance would mean defeat and degradation for the working class—forever.*

Then is peace a childish dream and is war to be an endless wrangle and blood-spilling nightmare—for the working class?

No—not necessarily.

We must resist.

But we should not resist first and only by physical force.

The working class must THINK—or they will have to struggle and bleed and weep and wait forever,—wait and whimper like babies in the woods for "some one" or some "good people" to come and "save" them.

The workers must *think till they find a form of social organization* in which the fundamental cause of war, that is, *class* robbery, will have *no opportunity,* and will therefore cease to exist.

What Dr. Ward calls the "spirit of aggression" will fade and finally expire when the *condition* (the parasitic opportunity) which *cultivates* the "spirit of aggression" is *destroyed.*

The founders of the American republic resisted fearlessly, by force too. But the working class in the United States at present should not, and cannot now, with advantage, resist by force and force alone, and that for very good reasons:

FIRST:—We of the working class in the United States have now for our own class defense another, and better, form of power, a form of power less dangerous, less expensive, quieter and more legal and therefore more strategic,—*a form of power that makes the capitalist class dread the awakening of the working class;* namely, our political power—our united ballots.

---

* ". . . Non-resistance would be fatal. . . . If ever war is done away, it will be when the spirit of aggression, not of protection, shall have been quenched." –Lester F. Ward: *Dynamic Sociology,* Vol. I., p. 684.

SECOND:—Until we are intelligent enough to strategically defend our class with our united ballots we shall be too dull, even if it should be necessary, to use force of arms successfully in defense of our class. It seems unwise to counsel the use of the ruder methods of armed force until, having developed the necessary intelligence, we have by trial *fairly tested our peace powers,* our political powers—our united ballots. (See special paragraph, page 303.)

THIRD:—We are not politically prepared,—that is, we are not legally in possession of the powers of government, and therefore we are not in strong position to protect our class with all our forms of power legally. And until we are prepared we shall be used and abused.

Thus it is evident we can not, with advantage, use physical force.

What must we do?

We must destroy capitalism and close the class struggle.

In all the variations of the struggles or wars of capitalism the working class are hired, flattered, fooled, or forced to do all the actual fighting.

This must cease—as soon as possible—as a preliminary.

This will cease—when the conscious workers successfully *explain capitalism and war* to the confused and deluded workers. War will cease when we have explained the national and international conspiracy of the capitalist class.

War will cease when we rouse the workers of the world *by explaining.*

By explaining we inform.

By informing we increase intelligence.

By increasing intelligence we increase self-respect and the passion for a greater life and for the freedom necessary for a greater life.

Therefore,

Explain—inside and outside the ranks—everywhere—in shop, mill, mine and on the farm.

Explain till emperors and presidents *dread their own conscripted and "volunteer" armies.*

Explain till murder for board and clothes and $16 a month looks vile.

Explain till young working-class men inside and outside the ranks see the light.

Explain till an advertisement for human butchers and military fists becomes utterly disgusting to the working class.

Explain till our class becomes class conscious—till it sees itself, sees its class interest and its class power.

Explain till our class can not be fooled, hired, flattered or forced to butcher or be butchered.

Explain till our class, like the capitalist class, understand the political method of class defense.

Explain till millions of the roused workers of all political parties clasp hands at the ballot box in a political party of their own class for the defiant self-defense of their own class.

Explain till our class clearly sees and proudly declares that we must destroy the capitalist class-labor form of society and *reconstruct society on a plan of rational mutualism.**

All such explanations, all such teachings tend powerfully to rouse the working class to a consciousness of themselves, make them eager to defend themselves, both on the *industrial* field and on the *political* field—with *all their forms of power.*

Chattel slavery has been destroyed. Certainly. Why not?

Serfdom has been destroyed. Of course. Why not?

Capitalism must be destroyed. Of course——

What! Shall we destroy the rich men, the capitalists?

No, of course not.

That would not be fair. Capitalists are capitalists *legally* —permitted by the working class.

By politically created laws and institutions capitalists are legally in position to rule and rob the working class.

And by politically created laws and institutions the ruling class shall cease to be in that position.

The *personal* destruction of thousands, or hundreds of thousands of capitalists would not in the least degree mend

---

* See Chapter Seven, Section 12.

matters. The children of chattel slave owners became slave owners by the politically created laws of inheritance. Just so the children of capitalists become capitalists through neither virtue nor vice of theirs—they become capitalists through politically created laws of inheritance.

The legal right to own privately the industrial foundations of society must be destroyed, legally. *If the capitalists should become anarchists and illegally resist legal methods they could not reasonably object to having their own laws against anarchists applied to themselves vigorously.*

Of course it is true that the capitalists fleece the workers of surplus value all the time, and many of the capitalists are malignant and cruel toward the workers and by a thousand persecutions invite their own personal destruction. Some of the capitalists have destroyed themselves, have committed suicide, to escape the disgrace of their crimes. Some capitalists are now in the penitentiary; many more capitalists should be in the penitentiary—as many of their own class confess; a far larger number of capitalists, if the laws were enforced, would promptly leave the country to keep out of the penitentiary—some have done so; and a large number of capitalists are also bribing juries and prosecuting attorneys in order to avoid the penitentiary; many prominent business men, trust magnates, have had the anti-trust law changed to enable them to more easily avoid the penitentiary—so President Taft said in Columbus, Ohio, August 19, 1907.*

------

* William Howard Taft: *Present-Day Problems*, pp. 162-63:—
". . . It is also true that had the Elkins bill never been passed, the same acts could and doubtless would have been prosecuted . . . under the Interstate Commerce Act of 1889 which the Elkins law supplanted. . . . Under the 1889 amendment, however, the individuals convicted could have been sent to the penitentiary, whereas under the Elkins Act the punishment by imprisonment was taken away. . . . The chief effect of the Elkins law had on these particular prosecutions . . . was . . . to save the guilty individual perpetrators from imprisonment.

"It was well understood that the Elkins bill was passed without opposition by, and with the full consent of, the railroads, and the chief reason was the elimination of the penitentiary penalty for

And the capitalist class outrage the working class in a thousand ways. This is all true. The multitude of capitalist outrages are sufficient to provoke revenge. But we do not seek revenge. Revenge is not fine. Revenge is not noble. Moreover we cannot escape war by means of revenge, and, still more important, rich men and women are not a *form* of society. They are *members* of society and they behave *naturally—under the circumstances;* that is, being a ruling class in a *class-form* society, they behave as masters.

Capitalism as a form of society must be destroyed.

---

unjust discriminations. . . . The imprisonment of two or three prominent officers of a railway company, or a trust . . . would have greater deterrent effect for the future than millions in a fine."

Theodore Roosevelt knows a good deal about the capitalist class. He wrote on pages 5, 6, 9, 10 of his book, *American Ideals,* as follows:

"The people that do harm in the end are not the wrong-doer whom *all* execrate. . . . The career of Benedict Arnold has done us no harm as a nation. . . . The foes of order harm quite as much by example as by what they actually accomplish. So it is with the *equally dangerous criminals of the wealthy classes.* The conscienceless stock speculator who acquires wealth by swindling his fellows, by debauching judges, and corrupting legislatures, and who ends his days with the reputation of being among the richest men in America, exerts over the minds of the rising generation an influence *worse than that of the average murderer or bandit,* because his career is even more dazzling in its success, and even more dangerous in its effects upon the community. Any one who reads the essays of Charles Francis Adams and Henry Adams, entitled *A Chapter of Erie,* and the *Gold Conspiracy in New York,* will read about the doings of men whose influence for evil upon the community is more potent than that of any band of anarchists or train robbers. . . . Too much cannot be said against men who sacrifice everything to getting wealth. There is not in the world a more ignoble character than the mere money getting American, insensible to every duty, regardless of every principle, bent only on amassing a fortune . . . whether . . . to speculate in stocks and wreck railroads himself, or to allow his son to lead a life of foolish and expensive idleness and gross debauchery, or to purchase some scoundrel of high social position, foreign or native, for his daughter. *Such a man is only the more dangerous if he occasionally does some deed like founding a college or endowing a church* which makes those good people, who are also foolish, forget his real iniquity." Italics mine. G. R. K.

Is it meant that we shall destroy the means of production—the mills, mines, forests, railroads and such things?

Certainly not. The means of production are material, mechanical things. They are not a form of society.

What then? Are we to "destroy society"? Are we to turn society upside down, inside out and "other end to,"—suddenly—"some dark night," so to speak?

Not at all.

Here is what we must do:—Rapidly, just as rapidlv as possible we must destroy the present class-labor form of society called capitalism,—and to do this we must *strike at and strike out* the foundation of the capitalist *form* of society.

But what is the foundation of this capitalist *class*-labor form of society?

As already pointed out, the foundation of capitalism is the institution of *private* property *in the means of production*.

The capitalists, the employers, the ruling class, stand legally between the means of production and the users of the means of production; thus a *legal obstruction* is raised between the workers and the things they work with in getting a living.

The capitalist class legally *control the conditions under which the workers may use the means of production*.

The capitalist class are in a legalized *parasitic relation* or connection *to the means of production*.

This *relation* is the key-stone in the arch of capitalism; this relation is the prime element in the present form of society.

This parasitic relation enables the capitalists to rule, rob and ruin the working class all the time everywhere.

This relation must be destroyed; this despotic, parasitic relation must be cut.

The capitalist class must be legally pared off, legally pushed off, legally shorn from, the chief material means of production—as PRIVATE owners.

Yes, this robbery, this organized, legalized robbery called capitalism—must be destroyed.

"The vast individual and corporate fortunes, the vast combinations of capital, which have marked the development of our industrial system, create *new conditions and necessitate a change* from the old attitude of the state and nation *toward property.*"*

The case, the circumstances, require *unflinching social surgery.*

You believe in surgery, don't you. Of course you do. Surgery is recognized the world over as a rational and necessary means of saving life, the life of the individual.

Well, *extend the application of the principle and practice of surgery to society*—to the social body.†

Parasites never voluntarily let go their grasp on the source of their lives, never voluntarily let go the living things from which they suck their livings. And the parasitic capitalist class will stick to the means of production, as private owners, till they are legally dislodged—shorn from the means of production. What is here written concerning social parasites should not be misunderstood as malicious reflection on the ancient slave owner or the ancient feudal landlord or the modern capitalist. In the course of human evolution the appearance and activity of social parasites has been—and is now—as natural as the appearance and activity of parasites in the lower animal world and in the vegetable world. And the effort to dislodge human parasites from society should be, as far as is humanly possible, *free from personal malice.*‡

---

* Theodore Roosevelt: in a speech at the State Fair, Minneapolis, Minnesota, September 3, 1901.

† "If the public economy of a people be an organism, we must expect to find that the perturbations, which affect it, present some analogies to the diseases of the body physical. We may, therefore, hope to learn much that may be of use in practice, from the tried methods of medicine." Roscher: *Political Economy*, Vol. I., pp. 85-86.

‡ It must be added for the sake of clearness (and fairness):

(1) That *some* members of the capitalist class detest the capitalist system; that these regret their unsocial relation to the social body; and that while they are living under the capitalist system they are in somewhat the same difficulty that a democrat is in Russia. One can *believe* in democracy in Russia, but he can not *practice* democracy under the autocratic form of Russian govern-

However, on the farm, in the care of plants and animals no matter how small or helpless or innocent or beautiful parasites may be which interfere with the wheat crop or the flock of sheep, the parasites must be dislodged—rigorously and promptly. And, in society, no matter how handsome, polite, pious, learned, philanthropic, or ancestrally distinguished and blue-blooded a human parasite may be who lives on the labor of the workers, that parasite, old or young, male or female, must dismount promptly, must be forced from the shoulders of the working class. Those who, at the time of social reconstruction, endeavor to defend themselves by polishing their family coat-of-arms and climbing their ancestral trees in search of credentials, will simply be making monkeys of themselves. They will be even more ridiculous than the Royalists in the American Revolution. Those of "gentle breeding" will have to learn the gentle art of getting a living by *producing* a living; that awful saying, "If he will not work, neither shall he eat," will mean more and more.

The working class must, then, legally, do whatever is necessary to protect themselves from the strangling clutches of the capitalist class.

And here is what is necessary:

The working class must themselves become *organized political authority,* must seize the powers of government—and thus secure legal control of sovereign political power which carries with it the *legal right** to control, or revise, or abolish, or reorganize industrial institutions; must thus secure the

---

ment. So under Capitalism: one may believe in industrial democracy, but he cannot practice it under an industrial despotism.

(2) That some members of present society belong partly to the capitalist class and partly to the working class.

(*The Theory of the Leisure Class,* a brilliant book by Dr. Thorstein Veblen, helpful in understanding social parasites, is urged upon the reader's attention. Also W. J. Ghent's *Mass and Class.*)

* "The government which has the right to do an act and has imposed upon it the duty of performing the act, must, according to the dictates of reason, be permitted to select the means."—Supreme Court of the United States, March 7, 1819. See Supreme Court Reports, Vol. 17, pp. 409, 430.

legal right (and power) to construct and inaugurate that industrial form of society which will destroy capitalism with its organized, legalized opportunity for class robbery, and which will, at the same time, substitute organized, legalized opportunity for every member of society to make a living without being robbed, opportunity to live without wasting and vulgarizing his life in a struggle against his fellow men. *And this destruction of unsocial capitalism and the construction, at the same time, in place of capitalism, the necessary social substitute, can be accomplished by the industrial reorganization of society on the following plan—*

The Plan of Rational Mutualism:

(1) The SOCIAL ownership of *the means of production.*

(2) The SOCIAL control of *the means of production.*

(3) Equality of OPPORTUNITY TO USE *the means of production,* under regulations made *by the workers themselves.*

(4) The production of goods primarily for SOCIAL SERVICE OF ALL,—instead of primarily for PROFITS FOR A PART OF SOCIETY.

(5) The SELF-EMPLOYMENT of all who are willing to do useful work,—by virtue of the fact of their joint ownership and joint control of the things the workers must collectively use in production, the reward of each to be undiminished by rent, interest or profits.

(6) THE POSSESSION AND CONTROL OF THE POWERS OF GOVERNMENT BY AND IN BEHALF OF THOSE WHO SEEK THE FREEDOM OF THE WORKING CLASS, BY THOSE WHO SEEK TO DESTROY THE TYRANNICAL CAPITALIST WAGE-SYSTEM AND THUS SECURE INDUSTRIAL LIBERTY.

This plan connects every life with the source of life.

This plan plants firmly the feet of all members of society upon the industrial foundations of society.

Safe.

Unafraid.

Free.

This mutualism in industry will not interfere with such private affairs as religious life, family life and social life,— any more than the mutual ownership of the public library now interferes with such private affairs.

Thus we must, in short, SOCIALIZE SOCIETY,—by socializing the *ownership,* socializing the *control,* socializing the *management,* and socializing the *purpose* of the industrial foundations of society.

This would be the destruction of that class-labor system called capitalism which now rests on the institution of private property in the means of production; and this would, *at the same time,* also constitute a rational substitute—social in its nature.

MUTUALISM would thus be in the STRUCTURE of society.

The purpose of this form of society would be a fundamentally social purpose, namely, the welfare of all the willing-to-be-industrious members of society.

The capitalist class, as such, would cease to exist.

The working class, as such, would cease to exist.

All—all the people would be in full, vital, unhindered, unrobbed connection with the industrial foundations of society, the chief material means of production. All people of proper age and condition of health would become workers. Industrial class lines would disappear. Industrial mastery would disappear. Industrial dependence would disappear.

This would be the foundation of industrial democracy.

This would be reorganization.

This would be revolution.

A revolution is a rapid, fundamental change in a *fundamental* institution.

The rapid *reorganization* of industry into the form called the *trust* is a revolution—now in process.

The trust magnates are revolutionists—*so far as it suits their economic interests.*

Revolutions are neither noisy nor bloody, *unless there is violent effort to prevent the growth of society.*

As to the matter of being afraid of revolutions: Why

should we clap our hands in praise of the American Revolutionists (who employed sword, rifle, bayonet and cannon in their revolution) and then harshly condemn the peaceful Socialists who stand for peace in all parts of the world and always urge the orderly methods of procedure in accomplishing the revolution (the fundamental change) they seek to effect.

Don't be afraid.

Fortunately millions of American school boys and girls are required to commit to memory the following words of splendid defiance and self-respect:

"We hold these truths to be selfevident: . . . That governments are instituted among men, deriving their just powers from the consent of the governed; that whenever *any form* of government becomes destructive of these ends (the inalienable rights . . . life, liberty and the pursuit of happiness) *it is the right of the people to alter or abolish it,* and to *institute* a NEW government, laying its foundation on such principles, and organizing its powers in such form as to *them* shall seem MOST LIKELY to effect their safety and happiness. . . . *When a long train of abuses and usurpations, pursuing invariably the same object, evinces a design to reduce them under an absolute despotism, it is their* RIGHT, *it is their* DUTY, *to* THROW OFF SUCH GOVERNMENT *and to provide* NEW *guards for their future security."*—American Declaration of Independence.

Don't be afraid.

"The State must from time to time readjust the relation of government to liberty. . . . As the people of the State advance in civilization, the domain of liberty must be widened."—Professor John W. Burgess, Head of Department of Political Science, Columbia University.*

Don't be afraid.

The time has come for the workers to use their *political* liberty to secure *industrial* liberty—to "widen the domain of liberty," to secure a fair race, to secure equality of opportunity.

---

* *Political Science and Constitutional Law,* Vol. I., p. 87.

Equality? Yes,—equality of opportunity. Certainly. Why not?

"A race that is fair requires an equal start. . . . The state must aim at perpetual renewal of the opportunities of life in every man and class of men."—Dr. John Bascom, Ex-President of the University of Wisconsin.*

Don't be afraid.

There will be no noise, no bloodshed; all will be orderly, legal and sociable—unless the capitalists anarchistically refuse to obey the law. In that case, of course, the roused, proud and powerful working class will do *whatever is made necessary* by the anarchistic capitalists.

BE IT REMEMBERED—DISTINCTLY:

THE ROUSED WORKING CLASS, ROUSED TO SELF-RESPECT, ROUSED TO CLEARNESS OF VISION BY THE STUDY OF THE FACTS, ROUSED TO REALIZE THE WRONGS THRUST INTO THE LIVES OF THE WORKERS PAST AND PRESENT, ROUSED TO SEE THEIR RIGHTS AND REALIZE THEIR POWER AS A CLASS,—SUCH A WORKING CLASS WILL BE A WHOLLY DIFFERENT CLASS FROM THE PRESENT MEEK, WEAK, CHEATED GRATEFUL SLAVES.

Don't be afraid.

We are weary of Antagonism.

We seek Mutualism.

The American Revolutionists said plainly in their Declaration that it is a DUTY to reorganize society, under certain circumstances.

We recognize our duty.

We make no cheap and noisy boast of insulting defiance.

We see our goal—Peace and Freedom.

We shall build Peace and Freedom into the Structure of Society.

We scorn any wheedler who would betray us from the correct, direct path to our goal.

We accept any challenge from those who would by force defeat us.

Social reconstruction—that is our plain duty.

* *Sociology*, pp. 45, 47.

Thus we of the working class must, to this extent, unify, —that is, mutualize, socialize,—society.

The class aggression of the capitalist class would cease with the disappearance of the capitalist class in the reconstructed society. And the class resistance by the working class would cease with the disappearance of the robbing of the workers in the reconstructed society.

Thus would disappear the unsocial clashing of class interests—the class struggle. And thus also would disappear the dominant motives for "foreign" wars and "civil" wars.

Thus the working class could remove war—both from the shop and from the battlefield.

Thus we would inaugurate peace simply by removing the cause of war.

Is a political party of the working class necessary for this political work of the working class?

To accomplish the work of industrial reconstruction we must first secure the political powers of government and thus secure the right, the legal right, and legal power to do this work.

A POLITICAL PARTY IS SIMPLY A LEGITIMATED ORGANIZATION WITH WHICH TO SEIZE AND USE SOVEREIGN POWER—TO BECOME AUTHORITY. (See page 280.)

The political power and privilege necessary to accomplish this industrial reconstruction of society—this political power and privilege—can be secured only by means of a political party; and that party must, of course, be a party *wholly committed* to this industrial *reconstruction* of society.*

---

* "It is the peculiarity of the social struggle that it must be conducted by a collective whole . . . EVERY SOCIETY [OR CLASS] MUST SECURE SOME SUITABLE ORGAN FOR CONDUCTING THE SOCIAL STRUGGLE.

"Thus the ruling classes, through their parliaments, exercise the legislative power and are able, by legal institutions, to further their interests at the cost of others. . . . Thus the rulers themselves forge the weapons with which the ruled and powerless classes successfully attack them and complete the natural process."— Gumplowitz: *Outlines of Sociology*, pp. 145-146. Italics mine. G. R. K.

Only a political party *of the working class* can be SIN-CERELY committed to this work of industrial reconstruction *for the working class.* INDEED, NO POLITICAL PARTY STAND-ING FOR ANY FORM OF CAPITALISM WILL PERMIT ITSELF TO BE SINCERELY COMMITTED TO THIS PROMPT, THOROUGH IN-DUSTRIAL RECONSTRUCTION.

Therefore, banded together in a political party of the working class the workers

must seize the political powers to make laws,

must seize the political powers to interpret laws,

must seize the political powers to enforce laws.

Then and then only shall we *be in position by legally possessing the power* to defend ourselves, our class.

Then and then only shall we be *in position* to destroy the parasitic class aggression, the class robbery, out of which grows the class struggle—the civil war in the shop, and the war, the civil war, of the toilstained brothers of the working class on the battlefield.

Then, and then only, shall we be in best position to declare war against war.

Then we shall cease forever to foolishly wet the earth with our blood and tears and cease to be robbed in the shop and factory; and then we shall claim our own, a greater life.

The only safety therefore for the working people in all lands is to organize themselves into a political party, an international political party, of the working class, *and patiently build their party big enough* for each national group of workers to seize the political powers of government in their own country—always, everywhere, loudly declaring war against war.

There is but one working class political party on all the earth. That party sincerely proclaims: "Freedom for the working class! No more war!" And loudly and patiently that party sounds an immortal call of brotherhood to all the workers on all the blood-stained earth:—"Workingmen of all countries, unite. You have nothing to lose but your chains; you have a world to gain."

That working-class party is the Socialist Party.

Already this working class party, loudly calling, "Freedom in the shop and freedom from the battlefield"—already this party is beginning to save the blood and tears and homes and joys of the working class.

Every working man and woman should learn—and teach the children to recite at school—the following page of history, four historic events:

FIRST EVENT: In 1847 two men, geniuses, wrote a very small, but powerful book.* The book was published in 1848. Kings, emperors, tsars and presidents have turned pale when their common people began to understand that small book. The first proposition in that astonishing book is: "The [recorded] history of all hitherto existing society is the history of class struggles." That is a great fact. Pack it into your mind. That sentence has opened wide the mental windows of millions of working men—and women. The last sentence of that book of social lightning is this:—"Workingmen of all countries, unite. You have nothing to lose but your chains, you have a world to gain!" That is a sublime call. That call has thrilled millions of weary working-class people. Every year it thrills millions more. *Some day that call will enter your soul.* Then you will know the meaning of this next event.

SECOND EVENT: In 1870 two distinguished crowned assassins sent hundreds of thousands of working men to the boundary between France and Germany to butcher and be butchered.† Even then—forty years ago—the *shrewdest* workers in Germany, France and other European countries realized what war meant for the *working* class. These men were banded together in the International Working-Men's Association. These keen, studious toilers warned the working class against the war. In 1870 they sent out this general announcement: "They (the members of the International Working-Men's Association) feel deeply convinced that whatever turn the impending horrid war may take, the alliance of the working classes of all countries will ultimately kill

---

* *The Communist Manifesto.*
† Reread Chapter Seven, Section 4.

war." The Paris branch of the International issued an address saying: "French, German, Spanish working men! Let our voices unite in a cry of reprobation against war. . . . Working men of all countries! Whatever may be the result of our common efforts, we members of the International Association of Working-Men, who know no frontiers, we send you, as a pledge of indissoluble solidarity, the good wishes and the salutation of the workingmen of France." The Berlin section of the International finely responded: "We join with you heart and hand in protestation. . . . Solemnly we promise you that neither the noise of drums nor the thunder of cannon, neither victory nor defeat, shall turn us aside from our work for the union of the workingmen of all countries." German delegates at Chemnitz, Saxony, representing fifty thousand workingmen also made noble reply: "We are happy to grasp the fraternal hand stretched out to us by the workingmen of France. . . . We shall never forget that the workingmen of all countries are our friends, and the despots of all countries our enemies."

The grand old International has become the Socialist Party of our day. The Socialist Party is indeed the political party of the working class.

In recent years election returns show in one country, the best educated country in Europe, this political party of the working class, the Socialist Party, with over three million four hundred thousand serious, loyal workingmen banded together voting solidly together. Every year a larger and larger number of them *take their seats in the world's leading legislatures.* In ten countries in Europe this party has from one to eighty members of the working class in the national legislatures in legal position to defend the working class. And right vigorously these brave working-class comrades have defended the working class in every possible way they could. With the increasing election victories of this working-class party, the working class have increasing power to defend themselves. And everywhere this party is down on war. The influence of this party has already been effectively exerted against war. The vast influence of this party against war is admitted by the most bitter and powerful enemies of the working class.

THIRD EVENT: In 1905-6 the Norwegian and the Swedish armies (working men, of course) were ordered to the front to butcher one another. They were assembled at the national boundary. Tens of thousands of homes were desolate. Fear was an agony in the hearts of a multitude of women and children. Reporters were present from all parts of the world to flash the news of the butchery around the earth. The capitalist coffin trust was exceedingly glad, business was about to pick up. Gilt-braided buccaneer commanders were about to shout: "Form! Fire! Charge! Slaughter!"

"Everything was ready"—it seemed.

Then something happened—something sublime and new in the sad and "somber march of mankind."

No sword was drawn.

No cannon roared.

No Gatling gun mowed down thousands.

No wild cavalry charged.

No hospital became a hell of cursing, groaning, screaming, mangled men.

Yet "everything was ready"—ready to defend the sacred honor of "royal" and "noble" coward parasites.

Everything was ready *except one thing*—the consent of the working class.

The conscripted *Socialist* soldiers in both armies and the *Socialists* everywhere throughout both countries had *passed the sign of working-class brotherhood* all through *both armies* and through *both countries:* "We working class men are brothers. Let us not slit the veins of our own class simply to satisfy the vicious pride of snobbish masters. Let us save our own blood and tears."

This international brothers' cry was like a splendid flash of lightning at midnight. Brothers saw brothers, working-class brothers, in the night, the midnight of capitalism. The soul of the working class in both these countries flashed response: "Brothers! Brothers! We understand!" The human race seemed to smile. The Swedish and the Norwegian soldiers mingled. These armed workers fraternized. Armed men embraced armed men. They shouted and wept—for joy.

They sneered at the frowns of their commanders. Proudly and promptly they refused to butcher and be butchered.*

That settled it. There was no war.

There can not be war unless the working class agree to it.

No working men were butchered, and the international misunderstanding had to be settled without opening the blood vessels of the toilers. For of course you know, reader, that the broadclothed capitalist snobs of these countries were too cowardly to fight the war themselves.

And now there are many more happy homes, happy wives, happy mothers and happy children in Norway and Sweden than there would have been if the humble working people of these two countries had permitted a precious lot of gilt-edged cowards to excite them and confuse them and then "sic" them at one another's throats.

FOURTH EVENT: Very recently, in 1906-7, the Socialist Party in Germany and France prevented war between Germany and France over the "Morocco affair." This is admitted even by distinguished European enemies of the Socialist Party. This threatened war might easily have cost five hundred thousand lives—working-class lives—and five billions of treasure and desolated hundreds of thousands of homes and darkened both countries with an international hatred lasting half a century.

But the Socialists blocked the game.

Again and again in their International Congresses the Socialists have protested against war and militarism as being, for the working class, nothing but a burden and a curse.†

---

* Fearing that the powerful suggestion might reach and rouse the slumbering working class the *capitalist* press of the world kept silent as an oyster on the behavior of the clear-visioned soldiers of Norway and Sweden. Only the *working*-class press properly reported the sublime event. (See Challenge, page 206 et seq.)

† For an excellent and convenient discussion of the Socialist Party's opposition to war and militarism, see Werner Sombart's *Socialism and the Socialist Movement*, pp. 193-211; Morris Hillquit's *Socialism in Theory and Practice*, pp. 296-302.

Political masters and industrial masters on all the earth —*these* recognize the Socialist Party as the Working-Class Political Party.*

You, my brother, should also recognize the Socialist Party as your own Working-Class Political Party.

Reread propositions numbered 1, 2, 3, 4, 5, and 6, p. 300.

The outline of industrial reconstruction there given in the six propositions is the outline of the constructive platform and program of the working-class political party, the Socialist Party, everywhere.†

Because the Socialist Party recognizes and points out the clash of class interests in the present class-labor system;

Because the Socialist Party proposes industrial freedom for the working class;

Because the Socialist Party proposes the destruction of the class-labor system called capitalism;

Because the Socialist Party proposes that every person who renders useful social service shall have the value of his service—undiminished by the modern legalized forms of filching, namely, rent, interest and profits;

Because the Socialist Party proposes that the working class band together and save themselves;

---

* "It is no easy task to detect and follow the tiny paths of progress which the unencumbered proletarian with nothing but his life and capacity for labor is pointing out for us. These paths lead to a type of government founded upon peace and fellowship as contrasted with restraint and defence. . . . From the nature of the case, he who would walk these paths must walk with the poor and oppressed, and can only approach them through affection and understanding. The ideals of militarism would forever shut him out from this new fellowship."—Miss Jane Addams, of Hull House, Chicago: *Newer Ideals of Peace*, p. 30.

† The class who despise you so thoroughly that they would be willing to have you murdered on the battlefield—*would these hesitate to tell you a lie?* Certainly not. And they have lied to you about "different kinds of Socialism," "Socialists don't seem to know what they want," etc., etc. But secretly the capitalists are worrying because they know that the Socialists of all the world *do* know what they want and also know how to organize the necessary power to get what they want.

For such reasons the Socialist Party is the Political Party of the Working Class.

The Socialists urge:

That no longer shall the workers whimper for the protecting wings of that strange political bird, that large male angel, called a "good man";

That no longer shall the workers childishly accept the treacherous advice from political stalking horses, called political "reformers," and "political saviors";

That no longer shall the workers rest in dull dependence upon the advice of eager-to-be-elevated capitalist "leaders of the people";

That no longer shall the workers go gullibly chasing after still-fed "statesmen" on election day;

That no longer shall the workers rest in dull dependence door of legislative halls teasing smooth, stall-fed capitalist "statesmen" for labor legislation;

That the workers band together and emancipate themselves from war, from the wholesale robbery, tyranny and blood-letting of Capitalism.

With heads and hearts and hopes together the working class should read together, study together, reason together, band together, struggle together, and altogether in a political party of the working class stand together and vote together and capture the power of government for the freedom and protection of the working class.

Let us respect our own working class.

Let us have faith in our own working class.

Let us protect ourselves.

"Let us get up off our knees—and our masters won't seem so tall."

Down with industrial despotism and its wars!

Up with industrial democracy and its peace!

(Before reading the following paragraphs examine last four pages of Chapter Six, paragraph headed: "A Special Warning to the Working Class of the United States.")

One more word here:

Brothers, beware!

With pride and defiance hold up your heads—and think.

Prepare to say: "WE REFUSE."

Beware. Another war is brewing.

"Another war is necessary!"—your betrayers will presently tell you.

True! From the capitalist's point of view another war will, indeed, presently be necessary; another war becomes more and more imperatively necessary—and for a new and increasing reason.

The much plundered working people are beginning to think. Thought is revolutionary. A thought is a file, a keen saw, with which a soul may escape from the gloomy dungeon of prejudice. Thought is intellectual nitro-glycerine for blasting the flinty mountains of prejudice. Thought utterly destroys mental rubbish. Thought kills what ought to die. Thinking slaves promptly become defiant and dare to do for freedom. Thought kills—kills slavery.

Thought, however, can still be prevented. Even the splendid thought of peace and freedom can still be strangled in a wild delirium called "patriotic" war. Hence every purchasable educated human thing with influence must play its prostitute part in resurrecting and perpetuating the ferocious thirst for war.

For capitalist purposes another war is necessary.

Therefore strangle brotherliness.

Therefore stifle man's grand sweet dream of peace.

A fat living of domineering idleness for industrial pirates and their pampered pets and shameless hangers-on is not much longer possible, unless the masters as usual can set the working people clutching at one another's throats, draining one another's sweat and blood in a hateful spasm of international epilepsy called "patriotic" war.

Therefore drug the working people.

Therefore read again to the weary multitude the goriest pages of history, and declare to them that an act must be soaked in a brother's blood before it is magnificent. The people must lust again for another savage storm of stupid wrath called war.

Therefore we see the war-flag of capitalism shrewdly waved before the bulging, easily inflamed eyes of the multitude: "Good fighters—war"; "young men not only willing, but anxious to fight—war"; "heroes, heroes—war"; "glory, military glory—war"; "noble, noble soldiers—war"; "ours the most improved arms in the world—war"; "greatest navy on earth—war"; "splendid victories—war"; "better militia—larger army—war"; "our national honor—war"; "we never surrender—war"; "America in the Orient—war"; "we must defend our foreign markets—war"; "see the brave boys behind the guns—war"; "send the fleets around the earth and dare the world to war"; "we are all ready for war, war, war";—over and over this oratorical flag, this Christless vocabulary of blood-spilling cruelty, on and on, year after year—till these disgusting phrases steam in memory with the spurting blood of the long-mourned slain.

Another war is necessary.

Therefore fill the trenches with the carcasses of citizens and with fixed bayonets march on—on—on to noisy glory, on to the red madness of the brutal battlefield. This is the pagan text of literary and oratorical hirelings before a nation of Christians and peaceful Jews; this is the loveless refrain bellowed before blushing school girls; this is the Alexandrian slogan before excitable, impressible boys; this is the gore-stained banner to be gallantly flaunted on holidays before the tear-wet eyes of the sad old widows and the hobbling cripples of the Civil War; this is the race-cursing call to ninety millions of people sick of stupidly disputing with sword and cannon, longing to embrace one another in caressing fraternalism. Hideous echoes of the cruel voice of Caesar, savage whoop from the tomb of Napoleon, the assassin of France, barbarous yell from the war-cursed plains of the long, long ago—this—yes, this is the sublime height reached by the average orthodox teacher and preacher of patriotism.

And from all parts of this thinly veiled despotism of foxy, industrial tsars, comes *enthusiastic approval of all such teach-*

ing;—approval from the profit-stuffed leeches whose pouting lips suck and tug at the veins of the toiling multitude; approval from the supercilious snobs at Palm Beach, Newport and Monte Carlo; approval from the editorial intellectual prostitutes of a subsidized press; approval from the "leading citizens" that roll contemptuously along carefully smoothed streets in rubber-tired carriages and from those who sneer through the palace car windows at the common "hired hands" who man the trains and keep the track in repair; approval from the masters who own the mills and mines and stick out their tongues in scorn at the hundreds of thousands out of work or on strike for a few cents more a day; approval from the "great business men" who search the earth for markets for goods produced by the sweating wage-slaves shrewdly kept too poor to buy what their own weary minds and their puffed and blistered hands create; and, saddest of all, approval from the millions of shame-faced wage-earners viciously seduced with ironically empty "prosperity" phrases, chloroformed with pompous military rhetoric, stupified with the proud strut and cheap swagger of "prominent" and "cultivated" vulgarians—yes, approval also from these modest modern slaves through whose veins seems to slip the inherited taint of long, low-bowing servitude.

Another war is "necessary."

Therefore from Mississippi to Minnesota and from Florida to Oregon there is a wide-grinning chuckle of lip-smacking satisfaction in the palaces and club-houses of America's industrial masters when the easily deceived multitude clap their calloused palms in thoughtless approval as the bribed orator makes fierce visaged War stalk with hypnotic fascination across the stage before the plain deludable people. The people's delight in arms is thus artfully deepened;—and thus and therefore both the walls of prejudice and the defiant fortresses of glittering steel—behind which the gorged masters of the multitude have for ages fattened and threatened in security—these fortresses of prejudice and force are with increasing diligence made stronger with every possible opportunity, made stronger by every possible means.

Another war?

Expect it and prepare for it by resolving not to go to the next war till the bankers and statesmen have been bleeding on the firing line for at least six weeks.

Yes—yes, it is true that the employers' fortress of riot-guns is still strong, defiantly strong. No doubt the rent-interest-and-profit game, the game of gouge and grab and keep, will be played securely yet a while by the plunder-bloated masters of our great and glorious country. Undoubtedly millions of our thoughtless young working class men are still ready for plutocratic Senators and Congressmen and uncrowned cruelty in the White House to craftily yell: "Sic 'em, boys, sic 'em."

But light breaks.

Everywhere, every day the toilers of the world listen— listen more respectfully, listen more intelligently, listen more gratefully to the glad new gospel of justice and peace.

The change comes and come it must. That cruel spell wrought over the mind of the multitude by the bribed orator, by the purchased writer, by the blood-lusting "man on horseback," and by the far-looking masters of industry—that spell will be, must be, broken. The iron shackles on the wrists and ankles of the toilers have already been broken. The wage-slaves' shackles also must be rended, not only the industrial, but the mental slavery of the modern workers must be destroyed.

And comes now swiftly forward that soft-toned, but all-conquering gospel of peace and freedom—freedom for the dumb, voiceless multitude, now deadened with the deafening roar of machinery, deadened with the stifling dust and withering heat of the mills, deadened with the poisonous gases in the mines, freedom for the multitude soon to be glad, happy, loving, laughing in the commonwealth of co-operation, of mutualism, of fraternalism—of Socialism.

Courage, courage. Put the strong shoulders of your twelve million ballots to the "stalled world's wheel" and push. Strike. March. Dawnward toward peace.

Know this, you toil-tormented horde: That shrewd juggler's word war—word with which the swinishly selfish masters have for ages seduced the gullible multitude into the ditches across which those same masters have then rolled on sneering, snickering and safe, that spell-working word reeking with the blood-rotting stench of centuries, that word war and all that that word war now stands for must be stricken from the language of brothers, struck from the affairs of mankind,—forgotten forever—forever replaced by the sweetening peace and the sane abiding power of warless Socialism.

Brothers of the working class, wherever you are on all the earth, let us all say, altogether:

Peace is patriotism to mankind.

We do not want other people's blood and we refuse to waste our own.

For thousands of years the ruling class have bled us pale. All cannon have always been aimed at us—by us.

We did not see. Our eyes were blinded with our own blood; our minds were paralyzed with lies.

But now we see. Now we understand. And therefore now we stand erect in self-respect. Now in sincere fellowship we extend the right hand of brotherhood to all the working men—and to all the women and to all the children —of the whole world; and to all these we promise:

We will not fight.

We refuse to plunge bayonets into one another's breasts.

We refuse to slay the fathers of tender children.

We refuse to murder the brothers and lovers of women.

We refuse to butcher the husbands of devoted wives.

We refuse to "Hurrah" over victories that break the heart and blind the world with tears.

We refuse the cheap rôle of Armed Guard—as the salaried assassins in the service of the plunder-bloated coward ruling class.

If the masters want blood let them cut their own throats.

CHAPTER ELEVEN.

A Short Lesson in the History of the Working Class.

(A very careful distinction should always be made between those who abuse and those who nobly use great offices and powers.)

"We have repeatedly pointed out that every social institution weaves a protecting integument of glossy idealization about itself like a colony of caterpillars in an appletree. For instance, wherever militarism rules, war is idealized by monuments and paintings, poetry and song. The stench of the hospitals and the maggots of the battlefield are passed in silence, and the imagination of the people is filled with waving plumes and the shout of charging columns."—Professor Walter Rauschenbusch, Rochester Theological Seminary.*

KNOWLEDGE OF THE HISTORY OF THE WORKING CLASS, WHICH INCLUDES THE HISTORY OF WAR, WILL CEMENT THE WORKERS INSEPARABLY TOGETHER—SOCIALLY, INDUSTRIALLY AND POLITICALLY, AND WILL THUS MANY TIMES MULTIPLY THEIR POWER FOR SELF-DEFENCE.

When the working class understand the history of the working class, a bronze monument erected in honor of a great general will look to the workers like a vote of thanks to the Superintendent of Hell, and an ornamental cannon in a public park will look like a viper on a banquet table spread for a feast of brothers.

In the public schools of the world the history of the working class is almost wholly neglected. No text-book gives the facts, and no teacher is permitted to tell the truth—clearly—about the martyrdom of labor since the dawn of class-form, "civilized" society. The union labor men and women of the world could with great advantage to the working class devote a few thousand dollars for the expense of a five-hundred-page book summarizing: The History of Labor—The Tragedy of Toil.

---

* *Christianity and the Social Order*, p. 350.

(At this point please reread first two pages of the preface of the present volume.)

The following pages are offered as suggestions for a half-hour lesson chiefly on the origin of the working class. It is suggested to the working class reader that he teach this lesson to the children of his family and of his neighborhood.

Now, no living thing can be understood without a study of its history, and the study of the history of a living thing requires special attention to the origin of the thing studied. The working class are a living reality, and in order to understand themselves the working class must study their class history—with the very special attention to their origin as a class.

Long, long ago—thousands of years ago—our ancestors lived in tribes. These tribes grew, expanded till finally the pressure of population forced the tribes to enlarge their territories; and thus the tribes trespassed—aggressed upon one another's territory.

This caused wars—intertribal wars.

This was the origin of war.

This led to the opening of hell—for the workers.

After a while a working class arose—and began to fall into hell. Here is the way it came about:

For a long time in these intertribal wars it was the practice to take no prisoners (except the younger women), but to kill, kill, kill, because the conquerors had no use for the captive men. When, however, society had developed industrially to a stage enabling the victors to make use of live men as work animals, *that new industrial condition produced a new idea*—one of the greatest and most revolutionary ideas that ever flashed in the human brain; and that idea was simply this:—A live man is worth more than a dead one, if you can make use of him *as a work animal.* When industrially it became practicable for the conquerors to make use of live men captured in war, it rapidly became the custom to take prisoners, save them alive, beat them into submission—tame them—and thus have them for work animals, human work animals.

Here the human ox, yoked to the burdens of the world, started through the centuries, centuries sad with tears and red with blood and fire.

Thus originated a *class* of workers, the *working class.*

Thus also originated the *ruling* class. Thus originated the "leading citizens."

Thus, originally, in war, the workers fell into the bottomless gulf of misery. It was thus that war opened wide the devouring jaws of hell for the workers.

Thus was human society long ago divided into industrial classes,—into *two* industrial classes.

Of course the interests of these two classes were in fundamental conflict, and thus originated the class struggle.

Of course the ruling class were in complete possession and control of all the powers of government—and of course they had *sense enough to use the powers of government to defend their own class interests.*

Of course the ruling class made all the laws and controlled all institutions in the interest of the ruling class—naturally.

Of course the ruling class socially despised the slaves—that is, despised the working class; this "upper" class felt contempt for the "lower" class—naturally; and thus originated the social degradation, the social stigma that still sticks to the working class, so clearly clings to the workers that, for example, the banker's daughter does not marry the wage-earning carpenter; the mine-owner's son does not marry the wage-earning house-maid; the rank and file of union labor are not welcome in the palatial parlors and ballrooms where the "very best people" are sipping the best champagne and are rhythmically hugging themselves in the dance; the servants, both white and black, in a high-grade (high class, "upper" class) hotel are not even permitted to take a drink of water at the guests' water fountain tho' the guest-list may include scores of blasé old reprobates, scores of polygamous parasites, scores of the most infamous, dollar-lusting, law-breaking disreputables in the world. The working class are indeed even yet openly or secretly despised socially by their "betters."

It was thus and there and then that, long ago, *in war,* originated the first class-labor form of society, the institution called slavery.* A class of despised human work animals and a class of domineering masters thus appeared; and these two classes developed, this METHOD OF PRODUCTION developed, to such vast proportions that this CLASS-labor system became the FUNDAMENTAL THING IN THE INDUSTRIAL STRUCTURE OF SOCIETY. It was in this manner that, long ago, one part of society climbed upon the shoulders of the other part of society and became parasites, social parasites, and as a class sunk their parasitic beaks into the industrial flesh of those who had become a working class. (Reread carefully the three quotations at the head of Chapter Ten. They are specially important.)

Of course the industrial blood of the workers tasted good to the masters—that is to say, the more work the slaves did the less work the masters had to do,—and that was lovely, for the masters, for the "leading citizens." The "leading citizens" knew they had a bright idea—just like a "leading citizen's" idea of course. The new idea became popular, extremely so—of course. The "leading citizens" were *so* pleased —with themselves and their "brainy" idea. They were "superior" people—their idea proved that, of course. At that point in human history a ruling class began to flatter themselves and talk in a loud and handsome manner about "the *best* people," "the *right to rule inferior people,*" "the progressive, enterprising part of society," and so forth. The "leading citizens" knew very well that they had a "good thing"—for the "leading citizens," for the upper class who thus became *so very pleasantly located as an upper class*—that is, upon the industrial shoulders of the "lower class," the working class. (Note carefully the quotation from Dr. Ward at Head of Chapter Ten.)

---

* It is true that even before this time woman occupied a servile position and virtually constituted an industrial class. See August Bebel's *Woman—Past, Present and Future.*

Very naturally the ruling class at once busied themselves *promoting and protecting* their new class-work plan, their new idea. The idea was *their* idea and it was such a splendid idea. Indeed slavery was such a perfectly delightful idea— for the rulers—that, being "gentlemen of push and enter- prise," they *eagerly studied the problem of developing ways and means of extending their new advantage.* They thought. They planned—to manage the new human mule.

Their first idea was—force.

Kick the mule—and rule.

An institution, an *armed* guard, was, therefore, promptly organized for holding down the slaves, the "lower class," by force,—to hold the toilers, as it were, by the wrists. But an armed guard was expensive, and it was expensive simply be- cause *one* armed guard could not hold *many* slaves to their tasks—by force. Now, the ancient slave-holding ruling class, like the modern capitalist ruling class, were, of course, eager to "reduce expenses and increase efficiency." Thus the rulers had another idea, a big bright idea. Mark well the masters.

Their second idea was—fraud.

Fool the mule—and rule.

The brilliant idea of using *fraud* in ruling slaves, that is, in ruling the working class, was simply this: to have an *unarmed* guard *teach* the human horse to "stand hitched," as it were, or, rather, to work like a trained horse without requiring an armed driver to whip him, to force him to his tasks. This unarmed guard was to hold the workers to their tasks by getting a grip on their minds, on their brains, rather than on their wrists.

This was more "refined."

This was also much cheaper. *This method has always been cheaper.* It is cheaper for this reason: One *unarmed* deceiver acting as a guard by holding the mind, the *brain,* of the workers, can hold to their tasks *hundreds of times as many* as one *armed* guard can hold by force. This was a most happy idea—for the ruling class.

A new era opened.

The ruler smiled at the deceiver. The deceiver smiled

at the ruler. They understood—each other, and agreed upon *"the best interests of society."*

Precisely so.*

Here originated the vile rôle of the intellectual prostitute, the cheap part of the chloroformer of the working class, the contemptible business of the professional palaverer. Here, right at this point in human history, the perfumed intellectual prostitute joined the blood-stained soldier,—in the ruler's service of *holding down the robbed and ruined working class.* The palaverer taught the toil-cursed workers to be obedient and grateful and humble and meek and lowly and contented, to "forget it" that they have poverty here and keep in mind that "it will be all right over there"—"up above" (over in behind beyond the stars) where they will be "richly rewarded, in the sweet bye and bye, for all their sufferings in this world"; taught them that they should not be "resentful," but "in patience bear all sufferings,"—bear even the agony of having their daughters raped by rulers, and their sons run through with spears.

Thus the toiler was kept in his "proper place" (at work) by the soldier and the palaverer, compelling and cajoling the domesticated human work animal.

They held him fast.

One seized his wrists, the other seized his reason; one used force, the other used fraud; one used a lash, the other used a lure; one used a club, the other used chloroform; one frowned threateningly, the other smiled seductively. With curses and cunning these two have taught the toiler LAW AND ORDER—THE LAW AND THE ORDER MADE BY THE MASTERS FOR THE MASTERS.

Both guards were "necessary"—in the business of robbing the working class. Both have served the ruling class long

---

* Professor E. A. Ross (Department of Sociology, University of Wisconsin) gently hints thus (*Social Control*, p. 86):

"Under the ascendency of the rich and leisured, property becomes more sacred than persons, moral standards vary with the pecuniary status, and it is felt that 'God will think twice before He damns a person of quality.' "

and well. Through the long sad centuries these three, the ruler and his two "standbys," the soldier and the palaverer, have ridden the human beast of burden, the working class. The mailed fist of the hired assassin and the soft voice of the bribed palaverer have held the worker utterly helpless while the ruler robbed him.

Both guards have been rewarded—with provender and flattery, with pelf and popularity. The whipper and the wheedler of the toiler, the slayer and the seducer of the working class, have been the specially petted patriots whose ignoble rôle has been to help defend the class-labor system.

The workers have been kicked and tricked for ten thousand years, but chiefly tricked, *betrayed into helpless consent and stupid approval.* The more fraud the less force.

Undoubtedly far more important than the physical conquest over the working class was the conquest over the mind of the working class. Undoubtedly the idea of teaching the slave to be a slave and to be satisfied with slavery and thus make the slave, the serf, the wage-earner, an AUTOMATIC *human ox to bear and draw the burdens of the world in brainless obedience and dull humility—undoubtedly that idea has done more solid service in the successes of injustice than any other idea ever born in the brain of tyrants.*

The ruling class have always carefully secured the services of many of the world's ablest men to play Judas to the carpenters—to the working class. Profound men, gifted men, trained men, eloquent men, enjoying the world's choicest food, blissfully happy with the world's finest wine, living in homes of comfort and splendor, dressed in softest raiment, many of these have traduced the slave, the serf and the wage-earner without shame. Tho the splendid Christ said: "The *truth* shall make *you free,*" these Judases have taught the working class that learning is a useless or an evil thing for the *working* people; * that the toilers' poverty is the will of

---

* Even great literatures, regarded as divinely inspired and boasted to be The Truth, have been kept from the *free* access of the people—the "plain people," too plain to *understand* the literature said to have *life* in it. Such literature has been hidden from the people for many hundreds of years—or "rightly divided" and diluted.

God, that unrewarded toil in this world would reap a *"specially* rich reward beyond the grave." These paid and powerful human things, palavering about the "dignity of honest toil," palavering about the "joy of the hope of good things beyond" (always *beyond*)—these themselves have been practical and careful to take cash-down-good-things for their collect-on-delivery services, careful to take a rich and prompt reward *here* and *now* in *this* world, while at the very same time they were advising and urging the slave, the serf, and the wage-earner to accept unsigned cheques payable in heaven.

Always this for the worker: *"Your* turn will come *next"* —that is, in the next world.

Following this vanishing lure, hundreds of millions of toilers have, as it were, walked barefoot on broken glass and lain down in their beds of misery *mentally paralyzed on the subject of justice.* Hundreds of millions of toilers have not only accepted these teachings; but, saddest of all, have been tricked into teaching these same things to their children.

Thus it was that almost the entire working class were tamed and trained for many centuries into spineless meekness, into the docility of humility—helpless—policed by prejudice and fear founded on *shrewdly perpetuated ignorance.*

"Slaves, obey your masters," has been taught in a thousand ways for ten thousand years by the stuffed prophets for the profit-stuffed rulers of the robbed and ruined workers of the world.

This perhaps will make it somewhat easier to understand the *present intellectual condition of the working class.* It thus becomes easier to understand why the workers were taught (and are taught now) to be "satisfied with their lot," taught the "identity and harmony of interests of capital and labor." This explains the meekness of the multitude, the docility of the majority, and their *political modesty.*

Sheepish meekness, self-contempt and prideless obedience long ago took the place of defiant and splendid rebellious self-respect—in the *character* and the *thinking* of the working class.

In every possible way the shackles have been riveted to the wrists and brains of the working class—what for?—*in order to perpetuate the class-labor system.* Under slavery, under serfdom and under capitalism, laws, constitutions, customs, religious teachings, secular teachings, and all the social institutions have been *shrewdly conformed or adjusted to* THE PREVAILING METHOD OF PRODUCTION for the PROTECTION of that method of production *in order thus to* SUPPORT THE CLASS *who, in the struggle for existence, have had* GROSSLY UNFAIR ADVANTAGE BY MEANS OF THAT METHOD OF PRODUCTION.*

Ferocious *wrongs* were studiously developed into vast *institutions.* For example, man-stealing and slave-breeding became the chief business of the mightiest of the ancient pagan societies, the Roman Empire, and was also a flourishing enterprise under the most highly developed modern Christian societies, the British Empire and the American Republic. Christian Queen Anne, of England, unrebuked by her "spiritual adviser," was a pious stockholder in a slave-hunting corporation composed of prominent and pious Christian ladies and gentlemen.† The Christian churches, colleges, newspapers, of the United States not long ago, North and South, were almost unanimous in their eloquent and pious defense of human slavery.‡ The business was emi-

---

* The inauguration of human slavery was a profound change in human relations—the greatest possible "change in circumstances"—down at the very foundations of society. Vast *fundamental* changes resulted—inevitably—in changed, and even *new*, institutions.

"Institutions must change with changing circumstances, since they are of the nature of an habitual method of responding to stimuli which these changing circumstances afford. . . . The institutions are, in substance, prevalent habits of thought with respect to particular relations and particular functions of the individual and of the community. . . ."—Thorstein Veblen: *The Theory of the Leisure Class*, p. 190. See quotation from Dr. Small at the head of Chapter Ten. Also consult Ross's *Social Control.*

† See Thomas's *History of the United States*, p. 68.

‡ See Hyndman: *The Economics of Socialism*, Lecture 1, Methods of Production.

nently respectable, the business of legally (and piously) sucking the industrial blood out of one's fellowmen—living like
a parasite,—the business of producing nothing and living
upon the results of the worker's labor-power.

Thus keep in mind: *

(1) The origin of the working class,

(2) The origin of the first class-labor system,

(3) The origin of the class struggle,

(4) The origin of the social degradation, the socially
"down-and-out" condition, the loss of social standing—of the
working class people,

(5) The origin and growth of the humility of the working class, of the sheepish meekness of the working class, the
meekness which to-day shows itself in the politics of most
working men—always suspecting and despising their own
working-class political party, always in our day tagging along
after some smooth, well-dressed crook candidates on capitalist class party tickets.

(6) The perpetuation of ignorance—in the working class.

(7) The origin of the intellectual prostitute, the moral
emasculate.

Now, help your satisfied fellow worker, help *him* understand *why he is satisfied.*

Without malice, without anti-culture prejudice, without
anti-religious hatred, without anti-church spite, but *with
knowledge of the naturalness of human behavior domineered
by economic necessity,* with knowledge of the great *historical
process,* with your vision clear, your heart kind, your courage
high, and your purpose fraternal—explain, explain this matter of meekness to your humble, contented wage-slave neighbor. Explain: That long ago the working man was forced
and taught to be docile and meek. Under slavery, later under
serfdom and still later under capitalism—for thousands of
years—he industrially, socially, and politically *surrendered.*
He was compelled to do so. He was taught to do so.

---

* And get these things into the minds of the children. If the
teacher at your nearest school does not know these things, have the
children teach the teacher.

He got the habit.

He had the manhood and the courage beaten out of him, kicked out of him—and coaxed out of him.

He lost heart.

He humbly took his place—as a chattel-slave class, as a serf-slave class, as a wage-slave class.

He has produced wealth.

He has reproduced slaves.

The wings of his aspiration have been clipped. He can hope no higher than a job—for himself. He hopes no higher than a job—for his children.

The top of the plans of his life is—toil.

And therefore even now as a wage-slave he teaches his own children to "respect their betters"—their employer masters.

He forgets.

He is so cringingly grateful for a job that he forgets he should have not only the right to breathe the air, the right to look at the sun, the right to read in the library, the right to walk on the highway, and the right to sit in the park,—but also the *right to work, the right to work unrobbed, the right to work under dignifying conditions,* and thus maintain himself on this earth at the *upmost levels of life,* enjoying the full result of his applied labor power,—and *without whining for permission to do so.*

He forgets.

He is still so very humble.

He is, under the wage-system, forced to obey orders all his life in the factory, the shop and the mine. He is thus habitually so obedient that he will obey any order. He prides himself on his obedience. Under orders he will even plunge a bayonet into the breast of his fellow workers—in the interest of the capitalist class. He forgets the thousand wrongs thrust into his weary life and into the life of his class.

He does indeed forget.

He is still in a dull, dumb slumber.

But he is *beginning to rouse* from the slumber of meekness—from the social damnation of brainless obedience.

He is beginning to study the history of his own working class; and therefore he is rousing, waking, rising.

Following are some additional short paragraphs on the history of the working class from books by distinguished writers and teachers. It is hoped that these quoted paragraphs will induce further working class study of working class history. These passages confirm the main points of this lesson. (See Chapter Twelve, Suggestion 4.)

Professor Lester F. Ward (Brown University) :*

"Still, the world has never reached a stage where the physical and temporal interests have not been largely in the ascendant, and it is these upon which the economists have established their science. *Self-preservation has always been the first law of nature* and that which best insures this is the greatest gain. . . . *All considerations of pride or self-respect will give way to the imperious law of the greatest gain for the least effort.* All notions of justice which would prompt the giving of an equivalent *vanish* before it. . . ."

Thus wrote Sir Henry Maine :†

"The simple wish to use the bodily powers of another person, as a means of ministering to one's own ease or pleasure, is doubtless the foundation of slavery."

And thus Professor W. G. Sumner (Yale University) :‡

"The desire to get ease or other good by the labor of another and the incidental gratification to vanity seem to be the fundamental principles of slavery, when philosophically regarded, after the rule of one man over others has become established. . . . It appears that slavery began historically with the war captive, if he or she was not put to death, as he was liable to be by the laws of war. . . . It seems to be established that it [slavery] began where the economic system was such that there was gain in making a slave of a war captive, instead of killing him. . . . The defeated [in war] were forced to it [slavery] and *learned to submit to it.* . . . It seemed to be good fun, as well as wise policy, to make the members of a rival out-group do these tasks, after defeating them in war. . . . Inasmuch as slavery springs from greed and vanity, it appeals to primary motives and is at once entwined with selfishness and other fundamental vices. . . . *It rises to an interest which overrules everything else.* . . . The motive of slavery is base and

---

* *Pure Sociology*, p. 61. Italics mine. G. R. K.

† *Ancient Law*, p. 164.

‡ *Folkways*, pp. 262-3 and 307. Italics mine. G. R. K.

cruel from the beginning. . . . The *interests* normally control life.
. . . Slavery is an instinct which is sure to break over all restraints and correctives. . . . It is a kind of *pitfall for civilization.*"

Here are a few lines from Professors Ely and Wicker (University of Wisconsin, Department of Economics) :*

"It follows from the need of larger territories [in the hunting stage] that war becomes an economic necessity wherever there is not an abundance of unoccupied land. This same condition of things gives us one of the causes of cannibalism. The pressure of increasing numbers bringing people continually to the verge of starvation, they fall, little by little, into the custom of eating enemies, taken in war. . . . Captives later came to be recognized as of use in serving their captors, and thus slavery succeeds cannibalism. . . .

"The Origin of a Working Class. Perhaps the most important result of the change which produced the agricultural stage was the growth of slavery as an institution. As we have said, slavery had its beginnings in the preceding periods [hunting and pastoral], but it is only in the agricultural stage that it becomes an important, almost a fundamental, economic institution. Tending the herds did not call for persistent labor, but the prose of tilling the soil is undisguised work, and primitive men were not fond of work. . . . It is not strange then that they should have saved the lives of men conquered in battle with the design of putting upon them the tasks of tilling the soil."

On the origin of slavery the eminent French sociologist, Gabriel Tarde, writes :†

"What do all our modern inventions amount to in comparison with this capital invention of domestication. This was the first decisive victory over animality. Now, of all historic events the greatest and most surprising is, unquestionably, the one which alone made history possible, the triumph of man over surrounding fauna [animals of the region]. . . . To us the trained horse that is docile under the bit is merely a certain muscular force under our control. . . . The idea of reducing men to slavery, instead of killing and eating them, must have arisen after the idea of training animals instead of feeding on them, for the same reason that war against wild beasts must have preceded that against alien tribes. When man enslaved and domesticated his own kind, he substituted the idea of human beasts of burden for that of human prey."

---

* *Elementary Economics*, pp. 27-33.
† *Laws of Imitation*, Parson's translation, pp. 277-79.

And this from Wallis:*

"But whatever its merits, the consideration of slavery intro-
duces a much larger subject—the place of class relations in social
development as a whole. In its material aspect, property in men is
an institution by means of which one class of people appropriates
the labor product of another class without economic repayment.
This relation is brought about [*also*] *by other institutions than
slavery.* For instance, if a class engross the land of a country and
force the remainder of the population to pay rent, either in kind
or in money, for the use of the soil, such a procedure issues, like
slavery, in the absorption of labor products by an upper class without economic repayment.

"We have observed the origin of the social cleavage into upper
and lower strata on this general basis at the inception of social
development. If we scrutinize the field carefully, it is evident that
one of the greatest and far reaching facts of ancient civilization,
as it emerges from the darkness of prehistoric times, as well as
one of the most considerable facts of subsequent history is just *this
cleavage into two principal classes.*"

Herbert Spencer has written:†

"The sequence of slavery upon war in ancient times is shown
us in the chronicle of all races. . . .

"Ready obedience to a terrestrial ruler is naturally accompanied
by ready obedience to a supposed celestial ruler; . . . Examination discloses a relation between ecclesiastical and political governments . . . and in societies which have developed a highly coercive
secular rule there habitually exists a high coercive religious
rule. . . .

"The Clergy were not the men who urged the abolition of slavery, nor the men who condemned regulations which raised the price
of bread to maintain rents. Ministers of religion do not *as a body*
denounce the unjust aggression we continually commit on weaker
societies."

Dr. Ward writes:‡

"Passing over robbery and theft, which, though prevalent everywhere, are not recognized by society, let us consider war for a
moment as a non-industrial mode of acquisition. In modern times,

---

* *American Journal of Sociology*, May, 1902, pp. 764-65. Italics
mine. G. R. K.

† *Principles of Sociology*, Vol. III., pp. 84, 92, 148, 448; Appleton's Edition, 1899. See also Lester F. Ward: *Dynamic Sociology*,
Vol. I., pp. 287-90. (Italics mine. G. R. K.)

‡ *Dynamic Sociology*, Vol. I., pp. 583-85.

most wars have some pretext besides that of aggrandizing the victorious parties engaged in them, although in nearly all cases this latter is the real casus belli [justification of war]. This shows that the world is so far advanced as to be ashamed of its motives for its conduct, but not enough so to affect that conduct materially. In olden times no secret was made of the object of military expeditions as the acquisition of the wealth of the conquered people. . . . We may regard war, then, strictly considered, as a mode of acquisition. . . . War, then, when waged for conquest, is simply robbery on so large a scale that in the crude conceptions of men it arouses the sentiments of honor."

In Dealy and Ward's *Text Book of Sociology,* pp. 86-88, is this luminous passage:

"The stage of race antagonism is reached and the era of war begins. The chase for animal food is converted into a chase for human flesh, and anthropophagous [cannibal] races arise, spreading terror in all directions. . . . The use of the bodies of the weaker races for food was, of course, the simplest form of exploitation to suggest itself. But this stage was succeeded by that social assimilation through conquest and subjugation. The profound inequality produced by subjugation was turned to account through other forms of exploitation. The women and the warriors were enslaved, and the system of caste that arose converted the conquered race into a virtually servile class, while this service and the exemptions it entailed converted the leaders of the conquering race into a leisure class.

"Such was the origin of slavery, an economic institution which is found in the earlier stages of all the historical races."

The next selected paragraph is from Professor Simon Patten (University of Pennsylvania), Ex-President of the American Academy of Political and Social Science:*

"The human hordes turned upon each other, and their prowlings about the precarious supplies of food evolved in the course of time the 'wars of civilization.' There was little peace where nature was most productive, and the conquering populations of the better lands, governing and protecting by conquest, built up whole states on the traditions and practice of fighting. . . . *Statesmen and philosophers set forth the necessity and beneficence of destruction. It was in such a world, where a man's death was his neighbor's gain, that* OUR *social institutions were grounded.* . . . Predatory

---

* *The New Basis of Civilization,* pp. 67, 69. Italics mine. G. R. K.

habits, which originated in the hunting of game, developed a zest for
hunting men as soon as conquests and the possession of slaves made
the agricultural resources of the valleys more desirable than those
of the mountain or upland plain. . . . The contests evolved social
institutions, which do perpetuate and conserve, and which do not
improve, man's adjustment to nature. Here arises the distinction
between the *social* institutions . . . and the *economic* institutions.
. . . The former establish status and the rights of possession and
exploitation; the other increase nobility of men and goods, promote
industry, and give each generation renewed power to establish
itself in closer relations with nature.

"The result of these conditions is two kinds of obstacles that
hinder advance. On the one hand are the obstacles economic, mal-
adjustments between man and *nature,* which forced men in the past
to submit to a poverty they did not know how to escape; and on
the other hand are the obstacles *social* which do not originate in
nature, but in those *past [social] conditions retaining present po-
tency* that have aligned men into antagonistic classes at home and
into hostile races abroad. The *economic* obstacles are being slowly
weakened by the application of knowledge, science and skill; but the
social obstacles will never be overcome until an intellectual revolution shall have freed men's minds from the stultifying social traditions that hand down hatreds, and shall have given to thought the
freedom that now makes industrial activity. *The extension of
civilization downward does not depend at present so much upon
gaining fresh victories over nature, as it does upon the demolish-
ment of social obstacles which divide men into classes and prevent
the universal democracy that unimpeded economic forces would bring
about.* The *social* status, properly determined by a man's working
capacity, has now *intervened between him and his relations with
nature* until OPPORTUNITY, which should be impersonal and self-re-
newed at the birth of a man, has dwindled and become partisan."*

Thus Professor Patten, tho a conservative and a non-
socialist, frankly points out the necessity of such social reorganization as will destroy the *artificial* barriers to equality
of opportunity for each to secure an abundance. And it is
certainly true, as Dr. Patten suggests, that we have arrived
at that stage in our knowledge of nature and in our industrial evolution, which renders industrial reconstruction of
society logically necessary—both to avoid war and to secure
industrial justice and freedom for the working class.

_____

* See discussion of parasites in Chapter Ten.

Anent this matter one of America's noblest and most scholarly women, Miss Jane Addams, writes as follows :*

"Existing commerce has long ago reached its international stage, but it has been the result of business aggression, and constantly appeals for military defense and for the forcing of new markets. . . . It has logically lent itself to warfare, and is indeed the modern representative of conquest. As its prototype rested upon slavery and vassalage, so this commerce is founded upon a contempt for the worker, and believes that he can live on low wages. It assumes that his legitimate wants are the animal ones, comprising merely food and shelter and the cost of its replacement."

Frederic Harrison thus :†

"Within our social system there rages the struggle of classes, interests, and ambitions; the passion for wealth, the restlessness of want. The future of industry, the cause of education, social justice, the very life of the poor, all tremble in the balance in our own country, as in other countries; this way or that way will decide the well-being of generations to come."

The wars of long ago originated because it was extremely *difficult* to get a living out of nature's store-house of supplies—when men were ignorant of nature's resources and ignorant of how to make nature yield abundantly. Those wars were due chiefly to ignorance of physical nature, due to our *inability to get into right relations* WITH PHYSICAL NATURE. But the wars of the present are carried on, and the wars of the future will be carried on, chiefly because of the following *combination* of circumstances:

(a) We have so much knowledge of nature's forces and resources that it is easy, now, to get livings from nature's store-house, easy to produce abundantly; and

(b) Under the *wage*-system the worker's power to produce abundantly is so much greater than his permitted consuming power that the surplus product becomes so large as to make a foreign market, a world-market, necessary; and,

(c) Since many nations have reached and more nations are rapidly approaching this stage of development in production, yet still remain under the wage-and-profit plan of

---

* *Newer Ideals of Peace,* pp. 115-16.
† *National and Social Problems,* p. 255.

distribution, THE WORLD MARKET IS INSUFFICIENT FOR ALL
OF THEM.

Hence there will be wars, if the working class permit them.

The future wars will be due chiefly to ignorance of social
nature, due to our *inability to get into right relations* WITH
ONE ANOTHER *industrially.*

War produced slavery, chattel slavery. Chattel slavery
evolved into serf-slavery. Serf-slavery evolved into **wage-slav-
ery.** And wage-slaves produce so much and are permitted to
consume so small a proportion of what they produce, that
the capitalists must order the wage-slaves to fight for a
foreign market for what the wage-slaves produce and the
capitalist employers do not consume or invest and the wage-
slaves are not permitted to consume. War thus originated
slavery and now slavery [wage-slavery] ends in war.

*War, conflict, struggle, Antagonism is in the social struc-
ture wherever there is slavery.*

Slavery is fundamentally unsocial—anti-social.

Now, the capitalist employer insists that the **wage-earner**
and the employer are in *proper* relation to each other. The
capitalist is satisfied to have had the first two class-labor
forms of society (slavery and serfdom) pass away. But he
accepts the *present* class-labor form of society (the wage-
system) as *correct;* it is satisfactory—to him. And he craftily has it taught in the high schools, colleges and universities
that the employer and the wage-earner are at present in proper
relation to each other.

The capitalist enjoys his own freedom *at the expense of
the worker's freedom.*

He is eager to have the wage-earner *believe* that he too is
free; and that, being free, he should be satisfied AND KEEP QUIET.

The capitalists explain that the wage-earners are free
because the wage-earners have the *privilege of making a contract,* a contract to *work for wages;* that the wage-earners
being thus at last free to make a contract, they have reached
their final status, an ideal status; and that thus (Blessed be
the Lord!) *evolution has finally finished its great work*—the
work is done and *well* done.

Capitalists and the intellectual flunkies of the capitalist class do all possible to have the world believe the following proposition:

THE EVOLUTION OF HUMAN RELATIONS IS FINISHED—PERFECT—IN INDUSTRY; AND, THEREFORE, THE WAGE-EARNERS ARE FOOLISH AND UNGRATEFUL TO BE DISCONTENTED, AFTER HAVING DEVELOPED TO THEIR PRESENT STAGE OF INDUSTRIAL FREEDOM.

Following is a sample of the familiar soothing congratulation on our having reached the present noble form of industrial freedom and civilization. Professor Fairbanks (Yale University) writes thus:[*]

"When captives taken in war could be utilized for work instead of being destroyed or eaten, a genuine means of production was secured. . . . Feudalism marked a decided advance on slavery. . . . The serf had certain interests of his own, not wholly identical with his lord's. . . . Then masters gradually learned that hired labor [the wage-system] was more profitable than forced labor, and the principle of serfdom, like that of slavery before it, had to give way to a higher form of organization for production [the wage-system]. . . .

"The laborer [at present under the wage-system] is bound to his master by no tie except such as he voluntarily assumes."

How frankly profits are admitted to have been the motive inspiring the origin of the wage-system.

And how entertainingly ridiculous is the last proposition quoted above. What cheap palavering about freedom. What clownish antics pleasing to the kings—the industrial kings. It certainly pleases the industrial Caesars to have the Professor turn intellectual sommersaults to induce the wage-slave to smile sweetly and admire the slave-bands on his own wrists. Are not those bands plainly marked *"Free"*?

Notice that Professor Fairbanks uses the words "master" and "bound" in referring to the relation between the employer and the "free-contracting" wage-earner.

A *free* man does not *voluntarily* BIND himself to a *master.*

With the lash of hunger cutting him and the wolf of want at the throats of his wife and children, the "free-con-

[*] *Introduction to Sociology*, pp. 136-39.

tracting" hired laborer, the wage-earner, promptly and voluntarily seeks an employer—"master," and "voluntarily" "contracts" to produce a dollar's worth of value for twenty or forty cents in wages and thus "voluntarily" degrades himself and thus "voluntarily" submits to have his wife and little children robbed of the abundant livings he wishes to provide for them. This is the freedom, the free contract, of the wage-system, the present (the third) form of *class*-labor system. This *glorious* freedom of the modern wage-slave is *easily* seen in the picture *opposite the title-page of this book.*

The "freedom" of the wage-earner in thus making a contract, with starvation behind him, vagrancy laws reaching for him, police, militia, soldiers, jails and bull-pens ready for him, this freedom is about as complete as that of a citizen facing an armed and threatening highwayman who commands, "Hands up!" The wage earner and the held-up citizen are free to comply, free to surrender and free to be robbed, and *also* free to decline *and take the consequences*—all "voluntarily" of course.

NO ONE IS FREE INDEED TILL HE IS FREE IN THE MOST FUNDAMENTAL ACTIVITY OF LIFE, THE ACTIVITY OF GETTING A LIVING.

In the evolution of mankind the worker has, in some parts of the world, secured:

Freedom to investigate,

Freedom of thought,

Freedom of assemblage,

Freedom of speech,

Freedom of the press,

Freedom of suffrage—for male workers,

Freedom of political party organization and association.

This indicates the stage at which we have arrived in the development of freedom for the working class. These *preliminary* forms of freedom are *the means with which, if we have pride enough, we shall secure freedom indeed—freedom in getting a living,* freedom from capitalist employers who, with soldiers and the lash of starvation, force us into wage contracts, freedom from the blue-blood social parasites who despise our common blood in social relations, suck our blood in industrial relations, and waste our blood in war.*

In the evolution of mankind the ancient free barbarian, taken prisoner in war, loudly and grandly protesting, became a chattel slave without any kind of freedom; the chattel slave became a serf without industrial freedom or any other kind in reality and completeness; the serf became a wage-earner, a wage-slave, without industrial freedom—that is, without the *fundamental* freedom, freedom in getting a living. However, in very recent times the wage-earner has come into the possession of several of those extremely *important forms of freedom with which he can defend himself* as soon as he has sufficient self-respect to do so.

Thus and therefore the QUESTION OF OUR DAY is this:

ARE THE WORKING CLASS PROUD AND KEEN ENOUGH TO USE THE FREEDOM THEY HAVE, TO SECURE THE FREEDOM THEY NEED MOST—NAMELY, FREEDOM IN INDUSTRY, FREEDOM IN GETTING A LIVING IN A SOCIALIZED SOCIETY, A SOCIETY WITH EQUALITY OF OPPORTUNITY FOR ALL, ALL OF US WITH OUR FEET FIRMLY PLANTED ON THE COLLECTIVELY OWNED INDUSTRIAL FOUNDATIONS OF SOCIETY, A SOCIETY OF RATIONAL MUTUALISM, WITH JUSTICE, PLENTY AND PEACE?

Reader, if you are with us in our peaceful struggle to win the world for the workers, start a fire—in your neighbor's mind (if he has one)—hand him a torch, a torch of truth. Let us shake hands and fight—the enemy—with light.

With the truth we shall halt the galloping cavalry, silence the cannon, "ground arms," and close the class struggle—in a co-operative commonwealth.

With a dollar's worth of literature you can reach a hundred brains.

It is your move.

---

* For a powerful argument showing the intellectual equality of the working class and the ruling class see Professor Lester F. Ward's *Applied Sociology.* The political foolishness of the working class is not due to lack of brains, but to lack of books—books that tell the truth, the truth that clears the vision and rouses the passion for freedom and points the way.—Suggestions, next chapter.

CHAPTER TWELVE.

More Suggestions and What to Read.

(1) Invite your pastor to preach against war, urge him to do so, and render him any assistance you can in the way of literature on war. Help get out an audience to hear the sermon. Urge others to do likewise.

(2) Inform your own children and other children concerning the class struggle and war, and urge them to talk about the class struggle and against war, at school. Teach them the cause of war. See also Chapter Eight, Section 20, and Index, "Recitations." *Rouse the children.*

(3) Wherever possible—in colleges, high schools, labor unions, fraternal organizations, women's clubs, churches, Sunday schools, at picnics, and so forth—have debates, declamations and essays on war. Help the debaters, writers and speakers, find literature on war, and, if possible, get the subject presented from a working-class point of view, showing especially the fundamental cause of war and what war always means for the working class.

(4) Have as many persons as possible call at your public library for books on war, and suggest books on war to be called for. Suggest books for purchase by your public library management. If the books you urge for the library are not purchased, *discuss* the reason. All the sociological works quoted in Chapter Eleven should be in your public library.

(5) Get articles and letters on war into your local newspapers and labor union journals.

(6) On the 30th of May, the 4th of July and other "great" days, when the blood-steaming praise of human butchery is poured forth by the noisy "patriotic" orators, pass around all possible literature helpful in counteracting the befouling suggestions commonly thrust into the minds of the people at such times. Chapter Two and other selec-

tions from *War—What For?* making an inexpensive sixteen-page booklet, may be had, printed separately, for such purpose.

It is possible to compel an entire community to think about the vast outrages against the working class. As long as the workers have the privilege of spreading the printed page, one of their highest pleasures and *powers* will be found in *forcing society to consider the case of the working class.* The first thing on the program in every community is to take the community by the shoulders, so to speak, and *compel it to consider the most vital subject of the hour.*

(7) A Ten-Dollar Cash Prize for the best essay or debate, or declamation on *war as a phase of the class struggle* by local school-children under eighteen years of age would create much interest in the vicious slaughter of men of the working class and in the new working class politics, if the proper literature were brought to the young people's attention. See Chapter Eight, Section 20, Suggestion (7).

(8) It would be easy to make here a pretentious parade of a discouragingly long list of books on war. But *War— What For?* is primarily for the class of readers who are usually too busy in the present warlike struggle for existence to find time to read a roomful of books on war. However, it is hoped that the present volume may also have readers with opportunity to make extensive studies of the subject. Such readers will find abundant bibliographies already prepared. Excellent book lists for the student of war are as follows:

(a) *The Political Science Quarterly,* December, 1900: over 200 titles, at the close of an elaborate article of great worth, "War and Economics in History and in Theory," by Edward Van Dyke Robinson.

(b) A pamphlet, *International Peace, a list of Books with References to Periodicals:* 600 titles with comment on contents, published by the Brooklyn Public Library, 1908.

(c) A well selected list of readings in *The Arena,* December, 1894.

Following is a list of pamphlets, magazine articles and books, directly or indirectly on the subject of social conflict, of which war is a phase. The list is short, tho' sufficient, it is hoped, to make a helpful beginning, a short reading course, for any one who would understand the subject of social conflicts, that is, would understand, not the science of war, but the cause, the meaning and results of class struggles and war.

There is a vast amount of worthless, or worse than worthless, literature on war: worthless because of the writers' neglect of the heart of the problem, namely, the *industrial structure* of all class-labor forms of society, with their *unsocial purpose and method of production,* resulting in the class struggle.

Whoever would understand war must give special attention: (1) to the *economic interpretation of history;* (2) to the *class struggle,* considered historically and currently; and (3) to *surplus value,* produced by the workers, but legally escaping from their control to the capitalist class—as a result of the institution of private ownership and private control of the collectively used means of production. The fact, the method, the purpose, and the result of the *legal confiscation* of that part of the world's wealth which the workers produce and are not permitted to enjoy—must have careful study. In the light of such studies, national and international policies, politics and war can be understood. And as war is thus understood we can make rapid headway against war. Pretty little speeches and essays on the beauties of peace, with "please-be-good" perorations,—such efforts, however carefuly prepared, tearfully punctuated, elegantly printed and prayerfully delivered, will result in—nothing. That is to say, occasional literary and oratorical snowballs ignorantly, gracefully and grammatically tossed in the direction of hell will have no effect on the general temperature of that warlike region. (See Index: "Another War," "The Hague Peace Conference," and "The Explanation.")

A Reading Course.

In the following list of readings those indicated by parenthesis thus () would serve as a shorter course.

(1) Kautsky: *The Capitalist Class; The Working Class; The*

Class Struggle; Ethics and the Materialistic Conception of History; and *The Road to Power,* Chapters 8 and 9.

(2) Simons: *The Man Under the Machine,* and *Class Struggles in America.*

(3) Marx: *Wage-Labor and Capital;* Marx and Engels: *The Communist Manifesto.*

(4) Massart and Vandervelde: *Parasitism—Social and Organic.*

(5) Myers: *History of Great American Fortunes,* entire work is an account of social parasitism in America; special references: Vol. II., pp. 127-38, 291-301; Chapters 11 and 12; Vol. III., pp. 160-176.

(6) Veblen: *The Theory of the Leisure Class.*

(7) Ross: *Social Control; The Foundations of Sociology,* pp. 219-23, 272-76; *Social Psychology,* Chapters on Suggestibility, The Crowd, and Mob Mind.

(8) L. F. Ward: *Dynamic Sociology,* Vol. I., pp. 565-597; *Psychic Factors in Civilization,* Chapters 33 and 38; *Applied Sociology,* pp. 224-295, 300-302, 307-313, 319-326; *Pure Sociology,* pp. 266-72; "Social Classes in the Light of Modern Sociological Theory," *American Journal of Sociology,* March, 1908; *Education and Progress,* Address delivered before the "Plebs" League, Oxford, England, August 2, 1909.

9 W. G. Sumner: *Folkways,* Chapter 6.

(10) Morgan: *Ancient Society,* pp. V.-VIII.; Pt. I. Chs. 1-3; and all of Pt. IV.

(11) J. O. Ward: *Ancient Lowly,* Chapter—"Spartacus."

12 Shoaf: *The Story of the Mollie McGuires.*

13 Hanford: *The Labor War in Colorado.*

14 ———: "Secret Army Guards New York Against a Traffic Strike," New York *Herald,* Mag. Section, March 20, 1910.

(15) Debs: *Class Conflict in Colorado.*

(16) Wright, U. S. Commissioner of Labor: *A Government Report on the Great Strike in Colorado.*

17 Darrow: *Speech to the Jury in the Haywood Case.*

(18) Untermann: *The Dick Militia Law* (U. S., 1903).

19 Commons: "Is Class Conflict in America Growing and Is It Inevitable?" * * * Carver: "The Basis of Social Conflict"; * * * Keasby: "Competition." *American Journal of Sociology,* March, 1908. See also Papers and Proceedings of the American Sociological Society, Vol. II., Special Topic: "Social Conflicts."

20 Small: *General Sociology,* Chapters 26 and 27.

(21) Shaler: "The Natural History of War," *International Quarterly,* Sept., 1903; also *The Neighbor.*

22 Ridpath: "Plutocracy and War," *Arena,* Jan., 1898.

(23) Jordan: "The Biology of War," an Address, Chicago,

1909, reported in *Unity,* June 10, 1909; *Imperial Democracy,* Chapters 1, 2, 3, and 7; *The Human Harvest; The Blood of the Nation.*

24 Chatterton-Hill: *Heredity and Selection in Sociology,* pp. 316-24. Thompson: *Heredity,* pp. 532-34.

(25) Jefferson: "The Peace-at-any-Price Men," *The Independent,* Feb. 4, 1909; "The Delusions of the Militarist," *Atlantic Monthly,* March, 1909.

(26) Charles Edward Russell: *Why I Am a Socialist.*

27 Tolstoi: *Bethink Yourselves; Patriotism and Christianity,* and *Thou Shalt Not Kill.*

(28) Robinson: "War and Economics in History and in Theory," *Political Science Quarterly,* Dec., 1900.

(29) Ghent: *Mass and Class.*

(30) London: *The War of the Classes; Revolution,* Chapter, "The Yellow Peril"; also, "Revolution," *Contemporary Review,* Jan., 1908.

(31) W. T. Mills: *The Struggle for Existence,* Chapters 4-23.

(32) Hillquit: *Socialism in Theory and Practice,* pp. 36-65, 153-167, 296-302.

(33) Spargo: *Socialism,* Chapters 4, 5, 6, and *Common Sense of Socialism,* Chapters 2-7.

(34) Ferri: *Socialism and Modern Science,* Chapter 7.

35 Seligman: *The Economic Interpretation of History.*

36 Boudin: *The Theoretical System of Karl Marx,* Chapters 1-5, 8-10.

37 Patten: "The Economic Causes of Moral Progress," *Annals of Amer. Soc. Pol. and Soc. Sci.,* Sept., 1892.

(38) Engels: *The Origin of the Family, Property and the State,* special attention to Chapters 8, 9; and *Socialism—Utopian and Scientific.*

(39) Hobson: *The Evolution of Modern Capitalism; Imperialism,* special attention to first six chapters; *The Psychology of Jingoism; The War in South Africa,* Part II.; and *John Ruskin—Social Reformer,* Chapters 3-8 inclusive, and Appendix 1.

40 Ferrero: *Militarism.*

41 Liebknecht: *Militarismus und Anti-Militarismus.*

42 Büchner: *Industrial Evolution* (Wickett's translation), Chapters 4-5.

(43) Robinson and Beard: *The Development of Modern Europe,* Vol. II., Chapters 18, 30-31.

(44) Weale: *The Coming Struggle in Asia,* special attention to Parts II. and III.

45 ———: "Peace on Earth," *Public Opinion,* Dec. 4, 1908, p. 635.

46 Schierbrand: *America, Asia and the Pacific.*

47 Harrison: *National and Social Problems,* Part I., Chapters 1, 6-11.

(48)   Strong: *Expansion*, Chapters 2, 3, 4.

49   Bolce: *The New Internationalism*, Chapters 1-6 inclusive, and 15.

50   Fisk: *International Commercial Policies*, Chapters 13-16.

51   Reinsch: *World Politics.*

52   Asakawa: *The Russo-Japanese Conflict.*

53   Kennan: "The Military and Political Memoirs of General Kuropatkin," *McClure's Magazine*, Sept. 1908.

54   Smith: *The Spirit of American Government*, Chapters 4, 11, 12.

55   McCabe and Darien: *Can We Disarm?*

56   Carver: *Sociology and Social Progress*, pp. 132-73.

57   Jaurès: "Socialism and International Arbitration," *North American Review*, Aug. 1908.

58   Broda: "The Federation of the World," *The International*, July, 1908.

(59)   Hervé: "Anti-Militarism," *The International*, July, 1908; *Anti-Patriotism; My Country—Right or Wrong.*

60   Edmondson: *John Bull's Army from Within.*

61   Mead: *Patriotism and the New Internationalism.*

62   Kampffmeyer: *Changes in the Theory and Tactics of the (German) Social Democracy* (Gaylord's Translation), Chapter 3.

(63)   Sombart: *Socialism and the Socialist Movement* (Epstein's Translation), Sixth Enlarged Edition, pp. 175-223.

(64)   Stoddard: *The New Socialism*, Chapters 14, 15.

(65)   Campbell: *Christianity and the Social Order*, pp. 176-230.

66   Warner: *The Ethics of Force.*

67   Wallace: *The Wonderful Century*, Chapters 19, 20.

68   (Anonymous:) *Arbeiter in Council.*

(69)   Walsh: *The Moral Damage of War.*

70   McLaren: *Put Up Thy Sword.*

(71)   Bloch: *The Future of War.*

72   Molinari: *The Society of Tomorrow.*

73   Brooks: *The Social Unrest*, Chapter 6.

(74)   Kim: *Mind and Hand*, Chapters 2, 17, 21, 22, 24.

(75)   Seidel: *Industrial Instruction.*

(76)   Eastman: *Work-Accidents and the Law;* Oliver: *Dangerous Trades.*

77   Addams: *The Newer Ideals of Peace.*

78   Anitchkow: *War and Labor.*

79   Cooley: *Human Nature and the Social Order*, Chapters 1, 3, 4, 7, 12.

80   Lloyd: *Man the Social Creator*, Chapters 1, 6, 11.

81   Kropotkin: *Mutual Aid.*

82   Bellamy: *Equality*, Chapters 22-27 and first half of 33.

83   Henry George: *Progress and Poverty*, Book 10, Chapter 3.

84 Amos: *Political and Legal Remedies for War*, Chapters 1, 2.

85 Charles Sumner: *Addresses on War.*

86 Fiske: *The Destiny of Man.*

87 Kelly: *Government and Human Evolution*, Vol. II.

(88) Barry: *Siege of Port Arthur—A Monster Heroism.*

(89) Sakurai: *Human Bullets.*

(90) Von Suttner: *Lay Down Your Arms.*

(91) Andreief: *The Red Laugh.*

(92) Zola: *The Downfall.*

(93) Wells: *The War in the Air.*

94 Channing: *Lectures on War.*

(95) Hugo: *Les Misérables*—the Battle of Waterloo; also *William Shakespeare*, Anderson's translation, pp. 294-312, 341-48, 384-95.

96 Sienkiewicz: *With Fire and Sword.*

(97) Crosby: *Captain Jinks—Hero*, and *Swords and Ploughshares.*

98 Mr. Dooley: *In Peace and War.*

99 Kipling: *Barrack-Room Ballads*—"Tommy."

100 Mrs. Browning: *Mother and Poet.*

The various "peace societies" have published considerable literature on war and peace—in most cases with good intentions, no doubt. However, there could be no peace between a chattel slave and a chattel slave's master; nor can there be peace between a wage-slave and a wage-slave's employer—if the wage-slave be awake; nor between the wage-slave class and the capitalist class. Until "peace societies" cry out against capitalism,—the heart of which is the wage-system,—until then their literature will be discouragingly ineffective.

Reread first page of Chapter Nine, paragraph beginning "The cash cost of militarism."

The one war sublime is: Light against Darkness.

The printing press is the machine-gun for the slaves against slavery.

It is a high privilege to make a human brain ferment—with facts.

THE END.

INDEX.